The PRIME **ORIGINS** Guide to

EXPLORING KRUGER

Your key to unlocking Africa's wildlife treasure

Brett Hilton-Barber and Professor Lee R Berger

ACKNOWLEDGEMENTS

The authors of this book acknowledge the efforts of South African National Parks and the South African government to develop and sustain this country's natural and human heritage. Sincere thanks are due to the staff and rangers of the Kruger National Park, to Eric de Jager and David Brenner of Tigers Eye who encouraged and supported this project from its inception. Thank you, too, to Lou Arthur for sharing his remarkable knowledge of the African bush, to Chris Patten of SANParks, Jackie Berger, Colin Bell, Doug Goetsch, Grant Vrey and Gary van Rensburg who went through early versions of the text. Thank you to Josie Grindrod, Nike Romano and Susie Joubert for their inspiration and practical suggestions, and to editor Margaret de Paravicini The authors are indebted to Wilderness Safaris for advice, feedback and access to photographic images, to Lazarus Makhitla of SANParks archives and to Africa Imagery for their assistance, and to all the photographers and illustrators who have contributed their work to the project, particularly Mike Poliza, Nigel Dennis, Albert Froneman, Heinrich van den Bergh and Roger de la Harpe. The animal illustrations are by Chip Snaddon and Walter Voigt, other illustrations by Louwra Marais and a special mention must be given to Francois Knight and Ryk Taljaard for the excellent maps. Our thanks to Gillian Black for design and layout. The authors would also like to thank Mark Read for his infectious enthusiasm about South Africa's wildlife, the staff at the various camps that supported the authors during the research phases of this book, in particular those at Ngala, Pafuri, Singita Lebombo, Imbali and Tinga, as well as Conraad de Rostner of Bongani. Other people whose support is appreciated include Tana and David Hilton-Barber, Bridget Hilton-Barber, Pauli and Murray Grindrod, Leslie Barbeau and Geraldine Abrahams.

Publisher
Prime Origins (Pty) Ltd
PO Box 15666, Vlaeberg 8018,
Cape Town South Africa
www.primeorigins.com
Trade enquiries 27-21-422-1634
brett@primeorigins.co.za

ISBN: 978-0-620-39228-0
First Edition published 2004
Second Edition published 2007

Design and Layout: Gillian Black
Editor: Margaret de Paravicini
Maps: Francois Knight & Ryk Taljaard
Illustrations: Chip Snaddon
Content advisor: Lou Arthur
Proof reader: Elizé Lübbe
Indexer: Mary Lennox
Photography: Michael Poliza, Nigel Dennis, Albert Froneman, Brett Hilton Barber, Dave Luck, Africa Imagery, SANParks, Heinrich van den Berg, Wilderness Safaris, Mark Tennant, Mike Myers, Colin Bell

Photographs of the Kruger Park for commercial purposes are available from Africa Imagery *africaimagery.co.za,* Albert Froneman *www.wildlifephotography.co.za,* Heinrich van den Bergh *www.hphpublishing.co.za* Nigel Dennis *www.nigeldennis.com,* and Michael Poliza can be contacted at *www.poliza.de*

Repro: Resolution
Printing: Paarl Print, PO Box 248, Paarl 7620, South Africa

Text copyright: Brett Hilton-Barber and Professor Lee R Berger
Published edition copyright: Prime Origins (Pty) Ltd

FOREWORD

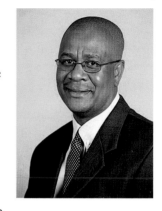

The paradox of nature lies in the relationship between certainty and unpredictability. There are things about the bush we take for granted, just as night follows day and each season slips into the next. However, we are increasingly aware of nature's deeper, less predictable elements, changes of a longer cyclical nature and those that are the consequence of human intervention.

The Kruger National Park is Africa's finest jewel like no other in the world. Visitors to the Park are met by a cast of characters as vast and intriguing as the African bush itself – elephants in tender courtship, wild dogs babysitting while the rest of the pack is out on the prowl, impalas sprinting away from danger lurking behind the bushes, the hyaena giggling on its way to the next leftovers and the lush vegetation that covers and nurtures the beauty of this unique landscape.

How do we manage and enhance pristine areas of wilderness while at the same time exposing them to the increasing number of tourists seeking a "back-to-nature" experience? This is the particular challenge facing SANParks in the management of one of the world's wildlife icons, the Kruger National Park. In this regard the preservation of the Park's biodiversity cannot be underestimated. Increasingly people are seeking a more holistic experience of the African landscape than the mere "safari" adventure.

In this sense *Exploring Kruger* is an excellent guide to the biodiversity of the Park as well as its human heritage. It goes beyond the conventional field guide in that it delves into both the behavioural and mythological elements of the Park's animal life and provides a backdrop of game ranger stories and historical human dramas that have shaped the character of Kruger over the years. In a sense *Exploring Kruger* is a celebration of the African landscape that gave rise to humankind's earliest ancestors whose traces are evident in parts of the Park. One hopes that the authors – Brett Hilton-Barber and Professor Lee Berger – succeed in their aim of raising people's awareness and enjoyment of Kruger so that the Park continues to occupy a special place in the national psyche for this generation and those to come. I would also like to use this opportunity to pay tribute to those past and present SANParks staff who have dedicated themselves to Kruger so that the rest of us may enjoy the experience.

Dr David Mabunda
Chief Executive
South African National Parks
Pretoria

CONTENTS

South-western foothills

Brett Hilton-Barber

Kruger's Trophy Five

A visit to Kruger is always lifted by seeing one of the Trophy Five, the big carnivores which live at the top of the lowveld food chain. These magnificent animals have each specialised in their own hunting style. Generally they avoid each other but their territories often overlap.

Lion *(Panthera leo)*

The biggest African cat is found in prides in mixed woodland and thorn thickets throughout Kruger. All other animals treat it with respect, apart from the hyaena which will attack lionesses and cubs. The highest concentration is in the game-rich areas around Satara, Skukuza and Lower Sabie.

Leopard *(Panthera pardus)*

Unlike the lion, this big cat hunts alone. It is mostly found in the dense riparian bush along the major watercourses, particularly the Sabie, Letaba and Luvuvhu rivers.

Cheetah *(Acinonyx jubatus)*

The least aggressive of the Trophy Five, the cheetah is often pushed off a kill by the other big carnivores. Cheetah are not common in Kruger and are restricted to the more open savanna, especially around Lower Sabie and Crocodile Bridge and in the central grasslands.

Spotted Hyaena *(Crocuta crocuta)*

A relative of the dog family, the spotted hyaena is a social animal found in small packs in mixed woodland throughout the Park, particularly around Skukuza, Lower Sabie, Crocodile Bridge and Satara areas.

African Wild Dog *(Lycaon pictus)*

These highly social dogs are an endangered species renowned for their stamina and collective hunting skills. The best place to see them is in the Phalaborwa Gate area, around Berg-en-dal, Crocodile Bridge and Skukuza.

Elephant

Brett Hilton-Barber

Introduction

HOW TO USE THIS BOOK

The *Prime Origins Guide to Exploring Kruger* is designed to enhance your visit to the Kruger National Park. The first part of the book provides an overview of the Park and its animal life with emphasis on the habitats that exist within the lowveld savanna. Part two is a regional guide that covers almost every road from Crocodile Bridge gate to Pafuri, detailing the habitat of the route and what one is likely to see. For each of the main seven areas in Kruger, we have recommended a top drive, sketched out what animals to look out for and listed the camps in that area. Interspersed throughout the text are content boxes:

 Vintage pointers relate to points of interest in human and natural history

 Habitat pointers relate to the landscape, including information on trees and shrubs

 Wildfiles are general interest boxes on animals and their interactions

 Explorer tips relate specific info that will enhance the tourist's experience

Part three highlights the activities Kruger has to offer and provides practical advice on how to make the most of the Park. Part four is a quick guide to camps and routes, rules and regulations.

 The Kruger National Park has

- The world's tallest land animal – the giraffe, which stands at 5,5m;
- The heaviest land animal – the elephant, which weighs up to 6 500kgs;
- The fastest land animal – the cheetah, which is capable of short bursts of 114km/h;
- The fastest antelope – the tsessebe, which can run at over 100km/h;
- The largest bird, the common ostrich which stands at 2m and weighs approximately 100kg;
- The fastest bird – the peregrine falcon, which can attain speeds of up to 300km/h during a dive;
- Two of the world's rarest fish, the lungfish and the killifish.

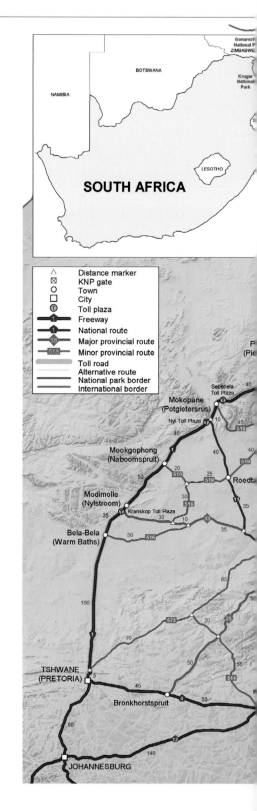

ZIMBABWE

MOZAMBIQUE

Beitbridge
15
Musina
(Messina)
35
40 508
525
30
525 Tshipise
40
Boabab Toll Plaza
523 70 524
25 524
35
Makhado
(Louis Trichardt) 70 521 Thoho-
yandou
81
55
578 90
Capricorn Toll Plaza
81 70
30 45
70 529
1 80
31 36 70
100 115
Tzaneen 71 30 60
35 20 10 Phalaborwa
Gravelotte 35
36 45 40
25 40 30
Hoedspruit Orpen
37 10 15 15
327 25
70 30 45
579 50 Klaserie 531
80 55 10 65
35 555 Pilgrim's Bosbokrand
45 37 36 Rest 533 30 30
rsdal 55 30 533 Graskop 25 536
578 45 535 10 Kruger
80 577 Lydenburg 37 Sabie 538 10 Phabeni
65 25 Hazyview Numbi
33 65 540 55 45 25
Dullstroom 10 Crocodile
145 35 20 Bridge
65 Waterval- Nelspruit 40 Malelane 40
555 Machado Boven 100 40 10
Toll Plaza 25 40 10 Komatipoort
Belfast 10 Machadodorp 5 Nkomazi Toll Plaza
Aiddelburg 85 50
65 Barberton
40 38 Badplaas
50
11 40 Carolina
endrina 36

LIMPOPO

NATIONAL

PARK

KRUGER

NATIONAL

PARK

MOZAMBIQUE

SWAZILAND

N

The Kruger National Park is one of Africa's premier game reserves, consisting of almost 20 000 square kilometres of woodland savanna, an area bigger than Wales or Israel, and almost the size of Massachusetts. It sits in the South African lowveld between the towering escarpment of the northern Drakensberg and the Mozambique coastal plains. Spanning a variety of savanna habitats, ranging from high-rainfall wooded mountains to semi-arid grassland plains, Kruger has within its borders an abundance of wildlife and a rich, but largely unexplored, human heritage.

Over time, Kruger will become the key partner in the world's largest game reserve, the 35 000 square-kilometre Greater Limpopo Transfrontier Park, which will include within its borders the neighbouring Limpopo National Park in Mozambique and Gonarezhou in Zimbabwe to the north.

Not only does Kruger embody the spirit of wild Africa but it is a window into the world that gave birth to humanity itself. We are, after all, a product of the African landscape. The wide open savanna grasslands and mixed bushveld of the Park are typical of the environment from which our earliest

The "Big Five".

Although the Kruger experience should not be reduced to a checklist mentality, it is thrilling to see the "Big Five" – those animals considered by 19th-century big game hunters to be the most dangerous animals to hunt. The "Big Five" are:

Lion (*Panthera leo*)

The most fearsome and cunning of the Big Five. Lions have perfected the art of collaborative hunting and have an uncanny ability to get extremely close to their prey before charging. This makes them extremely dangerous adversaries in the bush.

Leopard (*Panthera pardus*)

An elusive and discreet hunter, the leopard is a solitary animal that is active mostly at night. Leopards will generally avoid humans and will attack only when cornered, starving or injured.

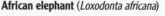

African buffalo (*Syncerus caffer*)

A mighty, muscular beast equipped with sharp horns which it can use to deadly effect. Wounded buffalo have been known to double back on their tracks to ambush the hunters pursuing them.

African elephant (*Loxodonta africana*)

Perhaps because they have been hunted for thousands of years for their ivory, elephants are aggressive towards humans who come too close. Size counts in the natural world and the elephant's strength, speed and its deadly tusks have cost the life of many a hunter in Africa.

White rhino (*Ceratotherium simum*)

The white rhino's claim to Big Five status is actually a tourist marketing ploy. The original Big Five rhino was the far more dangerous black rhino (*Diceros bicornis*), which has since been relegated to the Rare Five.

Lion

Heinrich van den Berg

Kruger's Big Six Birds

One has earned one's birding stripes in Kruger if one can tick off the Big Six. They are the:

Lappet-faced vulture (*Torgos tracheliotus*) – the largest Kruger vulture has a striking pinky-red head; it usually is the dominant scavenging bird at a kill; found throughout Kruger but mostly in the central grasslands.

Martial eagle (*Polemaetus bellicosus*) – a powerful bird of prey with distinct white chest covered in black spots; it has the largest wingspan of any raptor in Kruger and is found in mixed woodlands throughout the Park, particularly in trees growing along the drainage lines where prey is more plentiful.

Saddle-billed stork (*Ephippiorhynchus senegalensis*) – one of Kruger's rarities, distinguished by its multicoloured bill; found mostly in the riverine forests throughout the Park, but most often in the north, particularly around Letaba, Shingwedzi and the Luvuvhu area.

Kori bustard (*Ardeotis kori*) – uncommon grassland bird with noticeable crest; known for its elaborate courtship displays; found mostly in the central and northern Kruger savanna.

Ground hornbill (*Bucorvus leadbeateri*) – endangered but quite common terrestrial red-faced heavy bird; it is the most vocal of the Big Six and is found in small groups in woodland pockets throughout Kruger.

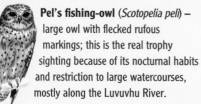

Pel's fishing-owl (*Scotopelia peli*) – large owl with flecked rufous markings; this is the real trophy sighting because of its nocturnal habits and restriction to large watercourses, mostly along the Luvuvhu River.

ancestors emerged some two-and-a-half million years ago. They would have regularly encountered many of the same animal species present in the Park today.

The Kruger Park has hot summers punctuated by rather erratic rainfall. The atmosphere is often humid and night temperatures are usually warm. Winters are generally temperate and dry, the crisp air turning surprisingly cool in the evenings.

From a visitor's perspective, the best time to visit Kruger is between late summer and spring (April and September). The winter months (June and July) are often the best game-viewing time when the vegetation thins out, allowing greater visibility.

During this time, animals are more likely to congregate around roadside water holes. The risk of malaria is at its lowest during the winter and spring months (from May to October) and the heat is not oppressive. For birding enthusiasts, summer (particularly January and February) is the best time to visit the Park as all the migrant birds have arrived and food is plentiful.

MALARIA

Malaria can be a risk during the summer rainy season, which falls roughly between October and April. This is especially true for lower-lying camps such as Lower Sabie and Crocodile Bridge and all camps in the north. Prophylactics should be taken in advance of visiting Kruger during malaria season and one should use a good insect repellant while in the Park. It is advisable for pregnant women and for children under the age of two not to visit Kruger in summer. The most vulnerable times are between dusk and dawn. Remember, however, that not every mosquito carries malaria. Should you develop flu-like, feverish symptoms within seven to 20 days of visiting Kruger, consult your doctor.

MALARIA HOTLINE 082 234 1800

Fives Alive

These days the "Big Five" is regarded as an outdated concept in conservation circles. It has its roots in 19th-century game hunter terminology and refers to the five most dangerous African mammals to hunt: the lion, leopard, elephant, rhino and buffalo. Although it is thrilling to see all of these animals, they do not constitute the Kruger experience. Indeed visitors should consciously avoid a checklist mentality in making sense of the bush. A more fulfilling approach is to appreciate the infinite number of multi-layered relationships between animals, plants and seasons. Kruger is a theatre of natural drama where there is always some action – sometimes subtle, sometimes obvious. Like the Lotto, there is always an element of luck. It's an ever-changing show where the age-old relationship between life, death and survival can be explored against the breathtakingly beautiful backdrop of African bushveld.

In attempting to move beyond the limits of the Big Five syndrome, some conservationists have suggested "alternative Fives", encompassing other rarities of the African experience.

The "Rare Five"

Aardvark (*Orycteropus afer*)

Black rhino
(*Diceros bicornis*)

Pangolin (*Manis temminckii*)

Roan antelope
(*Hippotragus equinus*)

Suni antelope
(*Neotragus moschatus*)

Elephant shrew
(*Elephantulus myurus*)

The "Little Five"
Red-billed
buffalo-weaver
(B*ubalornis
niger*)

Leopard tortoise
(*Geochelone pardalis*)

Ant lion
(*Myrmeleontidae sp*)

Rhino beetle
(*Scarabaeinae dynastinae*)

Southern Kruger

The Kruger Park south of the Olifants River is dominated by bushwillow and acacia woodlands, with vast stretches of grassland in the east and mountains in the south-west. The main rivers of the south are the Sabie and the Crocodile which forms the southern boundary of the Park. There are more animals in southern Kruger because the grasses are more palatable and there is a wider variety of habitats. The best game viewing is in the central grasslands, around Skukuza and in the south-east.

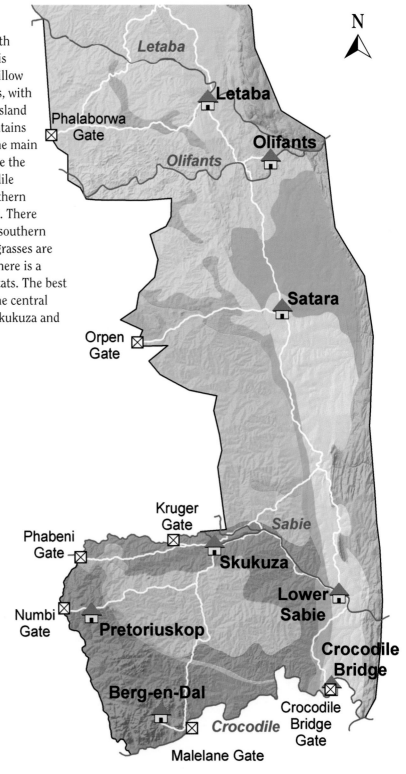

Open savanna
grassland on basalt

Pretoriuskop sourveld

Malelane mountain bushveld

Mixed woodland
and thorn thickets

Mixed woodland
with sweet grazing

Olifants rugged veld

Mixed thorn and
marula woodlands on granite

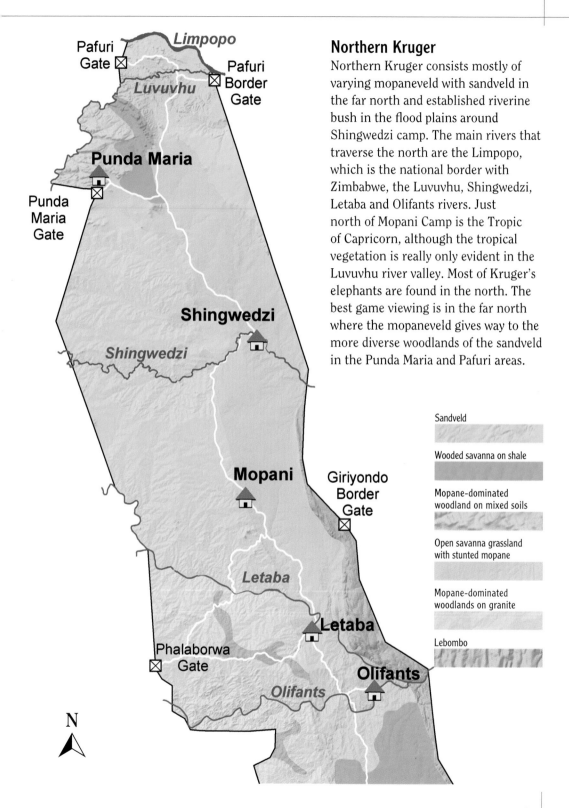

Northern Kruger

Northern Kruger consists mostly of varying mopaneveld with sandveld in the far north and established riverine bush in the flood plains around Shingwedzi camp. The main rivers that traverse the north are the Limpopo, which is the national border with Zimbabwe, the Luvuvhu, Shingwedzi, Letaba and Olifants rivers. Just north of Mopani Camp is the Tropic of Capricorn, although the tropical vegetation is really only evident in the Luvuvhu river valley. Most of Kruger's elephants are found in the north. The best game viewing is in the far north where the mopaneveld gives way to the more diverse woodlands of the sandveld in the Punda Maria and Pafuri areas.

Pafuri Gate

Limpopo

Pafuri Border Gate

Luvuvhu

Punda Maria

Punda Maria Gate

Shingwedzi

Shingwedzi

Mopani

Giriyondo Border Gate

Letaba

Letaba

Phalaborwa Gate

Olifants

Olifants

Sandveld

Wooded savanna on shale

Mopane-dominated woodland on mixed soils

Open savanna grassland with stunted mopane

Mopane-dominated woodlands on granite

Lebombo

N

Early days in the Kruger Park

SANParks

Kruger's modern history

The Sabi Game Reserve, the forerunner of today's Kruger National Park, was proclaimed in 1898 by the president of the Transvaal Boer Republic, Paul Kruger. The establishment of the 4 600 square-kilometre reserve between the Sabi and Crocodile rivers was in reaction to the disastrous depletion of game in the lowveld. Indiscriminate hunting during the mid-1800s and the rinderpest outbreak of 1896 had led to the local extinction of many species. In the face of virulent opposition from private landowners and hunters, he also proclaimed a second reserve, the Shingwedzi Reserve, which stretched between the Shingwedzi and Limpopo rivers. These original reserves would form the core of what would eventually become the Park of today.

Control of the region only became effective, however, after the end of the Anglo-Boer War when James Stevenson-Hamilton was appointed head ranger of both reserves in 1902. With a small force

of rangers, he rigorously enforced his mandate to let animals rule and make himself unpleasant to anyone getting in his way. He vigorously set about removing people from the demarcated reserve, including the indigenous populations who had lived in the area for hundreds of years, earning him his nickname of "Skukuza" ("he who turns everything upside down"). Stevenson-Hamilton's battle was not only against hunters and poachers, but against sheep farmers and mining entrepreneurs who had prior claim to the land. His vision of creating a national park that would be sustained by tourism came to fruition in 1926 when the Shingwedzi and Sabie reserves were merged and the 70 privately owned farms between them were purchased by the government to form a consolidated block of land – the Kruger National Park.

The Park was opened to tourism in 1927 and, after a slow start (only three cars entered the Reserve in that first year), Kruger soon turned into a popular destination. Within a decade, 3 600 kilometres of roads had been built and several camps established. By 1950, a research station and rest camp had been developed at Skukuza, transforming Stevenson-Hamilton's base into the "capital" of Kruger. By 1969, the Park was fenced in by 18 000 kilometres of wire and poles. In the 1960s and 1970s there was enormous pressure on the government to allow the northern part of Kruger to be mined for coal, but this was resisted and the Park was rededicated to conservation. In the 1990s, many activities and services were commercialised and a number of new private concessions were granted. In 2002, visitor numbers to Kruger topped the 1 million mark for the first time.

Ancient Kruger

Humankind's earliest ancestors lived and hunted in what is today the Kruger Park. The southern lowveld between the Drakensberg escarpment and the Mozambican border has been occupied by humans for at least the past 1 million years. This time period is particularly interesting because it occurs within the evolutionary framework of archaic *Homo sapiens* becoming modern humans – *Homo sapiens sapiens*. The evolution of the human brain is reflected in archaeological finds in the Park, showing the transition from the cruder stone tool kits of the Early and Middle Stone Ages to the more refined and aesthetic tools of the Late Stone Age. There is evidence of San hunter-gatherer occupation of the present day Kruger from approximately 6 000 years ago. Their legacy is in the rock art and engravings found in the Park (see page 122). Around the beginning of the first milennium Khoi herders from south-central Africa made their appearance in the Limpopo valley. From approximately 200 AD Bantu-speaking Iron-Age pastoralists moved into southern Africa from east Africa and established permanent settlements in the summer-rainfall areas. In more recent times, northern Kruger was a crucial cog in a major subcontinental pre-colonial trading network, known as the Thulamela culture. Although Thulamela itself is a relatively late site, dating from the 13th to the 17th centuries, there is evidence from Mapungubwe, further up the Limpopo Valley, that active trading with the coast began around 900 AD. Arab, Indian and possibly even Chinese ships docked on the Mozambican coastline to trade for gold, copper, ivory and animal skins from the southern African interior.

SANParks

Thulamela

Giraffe and red-billed oxpecker

Michael Poliza

PART 1

Understanding Kruger

The Kruger landscape

Habitats

Broadly speaking, Kruger can be described as mixed woodland savanna. Within this definition, there are a number of localised habitats ranging from dense riverine forest to treeless plains. Savanna is a Spanish term coined to describe the grasslands of South America, but it is applicable to Africa and Asia in describing an environment that consists essentially of interdependent grasses, shrubs and trees. Like the dynamic between two professional dancers – in which one alternately leads and the other follows – the ratio between grass and trees shifts according to the influence of seasons, climate and animals. This symbiotic relationship is the dance of the savanna.

However, there is far more botanical diversity than this description suggests because of the variation in climate, soil types and geology within the Park. In the Kruger savanna there are an estimated 2 000 plant species found in 30 specific botanical areas that can be grouped into 17 ecological zones. It is this "mosaic" composition of the landscape that enables the savanna to support more large animals than any other biome in the world. The relationship between animals and the savanna contributes to its sustainability. The Tropic of Capricorn is just north of Mopani, so one-third of the Park is tropical.

🍃 The Rhythm of Life and Death

Kruger is a landscape in which life and death are woven into the fabric of everyday experience. It is an environment beyond sentiment. Birth, growth and death are part of the same natural cycle. To experience the thrill of a kill is to access the core emotions of our African origins, to feel the horror and the power of circumstances beyond us. To come across death in the veld is a visceral reminder of our own mortality and a chance to marvel at the elegance with which death ensures that life is dispersed back into the environment. The bush is a reminder of our animal instincts of survival, competition and collaboration which are often disguised by what we call civilisation but are an integral part of our African heritage.

Dave Luck

Hippo skull

Habitat Map Key

Sandveld – restricted to the far north; predominantly sandy soils; diverse vegetation; baobabs very noticeable, dramatic sandstone ridges.

Woodland savanna on shale – mixed knob-thorn, marula and bushwillow woodlands and thorn thickets; good grazing; leadwoods along the drainage lines.

Mopane-dominated woodland on mixed soils – mopane and bushwillow species on low rolling hills; mopane takes stunted or tree form depending on soil conditions; elephants like this habitat.

Open savanna grassland with stunted mopane – open sweetveld grasslands, mainly on basalt, but low carrying capacity because of soils and low rainfall; very little woodland.

Mopane-dominated woodlands on granite – mopane in tree and intermediate form, mixed in with pockets of bushwillow and acacia species; lower game densities because of sourveld grazing.

Lebombo – low, arid rhyolite hills with euphorbia and succulents on the hill crests and woodlands and riverine forest in the gorges between the rocky outcrops.

Mixed woodland with sweet grazing – knob-thorn and marula woodlands, dense in places with pockets of grassland; good game-viewing habitat.

Olifants rugged veld – coarse stony soils with lots of black rock; mixed thornveld and woodlands with mixed grazing.

Mixed thorn and marula woodlands on granite – low, rolling hills with bushwillow and acacia species; sweeter grazing along the drainage lines and lots of marula trees.

Open savanna grassland on basalt – sweet, nutritious grazing on open plains; pans fill up quickly in summer; lots of large grazing herds and the predators that hunt them.

Pretoriuskop sourveld – large, granite domes and silver cluster leaf-dominated, high rainfall woodlands, sourveld grasses, favoured more by browsers than grazers.

Malelane mountain bushveld – tall, granite koppies with pockets of mixed knob-thorn sweetveld; high species diversity because of high rainfall.

Mixed woodland and thorn thickets – mostly along the lower contours of the catchment areas along the Crocodile and Sabie River; often good game viewing because of proximity to water.

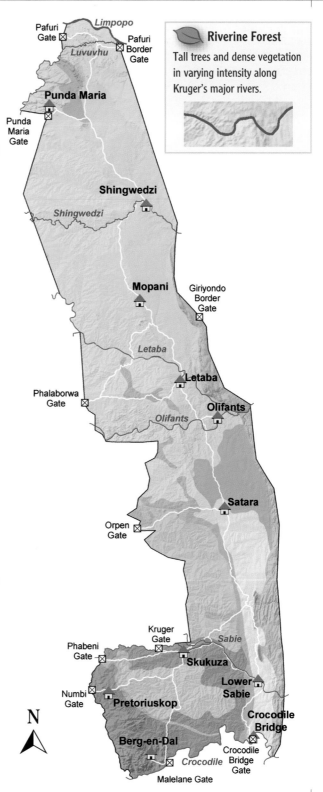

Riverine Forest

Tall trees and dense vegetation in varying intensity along Kruger's major rivers.

N

The Kruger calendar

Month	Traditional Shangaan Calendar	Weather
August	*Komkulu* The first stirrings of renewal are in the air as new buds appear on the trees and the sleeping wilderness becomes alive	Cool mornings and evenings, but temperatures and humidity rise during the day, more moisture; winds indicate spring is on its way
September	*Sekenwane* A time of keen anticipation as to when the marula trees will show their flowers – this determines the planting of crops	The month of spring; occasional showers but water is still scarce
October	*Kanamkulu* A time when the marula fruit begins to appear and the size of the harvest can be judged in terms of gallons of beer; the potential of the recently planted crop will be determined by the arrival of the rains	Usually the beginning of the rainy season, but can be very hot if rains are late
November	*iMpala* A time of promise and anxiety, such as that felt by the impala in the height of the lambing season; a time of relief if the rains come on time	Rainfall usually double that of October
December	*Nkokoni* The period of nourishment when the blue wildebeest gives birth to its young; a time to pull the year to a close and to celebrate life	Height of summer and the rainy season; days are hot and humid, often spectacular thunderstorms
January	*Hoho* A month of laughter and festivity, and full-time carousal as the marula fruit is ripe and being turned into beer and food is plentiful	Height of rainy season; days are hot and humid; good thunderstorms
February	*Mhlanga* The month when the grain should be tall and green like reeds waving in the wind	Hot and humid
March	*Jubamsoko* The month of rain and impenetrable bush; the time to cut back the vegetation along the paths	End of summer, generally the last major rains
April	*Mkwekwezi* A time of pleasantry when the first crops can be eaten and the heat of summer has abated	Seasonal shift towards autumn, noticeable drop in temperatures, occasional late-summer rains
May	*Sandwela* A busy month, the time of reaping and protecting one's crop against animals and thieves, a time when one is rewarded for hard work	Autumn gives way to winter; rainfall drops off dramatically
June	*Sheremela* The month of back-breaking activity when the soil has to be prepared for the new crop; much of this hard work is done by women	Winter; cool evenings and warm days; temperate climate that is generally wind free
July	*Konyane* A time of consolidation when the tilling has been completed and the last season's maize cobs are ripe, dry and secure in storage huts	Wind begins picking up a little

Landscape	Animals	Gate times	Sunrise – Sunset	Temps
Dry bush with little leaf cover; water scarce; veld prone to fire; wild-pear dombeya flowers; mopane is russet-coloured	Good game viewing at water holes	06h00–18h00	06h35–17h35	12–28
Weeping boer-beans flower in red; flowering knob-thorns and long-tail cassias give the veld a distinct yellow hue; marulas in flower	First migrant birds appear from the north, weavers begin breeding; Game still concentrated around water holes	06h00–18h00	05h54–17h50	12–28
New grass emerges on the savanna; bulbous plants begin appearing; magic guarri and sickle-bush flower; mopaneveld becomes green	Good game viewing as bush is still not too thick; birds engaged in courtship rituals and displays; steppe eagles begin to arrive	05h30–18h00	05h22–18h02	16–32
Vegetation more lush with tree cover returning and grasslands shift from yellow to green; white kirkia in flower; pans begin filling	Lots of young animals visible; woodland kingfishers make an appearance; predators concentrate on catching newborn animals	05h30 –18h30	05h00–18h22	16–32
Wild morning glory and flame lilies in flower; long-tailed cassia trees produce distinctive long pods	Wildebeest breeding season; lots of young animals everywhere in the bush; intense predator activity	05h30–18h30	05h00–18h33	18–34
Rain-dependent plants flowering, making landscape very colourful; marulas begin fruiting; combretums produce distinctive 4-winged pods	Animals spread over wider areas because of water availability, dung beetles prevalent; lesser spotted eagles arrive	05h30–18h30	05h19–18h52	18–34
Plants at their most nutritious; jackal-berries fruiting; numerous pans form on eastern grasslands	Waterbuck breeding; animals dispersed over wide areas; many nursery herds close to water	05h30–18h30	05h42–18h39	18–33
Vegetation dense; water plentiful; grasslands in full seed; baobabs begin fruiting	Kudu and buffalo breeding peak	05h30–18h00	05h57–18h13	18–33
Vegetation dense, many trees bearing fruit or seeds; red bushwillow is striking as it changes colour; mopane pods out	Most animals in peak condition; game spotting difficult; impala, wildebeest and warthog rutting season	06h00–18h00	06h11–17h41	13–28
White syringas in flower, wide range of autumn colours; kiaats seeding; water holes in mopaneveld dry out	Impala rut continues; internal migrations of animals towards warmer areas; white-backed vultures breeding; wild dog breeding	06h00–17h30	06h26–17h29	13–28
Grass cover recedes and many trees lose leaves; mopane in drier areas begins turning brown	Game begins concentrating around water holes	06h00–17h30	06h40–17h13	9–26
Mopaneveld changes colour as mopane leaves change colour from green to brown; potato bush begins flowering – distinct smell	Many winter birds fly from highveld down to the Park (eg stonechat)	06h00–17h30	06h42–17h23	9–26

Climate

Summers in Kruger are hot and punctuated by rain while winters are cool and dry. This is because Kruger is located within a high-pressure weather belt that covers much of the southern African interior. In summer, a southward shift of tropical circulations pushes aside the high-pressure cells, allowing moist air to be drawn in from over the Indian Ocean. This ensures that some 80% of rain falls between October and March and that, for the rest of the year, Kruger's climate is sunny and dry. In the local Shangaan-speaking traditions, thunderstorms are sometimes referred to as "male" rain while longer, softer, gentler showers are called "female" rain.

Rainfall in Kruger varies considerably. The mean average is approximately 500mm a year, but this varies from an annual average of 760mm in the high-rainfall areas of the south, which fall within the "rain shadow" of the escarpment, and as low as 210mm in the drier flatlands of the north-east. There is a longer dry and wet cycle lasting between seven and 11 years.

Rainfall is not only geographically erratic in Kruger, but is subject to regional fluctuations of "wet" and "dry" cycles that alternate between seven and 11 years. At the height of these "wet" years, there can be extensive flooding – as was the case with the floods of February 2000, which

Mountains in the mist

A major influence on rainfall in Kruger is the escarpment to the south-west of the Park, the northernmost extension of the Drakensberg range which rings the South African highveld. These craggy, granitic mountains act as a rain trap. Cool, moist air blowing inland from the sea meets the warm, dry air of the interior over the escarpment. Great clouds form above the mountains and deposit most of their load in the "rain shadow" of the eastern slopes of the escarpment and the granitic foothills of south-western Kruger.

Africa Imagery

Mountains in the mist

saw many parts of the Park closed down for several months. Climatic cycles are not predictable – Kruger's two worst droughts came within 10 years of each other. The first was during the early 1980s, the second in the early 1990s. On 26 February 1992, the temperature at Shingwedzi was 48°c, the highest ever recorded in the Park.

The other climatic determinant of the Park is its relatively low altitude. Most of the eastern plains are about 200m above sea level, while the altitude spikes to more

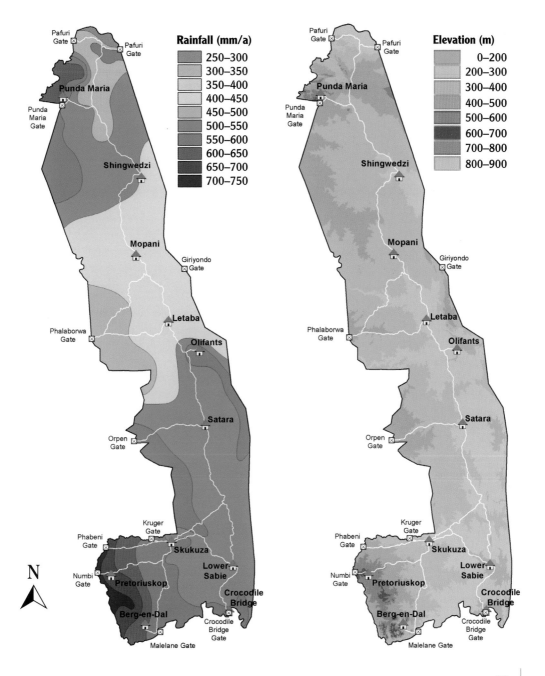

Terrapin

Nigel Dennis

than 800m in the south-western foothills between Pretoriuskop and Malelane. This, in part, accounts for Kruger's frost-free, subtropical climate. Within this temperate environment, there are a number of microclimatic zones that cut across the geological bands, contributing to the Park's incredible diversity of flora and fauna.

Average daily temperatures range from a maximum of 30°c (January) to 23°c (July), but extreme conditions can see temperatures soaring up to 46°c in summer and 35°c in winter. Average minimum temperatures are 18°c at night (January) and 8°c (July). Again, extreme conditions have seen temperatures fall as low as 7°c in January and -4°c in July. Frost occurs only very occasionally and is restricted to low-lying areas.

Climate shifts

Twenty million years ago, Kruger – like much of the African interior – was a more tropical environment. This was during the Miocene, a much wetter environment, dominated by dense rain forests and animals suited to an arboreal existence. However, from about 6 million years ago, global cooling resulted in a drier African climate, leading to a dramatic expansion in grasslands and the extinction of many forest-dependent animal species. This changing environment, described as a "species pump" by Kruger scientist Johan du Toit, saw a rapid evolutionary expansion of new grazing species and the predators that fed on them. Most of these savanna specialists – such as zebra, buffalo and lion – evolved in the grasslands outside of Africa and followed their habitat into new areas. Arid conditions meant that sea levels were lower than they are today and the major continents were easily crossed by the land bridges that linked them. Most of the antelope one sees today in Kruger enter the African fossil record approximately 2,5 million years ago. The diverse nature of the savanna has been described as a mosaic woodland environment, and its nutritional value enables it to support more large animals than any other biome in the world. Eland are among the most generalist of the savanna mammals, adaptable to deserts and the tropics. Impala too are highly adaptable, able to switch between grazing and browsing according to where the nutrients are. Klipspringer are one of the most habitat-specific savanna animals, restricted to the few rocky outcrops in the lowveld.

Albert Froneman

Leopard

Geology

Kruger's geology is relatively straightforward. The most basic component is the igneous granite which is made up of some of the oldest rocks in the world, the Kaapvaal Craton, formed approximately 3,6 billion years ago. Most geologists agree that these ancient granites, which scientist Bob Scholes describes as "the bones of the earth", were part of the core of the ancient supercontinent Pangaea. Over hundreds of millions of years, movements in the earth's tectonic plates resulted in the break-up of Pangea into Laurasia in the northern hemisphere and the southern land mass of Gondwanaland, a giant continent broadly made up of Africa, South America, Australia, Madagascar, India and the Antarctic. Gondwanaland existed for approximately 400 million years. A volcanic extravaganza led to layers of lava being spewed out over the lowveld, capping the granites and shales with sediments of basalt and rhyolite.

The subsequent separation of Madagascar from the African mainland from about 135 million years ago caused massive tilting and geological upliftment in eastern southern Africa. This is how the magnificent Drakensberg range was formed. The northernmost part of this mountain range is the escarpment that divides the lowveld from the highveld. The tilting exposed the ancient geological sediments as horizontal

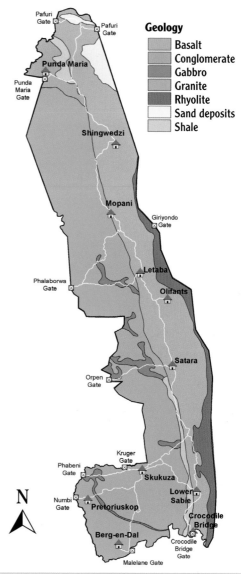

Geology
- Basalt
- Conglomerate
- Gabbro
- Granite
- Rhyolite
- Sand deposits
- Shale

N

🍃 **Geological Snapshot of Kruger**

Zone	Description	Type of Landscape
Granite/ Gneiss	Some of the oldest rocks in the world. Igneous, acidic, crystalline, slow weathering, relatively infertile, rich in silicone	Conical koppies, rolling hills, sandy soils of western Kruger
Ecca shales	Sediments from prehistoric swamplands. Layers contain fossils and coal. Shales are mixed with sandstone and erode fairly easily	Flattish plains with mixed grass
Basalt	Igneous, slow-eroding, acidic rock which supports shallow, rocky soils	Fertile, flattish plains of eastern Kruger; water pans
Rhyolite	Igneous, slow-eroding, acidic rock which supports shallow, rocky soils	The rocky hills of the Lebombo
Sandveld	Sandy, well-drained soils, protruding sandstone koppies	Rugged mountains around Punda Maria and Pafuri

The granite protrusions in south-western Kruger
are among the oldest rocks in the world

SANParks

Kruger's geological timescale

Timescale	Event
3,2 billion years ago	Granite formations
300 mya	Predominantly wet climate sees ecca shales get laid down on top of the granite
200 mya	Gondwanaland begins splitting up, intense volcanic activity lays down the basalt and rhyolite on top of the ecca shales
135 mya	Seismic tilt as southern Africa dips into the Indian Ocean
50 mya	Uplift during Miocene creates the Lebombo

bands that stretch from north to south across the lowveld.

The Lebombo, the ridge that runs on a north south axis on the western border of Kruger, was formed by a tectonic uplift approximately 50 million years ago. Generally, however, the past 100 million years have been free of geological cataclysm, and have allowed a more gradual shaping of the Kruger landscape, driven by water, wind and river erosion.

A twist in this geological tale comes in the form of the sandveld of Punda and Pafuri in the far north. The sands are geologically comparable to those of the Kalahari. Scientists believe the sandveld may have its origins in massive wind- and sandstorms that swept the subcontinent millions of years ago, carrying tons of soil into the sky and dumping them hundreds of kilometres away.

A good vantage point from which to appreciate the broad geology of Kruger is Mathekenyane Koppie, just south of Skukuza. Towering above the lowveld to the west is the escarpment, often shrouded by rain clouds. Below it are a series of tumbling granite foothills that extend across the south-western part of the Park. To the east is the younger geology – the flat plains of weathered basalt, and on the horizon the low, rhyolitic Lebombo Hills. To traverse the Park from west to east is to take a journey through geological time, from the evolution of some of the oldest rocks in the world (3,6 billion years old) to the most recent geological feature, the Lebombo (50 million years old).

Geology has a direct impact on game distribution. The older, more leached granitic soils of western Kruger are predominantly sourveld. They do not support the same number of animals as more nutritious sweetveld, which grows on the younger basalt plains that run in a broad band down eastern Kruger.

Human evolution in Africa

Africa is the birthplace of humankind. Every critical event in our physical evolution occurred on this continent before our ancestors inhabited the rest of the world.

Evolution is usually driven by changes in the physical environment. In this case, far-reaching climatic shifts between five and 7 million years ago resulted in the destruction of the great African forests and the rapid expansion of the savanna. Most scientists believe this led to a split in the primate lineage and the emergence of the apemen. Among them were the Australopithecines, who adapted to the emergent mixed woodlands by walking on two legs and utilising new food sources.

Of the many Australopithecine species that existed between three and 6 million years ago, one evolved into the genus *Homo*, some time between 2 and 3 million years ago. It is commonly accepted that, after 2 million years ago, a series of outward migrations saw *Homo erectus* populate the rest of the world. Since then, there have been several species of *Homo*, leading to the appearance, some 200 000 years ago, of *Homo sapiens sapiens*, the species that embraces all people on earth today. There is strong evidence that *Homo sapiens sapiens* evolved first in Africa.

Colin Bell

An early Stone-Age hand-axe found near the Luvuvhu River in northern Kruger

Kruger's grasslands – key to the savanna food chain

Grass is the foundation of the savanna food chain, with all animal species dependent on its nutrition either directly or indirectly. About one-tenth of the earth's 10 000 or so grass species occur in southern Africa, many of which are found in Kruger. Grasses are found to a greater or lesser extent in all the major Kruger habitats (see page 30–31). Simplistically, there are three types of grassland in Kruger – sweetveld, sourveld and mixed veld. Animals are most attracted to the palatable sweetveld, which is found mostly on the basaltic zone that runs down eastern Kruger. Typical Kruger sweetveld grasses are blue buffalo grass (*Cenchrus ciliaris*), finger grass (*Digitaria eriantha*) and stinking grass (*Bothriochloa radicans*). Grasses associated with sourveld are fibrous species such as fine thatching grass (*Hyparrhenia filipendula*) and yellow thatching grass (*Hyparrhenia dissoluta*).

Central grasslands
Albert Froneman

Veld type	Characteristics	Where in Kruger
Sweetveld	Most nutritious grazing because it occurs on rich soils with minimal leaching; palatable through most of the year and favoured by the main grazers; prone to overgrazing but recovers quickly	Low-lying, frost-free areas with less than 500mm of rain a year; mostly the eastern half of Kruger protruding west around Ship Mountain; Phabeni and Orpen
Sourveld	Poor in nutrients and often unpalatable because of granitic soils leached over millions of years; grazers eat it only in summer; slow to recover if overgrazed	Higher altitudes with more than 600mm of rain; western half of Kruger, particularly the mixed woodlands on granite and the south-western foothills
Mixed veld	Has both sweet and sourveld characteristics; game-carrying capacity is not as high as sweetveld but still popular among grazers	Transition zone between sweet- and sourveld; sweeter grazing is usually in the watercourses while the sour grazing is on the higher contours; occurs in a loose band running north to south through the mixed woodlands of central Kruger

NORTHERN SANDVELD

This complicated and diverse habitat is restricted to the far north of Kruger – around Punda Maria and west of the tar road to Pafuri, the Luvuvhu and Limpopo river valleys and a pocket along the north-eastern Lebombo. The sandveld has sandy, well-drained soils supporting a range of vegetation with no particular dominant species. Characteristic trees of the sandveld include the syringas – white kirkia (*Kirkia acuminata*) and mountain kirkia (*Kirkia wilmsii*), pod mahogany (*Afzelia quansensis*), nyala (*Xanthocercis zambesiaca*), southern lala-palm (*Hyphaene natalensis*), fever tree (*Acacia xanthophloea*) tree mopane (*Colophospermum mopane*), and, of course, the mighty baobab (*Adansonia digitata*).

MOPANEVELD

Mopaneveld is the most dominant ecosystem in Kruger, covering over half the Park's surface area. It stretches northwards from the Timbavati and Olifants rivers to the Luvuvhu valley and then in swathes up to the Limpopo. The mopane tree (*Colophospermum mopane*) is found in three main forms in Kruger – mopane woodlands (mostly the north-west of the Park) which are generally found on granite and gneiss, mopane shrubveld (mostly the central northern plains and the north-east) which is associated with basalt, and mopane thickets (restricted to the Punda Maria area) which are on ecca shales. Within the mopaneveld there are other tree species – particularly the bushwillows (*Combretum species*), knob-thorns (*Acacia nigrescens*), tambotis (*Spirostachys africana*) and apple-leaf (*Philenoptera violacea*) trees and shrubs.

SAVANNA GRASSLANDS

The eastern sweetveld plains that stretch south from the Olifants, through Satara and Tshokwane down to Lower Sabie are archetypal savanna grassland. They are home to large grazing herds and their predators. The broad expanse of savanna has a variety of palatable grasses such as blue buffalo grass (*Cenchrus ciliaris*), finger grass (*Digitaria eriantha*) and stinking grass (*Bothriochloa radicans*). There are large tracts of grassland with stunted knob-thorn acacia (*Acacia nigrescens*) punctuated by large trees, which are often restricted to the drainage lines. The most common trees in the central grassland are the knob-thorn, the umbrella acacia (*Acacia tortilis*), marula (*Sclerocarya birrea*), ebony jackal-berry (*Diospyros mespiliformis*) and red bushwillow (*Combretum apiculatum*). The open plains have dark, clay soils which are separated from the underpinning basalt by a layer of calcrete. This geology lends itself to water retention, so during the rainy season, vleis and pans form quite quickly along the drainage lines and remain with water well into the dry season.

MIXED BROADLEAF WOODLAND

The mixed broadleaf woodlands dominate large tracts of central western Kruger and the rolling ridges south of Skukuza. The main trees are the bushwillow or combretum species – red bushwillow (*Combretum apiculatum*), russet bushwillow (*Combretum hereroense*), large-fruited bushwillow (*Combretum zeyheri*) and the leadwood (*Combretum imberbe*) – as well as large marulas (*Sclerocarya birrea*), magic guarri (*Euclea divinorum*), pockets of knob-thorn acacia (*Acacia nigrescens*) and round-leaved bloodwood (*Pterocarpus rotundifolius*), which is also known as teak. The mixed woodland landscape is one of low, rolling hills on a geological bed of granite and/or gneiss. The upper contours consist of coarse, sandy soils with mixed grasses, while the footslopes and valleys between these hills consist of clay soils which can support large specimens of tamboti (*Spirostachys africana*), sycamore fig (*Ficus sycomorus*) and sausage trees (*Kigelia africana*). Within this mixed woodland there are pockets of grazing that sometimes open up into extensive, considerable grasslands, particularly around pans. The sweeter grasses generally are on the lower contours.

Brett Hilton-Barber

THORN THICKETS

Within the mixed broadleaf woodlands and along the Sabie and Crocodile river valleys are extensive thorn thickets. These can be almost impenetrable in some areas and are the favoured habitat of the rare black rhino. The thorn thickets consist mostly of acacias – particularly Delagoa acacia (*Acacia welwitschii*) knob-thorn (*Acacia nigrescens*), scented-pod acacia (*Acacia nilotica*), umbrella acacia (*Acacia tortilis*) and brack thorn (*Acacia robusta*). Within the thorny tangle of acacias are small-leaved sickle-bush (*Dichrostachys cinerea*), magic guarri (*Euclea divinorum*) and buffalo thorn (*Ziziphus mucronata*). The thorn thickets are usually associated with gabbro or gneiss.

Brett Hilton-Barber

LEBOMBO

The dry and rugged Lebombo range forms the eastern border of Kruger. The smallish, scattered rocks on the hills are mostly rhyolite which gives them their distinctly pinkish hue. The soils of the Lebombo are shallow and stony, and as this is one of the driest parts of Kruger, it is dominated by drought-resistant plants such as succulents and euphorbias – particularly the deadliest candelabra euphorbia (*Euphorbia cooperi*) and the naboom (*Euphorbia ingens*) which both have highly poisonous latex. White kirkia (*kirkia acuminata*), thickets of Lebombo ironwood (*Androstachys johnsonii*) and large-leaved rock figs (*Ficus abutilifolia*) are found on the hill crests, while the lower slopes have knob-thorn (*Acacia nigrescens*), raisin bushes (*Grewia species*), purple-pod cluster-leafs (*Terminalia prunioides*) and the ubiquitous bushwillow species. Marulas (*Sclerocarya birrea*) and round-leaved bloodwood (*Pterocarpus rotundifolius*) mark the transition to the basalt flatlands.

SOUTH-WESTERN FOOTHILLS

The foothills enjoy the highest rainfall in the Park, and often take the shape of dramatic granite outcrops, particularly around Pretoriuskop in the west and Berg-en-dal and Malelane in the south. The vegetation is mostly mixed woodland with sour grasses such as fine thatching grass (*Hyparrhenia filipendula*) and yellow thatching grass (*Hyparrhenia dissoluta*). Trees particularly associated with the Pretoriuskop area are silver cluster-leaf (*Terminalia sericea*) and kiaat bloodwood (*Pterocarpus angolensis*) while the Berg-en-dal area has most of the broadleaf woodland trees such as the bushwillow species and magic guarri (*Euclea divinorum*). There are large-leaved rock figs (*Ficus abutilifolia*) and mountain kirkia (*Kirkia wilmsii*) among the rocky outcrops. The grazing gets sweeter as the altitude drops and the soils are more claylike in the contour lines where sycamore figs (*Ficus sycomorus*), tamboti (*Spirostachys africana*), and ebony jackal-berry (*Diospyros mespiliformis*) thrive. There are often rare plant species because of the high rainfall and most of the drives in this habitat offer wonderful views over the lowveld.

Brett Hilton-Barber

RIVERINE BUSH

Riverine forests are found in varying degrees of intensity along all seven major rivers which bisect Kruger – the Limpopo, the Luvuvhu, the Shingwedzi, Letaba, Olifants, Sabie and Crocodile rivers. In addition it occurs on the banks of the major perennial rivers such as the Timbavati, the N'waswitsontso and the Biyamiti. The best examples of riverine forest are associated with the alluvial flood plains along the Shingwedzi, Luvuvhu and Limpopo rivers. This is because successive flood dumping has led to deeper soils which are more favourable to forest development. Trees of the riverine forests include the sycamore fig (*Ficus sycomorus*), leadwood (*Combretum imberbe*), ebony jackal-berry (*Diospyros mespiliformis*), Natal mahogany (*Trichilia emetica*), tamboti (*Spirostachys africana*), weeping boer-bean (*Schotia brachypetala*), apple-leaf (*Philenoptera violacea*) and nyala (*Xanthocercis zambesiaca*).

Long-tail cassia tree in flower

Albert Froneman

Kruger's trees

Kruger is a tree-lover's heaven. In all the regions, barring the mopane shrubveld, there are extraordinary trees – some 336 species in all. The riverine forests in the north of the Park and the granitic foothills of the south-west are home to some of the most magnificent specimens, while some of the baobabs north of the Luvuvhu River may be more than 4 000 years old.

Kruger has hardy trees – species that do well can withstand the vicissitudes of drought, over-browsing and periodic veld fires. Their distribution across the Park is primarily a consequence of the underlying geology, soil types and amount of rainfall. Many of Kruger's trees and shrubs have medicinal properties that have been used for hundreds of years by African communities. Traditional healers still make use of many of these plants in treating a variety of physiological and psychological disorders. Here are some of Kruger's most common trees, the animals associated with them and their medicinal qualities and other uses.

"Trees convey a sense of permanence and stability in our common experience . . . they have played a central role in Man's rituals from time immemorial and sacred groves, whether hidden in the depths of forests or growing prominently on some significant hillside, are as much part of the African landscape as anywhere else in the world." –Natural history writer Peter Borchert

Brett Hilton-Barber

MOPANE (*Colophospermum mopane*)

Characteristics
Deciduous tree that dominates the north; grows in tree, shrub and intermediate form; unmistakable "butterfly" leaves; mopaneveld becomes golden in winter

Animal associations
Elephant browse leaves and bark; other animals eat fallen leaves, lots of insects which attract baboons and certain birds

Traditional medicinal and other uses
Wood extracts used to cure venereal disease; good firewood

Brett Hilton-Barber

RED BUSHWILLOW (*Combretum apiculatum*)

Characteristics
Deciduous tree that dominates the south; grows in tree and shrub form; thin pointed leaves; four-winged pods visible in autumn and winter

Animal associations
New growth very attractive to browsers in spring, particularly giraffe, elephant, impala and kudu

Traditional medicinal and other uses
Good for furniture; leaves used in medicine for stomach disorders

Brett Hilton-Barber

KNOB-THORN ACACIA (*Acacia nigrescens*)

Characteristics
Deciduous tree that produces a magnificent creamy-yellow flower that announces the arrival of spring in the lowveld; knob-thorns pronounced on younger trees

Animal associations
Leaves and pods form the main diet for giraffe, elephants, kudu, impala and steenbok; giraffe and baboons love the flowers; many raptors use the bigger knob-thorns for nesting

Traditional medicinal and other uses
Used to make furniture, lightning conductors and fighting sticks

Briza

TAMBOTI (*Spirostachys africana*)

Characteristics
Semi-deciduous to evergreen that grows up to 18m; dark, rough bark that forms little rectangles on the straight trunk; narrow canopy; often grows in stands in brakwater areas

Animal associations
Porcupines are very fond of tamboti bark, especially in winter; leaves are browsed by black rhino, elephants, giraffe, eland, kudu, nyala, impala and bushbuck; fallen fruits are eaten by guineafowl and monkeys

Traditional medicinal and other uses
Poisonous latex used in fishing – dropped into pools to stun fish to make them easier to catch; never braai over tamboti wood as it can cause severe stomach pains; small amounts of the latex are used to treat stomach pains and diarrhoea and dysentery; sought-after wood for furniture

Brett Hilton-Barber

APPLE-LEAF (*Philenoptera violacea*)

Characteristics
Deciduous and semi-deciduous, drought-resistant tree with distinctive green-grey leathery leaves; beautiful lilac flowers in spring

Animal associations
Reliable winter-browsing tree for giraffe, elephant, kudu, impala, nyala; eland and Lichtenstein's hartebeest; also known as the "rain tree" because the ground around the tree is often damp – this is the result of falling secretions from aphids

Traditional medicinal and other uses
Roots are used in a variety of treatments – from curing colds to treating snakebites; wood used for fencing

Brett Hilton-Barber

MARULA (*Sclerocarya birrea*)

Characteristics
Deciduous tree that fruits from November to March; dappled bark makes it easy to identify

Animal associations
Favoured by wide variety of browsers, especially elephant and kudu, impala, baboons and monkeys; zebra eat fallen fruit

Traditional medicinal and other uses
Considered a sacred tree used in fertility rites; bark used in the treatment of malaria; potent alcohol can be brewed from fruit which is tasty and rich in Vitamin C

Briza

KIAAT BLOODWOOD (*Pterocarpus angolensis*)

Characteristics
Deciduous tree with distinct broad pods visible from late summer to mid-winter; yellow flowers in spring; rough dark grey bark; can grow to 30m

Animal associations
Elephant and kudu eat leaves, baboons and vervet monkeys browse on the pods and seeds

Traditional medicinal and other uses
Widely used for wood carvings and furniture; sap used to treat skin cuts and wounds and to treat eye cataracts; roots are used in concoction to treat blackwater fever and malaria; ashes of roots are used for asthma and tuberculosis; a liquid infusion of the bark is for headaches, stomach aches and piles

Brett Hilton-Barber

BAOBAB (*Adansonia digitata*)

Characteristics
Unmistakable deciduous tree with huge branches that appear root-like; brief flowering season in spring

Animal associations
Bark eaten by elephant; antelope chew on spongy wood to quench thirst; bats are part pollination agents

Traditional medicinal and other uses
Bark and leaves used to treat dysentery, malaria; drink made from fruit pulp is used to cure urinary problems and mild diarrhoea; leaves used to reduce fever; powdered seeds are a hiccup remedy for children

Brett Hilton-Barber

SYCAMORE FIG (*Ficus sycomorus*)

Characteristics
Semi-deciduous tree with yellowish bark; roots usually exposed; grows up to 35m with spreading crown

Animal associations
Browsed by a wide range of animals, including elephant, giraffe, kudu, bushbuck, nyala, impala and baboon; fallen fruit are eaten by bushpigs and warthogs

Traditional medicinal and other uses
Used as the base block for making fire by rubbing wood; mixture of bark and latex used to cure coughs and chest ailments; inner bark makes good rope; fruit is edible

Briza

EBONY JACKAL-BERRY (*Diospyros mespiliformis*)

Characteristics
Semi-deciduous to evergreen riverine tree; grows up to 25m; has dense crown and upright trunk with grey, fissured bark; flowers in early summer; fruits during winter

Animal associations
Fallen fruit eaten by jackal, kudu, impala and nyala; baboons and monkeys feed on fruit on tree; attracts lots of birds like green pigeons and brown-headed parrots

Traditional medicinal and other uses
Fruit used to treat internal parasites; extracts of bark and leaves believed to have antibiotic properties; leaves and bark used to disinfect wounds

SILVER CLUSTER-LEAF (*Terminalia sericea*)

Characteristics
Deciduous tree with hairy, silvery leaves; rough grey bark; spreading crown

Animal associations
Generally low nutritional value but browsers love young leaves; elephant and giraffe sometimes eat the wood; wildebeest known to eat fallen leaves

Traditional medicinal and other uses
Roots used to cure diarrhoea and treat pneumonia; extracts of bark used to cure poisoning and treat diabetes

FEVER TREE ACACIA (*Acacia xanthophloea*)

Characteristics
Deciduous and semi-deciduous tall tree with distinctive yellow-green bark

Animal associations
Elephants eat leaves and branches; baboons and monkeys eat flowers; trees often have weavers' nests

Traditional medicinal and other uses
Bark used for bringing down fever and treating eye infections

LEADWOOD BUSHWILLOW (*Combretum imberbe*)

Characteristics
Deciduous tree with extremely hard wood; recognisable by pale grey bark and location along drainage lines; four-winged pods in autumn

Animal associations
Leaves eaten by elephant, kudu, giraffe, and impala

Traditional medicinal and other uses
Revered as a mystical tree in indigenous folklore; leaves and flowers used to relieve coughs; good firewood

WEEPING BOER-BEAN (*Schotia brachypetala*)

Characteristics
Semi-deciduous to evergreen; up to 25m tall; dense clusters of bright red flowers from the start of spring to early summer

Animal associations
Baboons, kudu, giraffe and black rhino eat leaves; baboons also drink nectar from the flowers, which also attract lots of birds and insects

Traditional medicinal and other uses
A "morning after" tree – extracts of bark used for treating hangovers and heartburn

LARGE-LEAVED ROCK FIG (*Ficus abutilifolia*)

Characteristics
Deciduous tree with yellowish bark found on mountain outcrops; roots often visible across the rock face; grows up to 10m

Animal associations
Fruit eaten by baboons, monkeys, bushbuck, bushpigs, nyala and duiker

Traditional medicinal and other uses
Bark extract is a strengthening tonic for men

"The thorns of the tree Ziziphus mucronata *(Buffalo thorn) are spaced along the length of every branch in pairs. One of the pair points robustly outward and forward while the other curves back and inwards in the opposite direction. The Nguni African legend says the thorns tell us something about ourselves – that we must look ahead to the future …*
but we must never forget where we have come from."

Ian McCallum (*Ecological Intelligence* Published by Africa Geographic Books)

The animals

In essence, nature is a myriad of conflicting and collaborating relationships between different species of plants and animals. Almost every life form occupies some point in something else's food chain and each animal has come to dominate a particular niche in the environment where it can best get its food. The plant diversity of Kruger is the foundation for its rich animal life. That diversity is ensured by insects, which are themselves an important food source. Scientists have found that the biomass of insects per hectare in Kruger (approximately 2,5 tons) to be roughly equal to that of larger mammals. Some of the animal species you will see have been around long enough to outlive most of their enemies (aside from humankind). The ancestors of birds and crocodiles survived the mass extinction at the end of the Cretaceous (65 million years ago), which marked the end of the age of reptiles and the rise of mammal dominance.

The animal life of Kruger today is largely a response to widespread climate change that led to the aridification of Africa at the end of the Miocene, 6 million years ago (see page 24). Forest-dependent species gave way to those animals that could adapt to wooded grasslands. These changes favoured a collective approach to survival rather than an individualistic one, and by implication, the best communicators lived longer. Herd behaviour is often derided as a concept but it's a very succesful evolutionary adaptation.

The relationship between animals that we humans most identify with is that between the hunter and the hunted. An indicator of where a mammal stands in the food chain is in its eyes. Hunters' eyes are at the front of their heads so they can focus on their prey; the hunted have eyes on the sides of their heads so they can scan the widest area for danger.

Hunters, of course, range across the genera – the pied kingfisher or the African rock python, for instance, are formidable hunters in their own environments.

Spotted hyaena

Brett Hilton-Barber

> In the grasslands there is safety in numbers. Savanna grazers tend towards herds as a security measure. This is also why there are often mixed herds of grazers. The more sets of eyes, ears and nostrils there are, the less chance of being caught unawares. The more animals there are, the lower the individual risk profile. Impala, zebra, wildebeest, elephant and buffalo all evolved into herd animals with collective defence systems. The hunters – humans included – responded by developing collaborative hunting techniques.

Albert Froneman

Elephant

Contrary to popular belief, in most situations, hyaenas hunt more than they scavenge. Research has also demonstrated that lions steal more from hyaenas than hyaenas steal from lions.

Wilderness Safaris

Hyaenas robbing lioness of a kill

The hunters

Kruger is probably most famous for its large carnivores, the big flesh-eating cats (lion, leopard and cheetah) and dogs (hyaena and wild dogs). These carnivores evolved from a mongoose-like ancestor some 40 million years ago and include in their lineage domestic dogs and cats.

Carnivores became particularly dominant in Africa during the past 3 million years as climate changes led to the development of large swathes of savanna grassland over the continent. The opening of grassland led to the arrival of many new species of animals, particularly large herds of grazers that depended on safety in numbers rather than their ability to hide from predators.

Predators, in turn, relied more on collaborative hunting to generate a surplus of food. How the surplus was disposed

created hierarchies and strengthened social bonds. Because there was more food than the parents could consume, carnivore offspring could remain part of the family unit for a longer time, thereby increasing their chances of survival.

The dominant large mammal predators in Kruger are lions, hyaenas, leopards, cheetah and wild dogs, each of which occupy slightly different habitats or ecological niches that are suited to their food acquisition needs. They are found throughout the Park, but are more easily seen in the game-rich grasslands of central and south-eastern Kruger.

According to scientist and natural history writer Bob Scholes, who has studied the relationship between the hunters and the hunted, these predators kill a combined total of approximately 76 000 larger animals a year in Kruger.

Predators

Lion (*Panthera leo*)
Favoured prey: Wildebeest, buffalo, giraffe, zebra, porcupines and warthogs
Estimated numbers in Kruger: 2 000
Hunting techniques: Hunt collectively and individually, one animal sets up the charge and drives the prey towards other members of the pride who then pull off the ambush; lions are also effective scavengers
Where best to see them in Kruger: Central Kruger around Satara, also around Skukuza, Lower Sabie and Crocodile Bridge

Hyaena (*Hyaena brunnea* and *Crocuta crocuta*)
Favoured prey: Impala, wildebeest, waterbuck and kudu
Estimated numbers in Kruger: 2 000
Hunting techniques: High-stamina hunters that will collectively isolate their victim, chase it and disembowel it; they are also effective scavengers
Where best to see them in Kruger: Throughout Kruger but mostly in central savanna and around Skukuza

Leopard (*Panthera pardus*)
Favoured prey: Impala, bushbuck, reedbuck, waterbuck, monkeys, jackals, francolins, snakes and insects
Estimated numbers in Kruger: 1 000
Hunting techniques: Hunts mostly at night although leopards will seize any opportunity for a kill; solitary hunter; drags its prey into trees
Where best to see them in Kruger: Riverine forest throughout the Park; highest populations are along the Sabie River, also sometimes on rocky outcrops

Cheetah (*Acinonyx jubatus*)
Favoured prey: Impala, kudu, waterbuck and reedbuck
Estimated numbers in Kruger: 200
Hunting techniques: Stalks its prey to within a short distance and then charges at it, using its advantage of speed. Eats quickly because it cannot guard carcass against scavengers
Where best to see them in Kruger: Mostly open savanna woodland in central Kruger, also common around Lower Sabie and Crocodile River in the south

African wild dog (*Lycaon pictus*)
Favoured prey: Impala, kudu, waterbuck and reedbuck and other small game
Estimated numbers in Kruger: 400
Hunting techniques: A pack will try to isolate an animal from the herd and then chase it in relays, snapping at the animal until it is exhausted and falls from shock or loss of blood
Where best to see them in Kruger: Mixed woodlands and open savanna throughout Kruger but more common in the south-west

Nigel Dennis

Lion

Nigel Dennis

Lions

One of Africa's most unforgettable experiences is hearing the roar of a lion at night. When *Ingonyama* (Swazi) or *Nghala* (Shangaan) announces his presence with a deep roar that reverberates through the dark bush, everything within a five-kilometre radius pauses to take note.

A thousand years ago, they roamed as far afield as southern Europe, the Middle East and Asia, but they are now found mainly in Africa and are generally restricted to the bigger game reserves.

Lions have always had an association with royalty and leadership. Their power is reflected in their impressive size and the fact that their lifestyles allow them to sleep a lot – up to 18 hours a day. They are awesome animals, with males weighing up to 225kg and females up to 150kg. The lion's average lifespan in the bush is probably around 15 years.

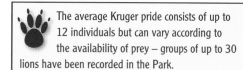

The average Kruger pride consists of up to 12 individuals but can vary according to the availability of prey – groups of up to 30 lions have been recorded in the Park.

Lions are the biggest, and most social, of the African cats, living communally in prides. Pride leadership often shifts between several individual animals – male and female – but the social structure of the pride hinges around the bond between related lionesses, who collaborate in all tasks, from raising cubs to hunting. Male lions come and go – often in spectacular battles over territory or individual dominance – but the pride cohesion remains unaffected, firmly under female control.

Lions favour open woodlands and thick scrub, the type of landscape that allows them to get as close to their prey as possible without being seen. In Kruger, the best chance of lion sightings is where the big

Lions at dusk

Heinrich van den Berg

41

Lions hunt mostly at night

Heinrich van den Berg

game herds are – in the grasslands around Satara and Lower Sabie and the woodland and thorn thickets around Crocodile Bridge and Skukuza. As a rule, they hunt mostly at night and rest during the day but are often active at dawn and dusk and on cooler days. During the day they rest in thorn thickets, often near water holes.

Lions are believed to feed every three or four days, and need on average between 5kg and 7kg of meat a day. But they can go without food for more than a week and then tear into prey, eating up to 50kg of meat at a time – that's almost a quarter of the animal's body weight. Former Kruger Park information officer PF Fourie says that, in his experience, each lion in Kruger kills approximately 15 animals a year.

Lions hunt either collaboratively or by themselves. Collaborative hunting usually involves the males approaching the intended prey upwind with the intention of driving it towards lionesses hiding in the bush downwind. Lions are not as fast as most of their prey so they rely heavily on the element of surprise when hunting. They will attempt to get to within 30m of their prey before charging. They don't have the inclination for a long chase and will not pursue their prey very far if the first attack fails.

In a successful hunt, the prey is knocked off balance, dragged down and then killed with a bite to the back of the neck or the throat. In some cases, a kill can be a bloody, drawn out procedure. Buffalo have been known to fend off lion attacks for hours before succumbing to loss of blood and energy. The strongest male lion will eat first, followed by other members of the pride. Lionesses will feed themselves first, with cubs getting the scraps.

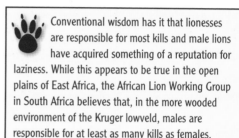 Conventional wisdom has it that lionesses are responsible for most kills and male lions have acquired something of a reputation for laziness. While this appears to be true in the open plains of East Africa, the African Lion Working Group in South Africa believes that, in the more wooded environment of the Kruger lowveld, males are responsible for at least as many kills as females.

Lion and waterbuck

Albert Froneman & Brett Hilton-Barber

popular belief, lions are not so fond of impala.

Kruger researchers suggest male and female lions may also have different prey preferences, with males being more disposed towards hunting buffalo, while lionesses prefer zebra or wildebeest. Another fact not commonly appreciated is that lions are not just hunters, but scavengers as well, often chasing smaller predators – like cheetah – off their kills. In some instances, up to 50% of a lion's diet can come from scavenging rather than hunting live prey.

During periods of drought, lions sometimes go on a killing spree when they come across herds of weak animals. During the particularly bad drought of 1964, a pride of lions killed 15 buffalo near Punda Maria – far more than they could have eaten.

What do lions eat? The short answer is quite a lot. In Kruger, lions have a broad diet with 37 animal species on the menu, including ostriches, quelea nestlings, tortoises and small crocodiles. Their preference is for buffalo, giraffe, zebra and wildebeest among the bigger animals, and porcupine and warthog as smaller game.

Natural history artist Charles Astley Maberly – who rode through the Park on his bicycle sketching the wildlife in the 1920s – said that, in his experience, lions had a particular preference for waterbuck. This was confirmed by a 1960s study by former Kruger Chief Ranger Tol Pienaar who measured the kill rate of lions in the Park against the relative abundance of particular prey. He found that, although lion killed relatively few giraffe, giraffe meat accounted for almost a third of the average lion's diet. His study also found that, contrary to

The territorial behaviour of lions is complicated because prides split up and re-unite, and hunting grounds shift as the seasons change and the game moves around. At any one time, a pride's territory in Kruger measures approximately 10 square kilometres. Territories may be defended vigorously by both males and females, but there are instances when prides share the same overlapping hunting zone yet deliberately avoid confrontation.

Clashes occur between prides when game migrations force lions to move beyond their territories in search of food,

 Lions sometimes become the victims of their intended prey. In Kruger, there have been instances in which lions have been killed by giraffe, buffalo, kudu, snakes and even porcupines.

or when nomadic males challenge pride hierarchies. Fights can take the form of symbolic aggression displays and/or ferocious physical clashes that often result in the death of one or more participants. If the challengers win, the defeated males are expelled and, in turn, become nomads themselves. The lionesses accept the new regime. Usually the conquering males kill all the cubs of the conquered pride. Within days of this infanticide the females come into oestrus and are ready to raise a new litter of the conquerer's cubs.

Scientists believe that territorial challenges are good for the survival of the species – they ensure diversity in the gene pool and dominance of the strongest genetic characteristics.

Lionesses typically give birth to litters of between two and four cubs. They are kept hidden in the bush for about six weeks. During this time, the lioness hunts exclusively for her cubs. Males provide no help. By the time they are two years old, cubs will have learnt to hunt for themselves. At this time, male cubs are expelled from the pride while females are nurtured within it. These young males often form groupings of nomadic bachelors and either find new territories or challenge males in existing prides, and so the cyclical struggle for dominance goes on.

Lions have accounted for fewer than 20 attacks on humans in Kruger's century-old history. However, they are probably more dangerous now than they have ever been. Former Kruger head ranger Bruce Bryden believes that lion attitudes towards humans changed significantly after the political turmoil of the 1970s when many Mozambican refugees crossed Kruger on foot. Since then, he believes, lions have increasingly lost their fear of humans and consider them fair prey.

🐾 Anatomy of a lion kill

Lions hunt either alone or in prides. In collaborative hunts, it is usually the lioness who initiates the kill. Lions stalk their prey and, when close enough, attempt a short charge on their prey, trying either to pounce on their target or knock it over. They then kill their victim by breaking its neck or suffocating it by clamping their jaws around its throat.

The stomach is usually the easiest point of entry into the carcass, and this is the route most often taken by lions. It also gives them direct access to some of the most nutritious parts of the body, such as the kidneys and liver of the prey. Lions usually rest after an initial feed, lying a short way away from the carcass so that they can still defend their kill against scavengers.

Lion with a kill
Wilderness Safaris

Lappet-faced vulture
Michael Poliza

In a short time vultures are certain to begin to arrive. The first are usually the white-backed vultures and then come the lappet-faced and others. Scavengers like hyaenas and jackals will be attracted by the vulture activity and will patiently wait at a safe distance until the lions have had their fill. It can take over 24 hours before lions abandon their carcass and spectacular fights may occur among scavengers for the last scraps of food.

Leopard with a kill

Nigel Dennis

LEOPARDS

Leopards are the least social – and perhaps the most beautiful – of the African big cats. They usually keep to themselves, lurking in dense riverine bush or around rocky koppies, emerging to hunt late in the afternoon or at night.

Ingwe is a graceful animal with an elongated body, relatively short legs and a long tail. After the lion, it is the next-biggest African cat with an average body mass of between 60kg and 70kg, standing about two-thirds of a metre tall at the shoulder. Leopards in the wild may live up to 15 years. Unlike the lion, the leopard is a silent creature, only occasionally emitting a cough-like call.

The leopard's hunting technique is to either ambush its prey or to stalk it. In either instance, it tries to get as close as possible to its target. It then makes a brief and explosive charge (up to 60km/h), pouncing on its prey and dispatching it with a bite to the neck. Leopards do not have

the aptitude to chase their quarry over any kind of distance and will give up if the initial element of surprise is lost and the intended victim gets away.

Leopards are capable of carrying animals heavier than themselves and will often drag their prey into the fork of a tree several metres off the ground. This tree "lardering" protects the carcass against scavengers and allows a few days of undisturbed feeding.

These big cats eat a variety of food, from wildebeest to fish, but most of their diet comes in the form of antelope. In Kruger, impala appear to be the mainstay of the leopard.

Baboons and leopards appear to be ancient enemies. Leopards will often stalk baboons sleeping in the trees at night, and

 Leopards can survive for long periods without drinking, satisfying all their moisture needs from their prey.

Leopard

Heinrich van den Berg

Leopard and a baboon

Albert Froneman & Nigel Dennis

try to carry off one of the troop. There has been a case recorded in which a leopard that tried to attack a baboon in broad daylight was torn to pieces by the rest of the troop, which quickly came to the shrieking primate's defence.

Researchers believe that each individual leopard accounts for approximately 20 kills a year in Kruger. Leopards eat on average about a third of the carcass of the animal they kill and this works out at roughly 400kg of meat per leopard each year. This means that leopards probably need just over a kilogram of meat a day.

A leopard will often lick the fur off the carcass of its prey before it feeds, starting with the thighs or the chest.

Leopards are highly adaptable creatures, capable of living in semi-desert conditions as well as dense subtropical bush. Their territories can also vary in size from 10 square kilometres – which is probably the norm in Kruger – to several hundred square kilometres. The animals scratch trees and use urine to mark their turf. A male will defend his territory against other males, but will share territory with females.

Male and female leopards spend only a brief time together while they are mating and then go their separate ways. The female will then raise the cubs on her own.

In Kruger, the best place to see leopards is along the riverine bush of the Sabie River.

> Leopards can make extraordinary kills. In one case a leopard climbed into a tree carrying a 125-kg juvenile giraffe, while in 1981 a baby elephant skeleton was found in the fork of a tree, presumably killed by a leopard.

The difference between leopards and cheetahs

	Leopard	Cheetah
Physique	Robustly built with more powerful appearance; bigger head and more muscular limbs	Slender build with small head and an elongated body; slightly dog-like appearance
Markings	Bigger rosettes rather than spots; no "tear mark" stripes down the face	Smaller spots; distinctive "tear lines" down either side of the nose
Hunting techniques	Ambush or stalk prey, pouncing when close enough	Stalk prey and then make a 60m to 100m charge, knocking the fleeing animal off balance
Claws	Retractable	Retractable as a cub but non-retractable as an adult
Tail	Shorter	Longer, heavier
Habitat	Dense bush and wooded koppies	Open savanna

Leopard

Cheetah

Nigel Dennis

Cheetah

Heinrich van den Berg

CHEETAHS

The Cheetah's body is built for speed. *Ndloti's* (Shangaan) legs are relatively long compared to its greyhound-like body; it has a big heart and lungs and wide nasal passages. It is the fastest land animal, timed running at speeds of up to 114km/h. While the lion and the leopard rely on getting close to their intended prey before breaking cover, the cheetah's speed gives it an advantage in the more open savanna. Cheetahs are slightly taller than leopards but not as bulky, probably weighing between 40kg and 60kg. Although cheetahs are members of the cat family, they have dog-like non-retractable claws. This limits their tree-climbing ability but gives them a speed advantage when charging.

Typically, a cheetah will start a charge 60m to 100m from an antelope and, within seconds, will be racing at full tilt. If the buck is alerted in time, it will attempt to throw the cheetah off its trail by zigzagging and dodging between trees and shrubs. Using its long, heavy tail as a stabiliser, the cheetah will single-mindedly pursue its intended prey, trying to anticipate which way it will turn. At the right moment, it will knock the antelope off balance and grab it by the throat as it falls. Because of the relatively small jaws and teeth, cheetahs are not as effective in killing their prey as quickly as lions or leopards, and it can take between five and 25 minutes for its prey to die.

The element of surprise in hunting is as important for cheetahs as it is for other big predators. While its speed gives it an edge, the cheetah's vulnerable point is its

 Despite their speed, cheetahs still rely heavily on the element of surprise. Experts believe that a cheetah has a one-in-10 chance of catching an animal that isn't taken by surprise, and that this rises to a one-in-two chance if the quarry is caught off-guard.

Michael Poliza

Cheetah brothers

Cheetahs are the most timid of the big cats and there is no record in southern Africa of a cheetah ever having attacked a human.

Cheetah

Heinrich van den Berg

stamina. It will manage to run at top speed for only about 250m before it needs to catch its breath. After a high-speed chase, the cheetah desperately needs to rest for about half-an-hour – even before it eats its prey. This is when cheetahs are at their most vulnerable. They are often robbed of their kill by lions or hyaenas during this recovery spell. If the cheetah is unmolested, it normally devours its prey at the kill site.

A cheetah's food tastes are not as broad as that of the leopard, and it concentrates mostly on small and medium antelope. In Kruger, impala make up 70% of the cheetah's diet, although it is known to go after the young of larger animals, as well as warthog, ground birds, porcupines and hares. The cheetah's kill rate is hard to determine, but the consensus amongst Kruger rangers is that each cheetah kills between 30 and 150 animals a year, depending on its size, hunting frequency and the condition of the veld. Experts believe a single cheetah ideally needs

between one and three kilograms of meat a day to stay in shape.

There has been some scientific discussion as to whether they should be classified as part of the dog family because of their non-retractable claws, but they exhibit too many cat-like features, including the ability to purr loudly. Cheetahs cannot roar but can growl and spit like a cat and sometimes they make a peculiar chirping noise.

Unlike lions and leopards, cheetah don't define a territory to defend. They have a home range which they mark with urine, but will not actively fight off other cheetahs. Socially, cheetahs are somewhere on the scale between lions and leopards. They do not form prides as lions do but small groups of between four and six cheetahs can be common, particularly groupings of brothers. However, up to half the cheetahs of Kruger operate on their own.

Cheetah probably live for between 12 and 15 years in the wild. Unlike most other major carnivores, they hunt during the day.

HYAENAS

Mhisi (Shangaan) the hyaena is a shaggy, untidy and opportunistic carnivore with a distinctive, sloping back. It is a member of the dog family, weighing around 60kg (males can be heavier) and standing at about 80cm at the shoulder.

Almost all hyaenas in Kruger are the spotted hyaena. They are found throughout the Park with the highest concentrations around Satara, Skukuza thorn thickets and the Crocodile Bridge area. The brown hyaena has been recorded in the mopaneveld near Letaba and in the northern sandveld, but its status in the Park is uncertain. Generally, the brown hyaena is found in southern Africa's more arid environments.

The spotted hyaena hunts and scavenges by night and is closely connected in African folklore with the supernatural world. Anyone who has heard the sound of hyaenas in full cry around midnight would understand the animal's association with the

 Spotted hyaenas have the reputation of being scavengers, but studies have shown that, in Kruger, they tend to hunt more than they steal. Indeed, they are the second major group of predators in the Park after lion, probably accounting for more animal kills than leopard and cheetah combined.

dark arts. Unlike the honest, authoritarian roar of the lion which resonates with purity and strength, the "laughing" hyaena's utterances are hysterical and mocking, an eerie human-like giggling shriek that would not be out of place in a mental asylum. It's body parts command a premium price on the local *muthi* market, particularly the tail, ears, whiskers, lips and genitals.

As a general rule, hyaenas hunt more when they are the dominant carnivores in any particular habitat and tend towards scavenging when there are lots of other predators around. They are chancers of note, often taking great risks to snatch meat

Heinrich van den Berg
Hyaena with pups

🐾 Hyaenas have tremendously powerful jaws, capable of crushing the thigh bone of a buffalo in one movement. If they are hungry, they will gorge themselves, eating up to a third of their own weight (15kg) at a single sitting!

away from lions, and often being mauled to death in the process.

Hyaenas are mostly social, living in clans of between 10 and 40 animals, led by a dominant female. Social structures can be quite loose, however, with clan members shifting allegiances, breaking up and reforming. They are territorial, marking their hunting ground through communal defecation. Their territories vary in size depending on the amount of prey in the vicinity as well as the number of competing clans. The territory itself is not vigorously defended, but hyaena clans will respond aggressively to other predators moving into their area.

Although hyaenas sometimes hunt alone, they mostly hunt in packs. They have an almost uncanny ability to seek out the most vulnerable animal in a herd and isolate it from the others. Hyaenas are designed for the long haul and, as Kruger mammal expert Heike Schutze says, "they are high-stamina hunters relentless in the pursuit of their prey once they have tasted blood".

Hyaenas are capable of short charges of up to 50km/h and can maintain a steady, fast pace in pursuing prey over several kilometres. Their prey usually succumbs to exhaustion and is pulled down and disembowelled by the pack.

In packs, hyaena go for big game – wildebeest, zebra and kudu and, very occasionally, buffalo. When they hunt alone, they go for smaller animals such as baboons, guinea fowls, ostriches, snakes and tortoises.

There is no love lost between lions and hyaenas. Each will attack and kill the other's cubs, or elderly or sick individuals. Hyaenas seem far less intimidated by lionesses than by lions, and are occasionally bold enough to try to bully lionesses off a kill if there are no males around. A ranger at Letaba noted this animosity between hyaenas and lionesses as far back as 1937 when he witnessed three hyaenas chase a lioness up a tree.

Hyaenas are known for their cunning. They reputedly watch the skies for circling vultures to help them locate kills. They follow the path of least resistance in getting food and, as a result, have become quite ingenious – they've been seen trying to scoop out fish at drying water holes during times of drought.

Hyaena

Brett Hilton-Barber

Hyaenas

Brett Hilton-Barber

African wild dog
Albert Froneman

African wild dogs

Mark Tenent

AFRICAN WILD DOG

The African wild dog is an endangered species, with only four remaining populations in Africa, one of which is in the Kruger Park. Their survival is dependent on the pack. A wild dog by itself is not that much of a threat to other animals, but a pack is a different story. Wild dogs have the most structured social order of the carnivores, living in packs led by a dominant male and female. All other members of the pack play a subordinate role to the alpha pair. Pack sizes in Kruger vary from about 11 in the south to nine in the north, although groupings of up to 30 dogs have been recorded.

Budaja (SiSwati), or *Dalerwa* (Shangaan), tends to shy away from areas dominated by lion and hyaena. There are an estimated 250 wild dogs in Kruger, so seeing them is a matter of luck. They can roam over long distances – up to 250 square kilometres – and may travel over 50km in a single day looking for food. They

are most commonly seen in the Skukuza, Pretoriuskop, Malelane, Phalaborwa and Tshokwane areas and around Punda Maria.

Wild dogs are masters of the collective approach to hunting. A hunt begins at sunrise or sunset when the dogs perform an elaborate greeting ceremony, sniffing and licking each other, wagging their tails and twittering aloud. They make a range of chattering sounds and have a distinctive long-distance greeting call – a sharp *Hoo* – that can be heard up to four kilometres away. During the hunt itself, however, they are silent. Occasionally, they hunt at full moon.

Wild dogs will fan through the bush looking for a herd of antelope. More often

 Wild dogs have often been regarded with horror by humans because of their seemingly cruel hunting techniques – death does not come quickly to the victim, which will first be run to exhaustion and then die from a loss of blood while being devoured.

Wild dogs are high-stamina hunters, capable of maintaining a 40km/h pace over five kilometres and increasing this to bursts of more than 60km/h for short distances. The pack splits up during the hunt, with some dogs trying to drive the fleeing prey in a circle towards the others. If this fails, they press on with determination, taking it in relays to increase the pace, nipping and tearing at the fleeing victim each time it slows down. They literally run their quarry to exhaustion. Once the animal collapses, the dogs immediately begin feeding, even before their prey has died from loss of blood.

Unlike hyaena, which feast noisily and chaotically, wild dogs are restrained and orderly at the kill. The young feed first, followed by the subordinate males and females, with the alpha pair eating at any time. Each dog awaits its turn, and if there is not enough food to go round, the hunt begins again. Subordinate females support nursing wild dog females who remain at the den. They will stuff themselves with food and then go back to the den to regurgitate the remains for the mother and her young to eat.

African wild dog

Nigel Dennis

than not, this will be impala. Once they have located a herd, the most vulnerable member is singled out – usually a female and young antelope. A subordinate male wild dog usually starts the hunt by trying to isolate the animal from the rest of the herd. Once the target has been identified and separated, the alpha male takes over the lead of the hunt and the deadly endurance race begins.

The average litter size for the wild dog is between four and eight puppies. They suckle for the first three months of their lives before being taught to hunt.

Wild dogs hunt every day as they require more meat relative to their size than lions do. Eighty percent of their diet consists of impala, but they do attack bigger game as well, including wildebeest, kudu, waterbuck, reedbuck and sometimes zebra.

Wild dogs appear to have an interesting relationship with crested francolin. They allow these game birds to come into the dens to clean up scraps of meat and, in return, the francolin act as guards, sounding the alarm if any danger is about.

Smaller predators

Besides the large predators, there are a host of smaller carnivores such as jackals, caracals, servals, civets and genets. These are most likely to be seen early in the morning or late in the evening, and it is highly recommended that one takes advantage of the night drives offered by almost all of the camps for the insight one can get into the world of the small predators.

Of these smaller carnivores, the spotted genet can most often be seen around the camps as it appears to be quite familiar with humans. The civet, too, can often be seen in the central camps, particularly around dustbins and braai areas. Both species are ardent predators of birds.

BLACK-BACKED JACKAL (*Canis mesomelas*)
Characteristics: Predominantly noctural scavengers that lie about during the day; they are often solitary animals but gather in groups around a kill; they can be very noisy
Favoured prey: Carrion killed by larger predators, but also hunt small animals, birds, hares and insects; sometimes eat wild fruit and birds' eggs
Where best to see them in Kruger: Open savanna and light woodland throughout Kruger

CARACAL (*Felis caracal*)
Characteristics: Reddish-brown robust cats with distinctive long tufts of dark hair on their pointed ears. Eyes are bright yellow; mostly solitary animals, hunting at night
Favoured prey: Preys on small animals, particularly rodents and dassies, hares, small antelope, occasionally birds and lizards
Where best to see them in Kruger: Variety of habitats but prefers open savanna where there are rocky outcrops

SERVAL (*Felis serval*)
Characteristics: Tawny yellow spotted cat that looks like a small cheetah; hunts mostly at night when it can be very noisy; sleeps in thick bush during the day
Favoured prey: Mostly birds and rodents, sometimes small antelope
Where best to see them in Kruger: Thick riverine bush along most of Kruger's rivers

AFRICAN CIVET (*Civettictis civetta*)
Characteristics: Cat-like animal with distinctive black band across face and throat; they are solitary and nocturnal, lying in thick grass during the day; despite being cats, they are not tree climbers
Favoured prey: Wide variety of foods including carrion; prey on young buck, rodents, reptiles, birds, insects, eggs and occasionally eat wild fruit and berries
Where best to see them in Kruger: Found in mixed woodlands in drier areas of Kruger; best chance of seeing them is on a night drive

GENET (*Genetta genetta and Genetta tigrina*)
Characteristics: Two species of this feline-like creature are found in Kruger – large-spotted and small-spotted varieties; both are nocturnal hunters and agile tree climbers
Favoured prey: Birds' eggs, birds, lizards, snakes and insects, rodents and other small animals; big threat to poultry outside Kruger.
Where best to see them in Kruger: Both species are found mostly in southern Kruger – night drives are the best opportunity for seeing them

AFRICAN WILD CAT (*Felis lybica*)
Characteristics: Similar in appearance to domestic cat but more robust; shy, nocturnal animals
Favoured prey: The young of small antelope, rodents, hares, birds, small reptiles, insects
Where best to see them in Kruger: Dense bush and long grass throughout Kruger

Note that illustrations are not to scale

Wounded buffalo

Brett Hilton-Barber

Grazers

The distribution of animals in Kruger depends largely on the time of year and the quality of grazing in each area. Migration patterns have been substantially altered by the removal of fences between western Kruger and the adjoining private reserves. Game roams over a far wider area, particularly in summer when grazing is plentiful and there is widespread water.

During times of drought when the grass cover is poor, there is a general decline in animal numbers. During seasons of abundant rainfall, the opposite is true. Animal populations are, therefore, continually shifting according to southern Africa's wet and dry cycles.

Zebra and wildebeest appear to have a close social relationship, and of all the grazers appear most prone to seasonal migration. Long-term patterns in Kruger show that these animals generally graze around Satara in summer and then migrate southwards towards the Sabie River for winter.

On the savanna, there is safety in numbers, which is why one often sees different herds of animals mingling together. The more animals there are, the less chance of an individual being eaten by a predator. Grazing animals also make the most of their collective strengths – for instance, zebra have very good eyesight, while wildebeest have excellent hearing, which boosts the survival chances of both species against danger.

The hunted

All in all, large and small predators account for relatively few of the total number of animals in the Park. They are significantly outnumbered by herbivores, which can be broadly classified as either grazers or browsers, although many species do both. Grazers, like buffalo, depend on the grass for their nutrition while browsers, like the giraffe, have a diet based around leaves.

In times of drought when grasses disappear, the distinction between the two can become blurred, as animals will eat any nutritious plant that they can. In fact, the two most successful mammals in the Park – elephant and impala – have adapted to both grazing and browsing conditions.

Generally, grazers need water at least every two days while browsers get most of their moisture needs from eating green leaves and are less dependent on regular water intake.

Zebra

Nigel Dennis

Grazing species often eat different parts of the grass and, therefore, do not compete directly for food. There is also inter-species communication relating to water – wildebeest are very responsive to rain and can sense it falling up to 25km away, and thus often lead other animals to water and fresh grazing.

Grazing animals also help rejuvenate the veld by eating the grass. Buffalo, in particular, play an important role in sustaining the quality of grass. Because they can digest long, fibrous grasses, they often clean up old grazing areas and open the way for new growth.

Elephants, too, are conservationists, despite their reputation as being destructive, wasteful eaters. They can consume up to 250kg of grass and leaves a day, much of which is recycled into the environment. Many seeds are germinated by passing through the digestive system of the elephant, while the dung is also a handy source of manure for the veld.

Nonetheless, elephants are a source of ongoing controversy in Kruger with many scientists believing that the long-term prospects of the Park are severely compromised by the relatively high elephant population. Since the mid-20th century, there has been a substantial decline in the number of trees in the eastern grasslands, a decline attributed mostly to destruction by elephants.

Warthogs help aerate the soil when they use their tusks to root about for bulbs or rhizomes.

The Tsessebe is reportedly the fastest antelope in Kruger. This awkward-looking antelope is believed to be able to run at speeds of over 100km/h. Tsessebe also have great stamina and can gallop – at a gentler pace – for many kilometres.

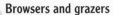

Browsers and grazers

ELEPHANT (*Loxodonta africana*)

Characteristics: Largest land mammal, big males can be 4m tall and weigh three-and-a-half-tons; its heart alone weighs 25kg; lifespan of approx 60 years; browses and grazes; seldom strays more than 80km from water; can drink up to 200 litres/day and eat 250kg of dry matter; approximately 12 000 elephant in Kruger – over-population is an environmental concern

Behaviour: Matriarchal social order with females looking after nursery herds and separate male bachelor herds; strong family bonds; may get extremely aggressive and charge when irritated or protecting young

Where best to see them in Kruger: Grazer and browser; Riverine forest and mixed woodlands of northern Kruger, particularly around Olifants/Letaba, Shingwedzi and Pafuri areas; two-thirds of Kruger's elephants are north of the Olifants River, with the next-biggest populations around the Sabie River; much less common in the extreme south

GIRAFFE (*Giraffa camelopardalis*)

Characteristics: Tallest animal in the world with toe-to-head height of up to 3,5m in males; males can weigh up to 1,9 tons; each giraffe has unique patch pattern; tongue is 45cm long; mostly browsers favouring acacia and combretum species; lifespan approximately 20 years; they are capable of galloping at 55km/h for brief periods; approximately 9 000 in Kruger

Behaviour: Solitary or in mixed herds led by dominant male; young males sometimes form small bachelor herds; often associate with other animals; main form of defence is a well-aimed kick, which is powerful enough to kill a lion

Where best to see them in Kruger: Browser; mixed acacia woodlands; Satara and Crocodile Bridge areas have biggest populations of giraffe in Kruger; very few giraffe north of Letaba River

WHITE RHINO (*Ceratotherium simum*)

Characteristics: Second-largest land mammal after the elephant; male white rhinos weigh up to 2,4 tons with a shoulder height of 1,9 metres; both male and female have two massive horns protruding from nose; poor sight but good sense of smell; can run at up to 50km/h; approximately 5 000 in Kruger

Behaviour: Fast grazers active in early morning and late afternoon, sluggish during the day, average herd size in Kruger is two to three individuals, either a bull and cows or nursery herds; like to wallow in mud; can be very dangerous and charge when disturbed

Where best to see them in Kruger: Grazer; mixed woodland with sweetveld grazing; mostly limited to the south between the Sabie and Crocodile Rivers, smaller populations around Letaba and Shingwedzi

BLACK RHINO (*Diceros bicornis*)

Characteristics: Distinguished from the square-lipped, white rhino by its hook lip and smaller size; males weigh up to 1,5 tons and stand up to 1,6m at the shoulder; can run at speeds of up to 50km/h; approximately 350 in Kruger

Behaviour: Shy browser that rarely emerges into the open; usually solitary but sometimes gathers in groups at water holes; not often seen in Kruger

Where best to see them in Kruger: Browser; Thorn thickets and dense bush in southern Kruger, particularly between Skukuza and Pretoriuskop and also south of Lower Sabie.

HIPPO (*Hippopotamus amphibius*)

Characteristics: Third-largest land mammal; barrel-like body covered with naked grey-brown skin; adults have huge incisors up to 60cm long; lifespan of between 50 and 60 years; approximately 3 000 in Kruger

Behaviour: Nocturnal grazer spending days in the water; can submerge for six minutes at a time; occurs in mixed herds of between five and thirty individuals led by a dominant, territorial male; one of Africa's most dangerous animals as it attacks when surprised or challenged

Where best to see them in Kruger: Grazer; permanent rivers and water holes throughout Kruger

WARTHOG (*Phacochoerus aethiopicus*)

Characteristics: Pig-like animal with extended snout and tusks; grey skin with a bristly manei; males weigh up to 150kg and stand 80cm high; approximately 3 800 in Kruger

Behaviour: Grazer and rooter of bulbs; usually found in small families of two sows and their piglets; average herd size in Kruger is two to five; males are usually solitary; loves mud baths; little fat on body so hates cold weather

Where best to see them in Kruger: Grazer; open savanna, particularly around water holes and marshy areas, common throughout Kruger

BUFFALO (*Syncerus caffer*)

Characteristics: Thin-coated, bull-like animal with distinctive, large w-shaped horns, males can weigh up to 870kg; mainly grazer, eating course grasses; can run up to speeds of 55km/h; approximately 29 000 in Kruger

Behaviour: Average herd size in Kruger is 250, consisting of smaller clans dominated by one or more older bulls; young bulls form bachelor herds; old bulls often solitary; buffalo mix easily with other grazers; dangerous when cornered; known to kill lions with their horns

Where best to see them in Kruger: Grazer; open grasslands, particularly sweetveld around Satara and Orpen, as well as river valleys and around permanent water sources throughout the Park

ZEBRA (Burchell's) (*Equus burchellii*)

Characteristics: Unmistakable black and white striped grazer; each pattern is unique to that individual; males weigh up to 340kg and stand 1,4m at the shoulder; can gallop at speeds of up to 65km/h; lifespan of up to 25 years; approximately 33 000 zebra in Kruger

Behaviour: Found in herds of varying sizes from three to five with dominant male, up to groupings of 50 in the open grasslands; communally grazes with other species

Where best to see them in Kruger: Grazer; open sweetveld grasslands but also occur throughout Kruger

WILDEBEEST (Blue) (*Connochaetes taurinus*)

Characteristics: Dark grey bovid with pronounced shoulders which in males are up to 1,5m high; males weigh up to 290kg; predominantly grazer; approximately 17 000 in Kruger

Behaviour: Average herd size in Kruger is between four and six individuals led by a dominant bull; clans often join in larger groupings; social grazer often with impala and zebra; very keen nose for water

Where best to see them in Kruger: Grazer; open grassland and lightly wooded savanna throughout Kruger

KLIPSPRINGER (*Oreotragus oreotragus*)

Characteristics: Small antelope with grizzled light brown coat; male has short straight horns; female does not carry horns; male and female the same size weighing up to 15kg and standing 60cm tall

Behaviour: Grazers usually found in pairs; mostly active in early morning and late afternoon; often freeze in the face of danger before bounding off; no predator can catch them once they get into rocky terrain

Where best to see them in Kruger: Browser; very habitat-specific to rocky outcrops and bouldered landscapes, particularly in Lebombo and south-western foothills

STEENBOK (*Raphicerus campestris*)

Characteristics: Smaller than a duiker with y-shaped marking on its nose; male and female same size weighing up to 15kg and standing 55cm at the shoulder; lifespan up to 10 years

Behaviour: Solitary woodland browser, occasionally grazes; sometimes found in monogamous pairs

Where best to see them in Kruger: Browser; open woodlands in hilly country, particularly visible in sandveld around Punda and Pafuri

Note that illustrations are not to scale

COMMON DUIKER (*Sylvicapra grimmia*)

Characteristics: Small antelope with dark, tufted crest on head and dark stripe down muzzle; only rams carry horns; rams can weigh up to 21kg and stand approx 60cm high; lifespan up to 10 years

Behaviour: Solitary woodland browser, active by day and night; has very effective zigzag run to shake off predators

Where best to see them in Kruger: Browser; mixed woodlands throughout Kruger

IMPALA (*Aepyceros melampus*)

Characteristics: Most numerous antelope in the Park with over 130 000 adults at any one time; grazers and browsers; only rams have horns, they weigh up to 80kg and stand just under 1 metre tall ; graceful in movement, impalas can leap over a three-metre fence and can run in bursts of up to 80km/h; favoured prey of many predators

Behaviour: Single rams have harems of 10 ewes on average but herds can swell to over 50 after lambing season; young males leave to form bachelor herds; alpha males often challenged during rutting season in late summer

Where best to see them in Kruger: Grazer and browser; open savanna grassland but also common in mixed woodlands throughout the Park; uncommon in mopaneveld

KUDU (*Tragelaphus strepsiceros*)

Characteristics: Males have large spiralled horns, weigh up to 300kg and stand 1,5m at the shoulder; females don't have horns; both have white stripes down their grey flanks; mainly browsers favouring bushwillow and acacia species; approximately 5 000 in Kruger

Behaviour: Dominant male accompanied by three to five females; young males form bachelor herds; when they flee their raised tails flash a white signal for others to follow; can use huge horns as deadly defences when attacked

Where best to see them in Kruger: Browser; thick woodlands in hilly country, common in riverine forest areas, common in south-western foothills and woodlands in the Sabie River catchment area

ELAND (*Taurotragus oryx*)

Characteristics: Largest antelope with distinct shoulder hump, males weigh up to 940kg and stand 1,8m at the shoulder; both sexes have horns; they can run at speeds of up to 40km/h and comfortably trot for longer distances at half that speed; amazing jumper capable of clearing a 2m fence; approximately 300 in Kruger

Behaviour: Grazer and a browser, small herd sizes in Kruger of between two and five animals; tend to graze at night when the water content of plants is higher; one of the gentlest animals and will not charge even if cornered

Where best to see them in Kruger: Grazer and browser; savanna plains and mixed woodlands throughout Kruger; can exist easily in very arid areas

NYALA (*Tragelaphus angasii*)

Characteristics: Similar to kudu except that males have white nose bands, shaggy coats tipped with white and light legs; only males have horns; males weigh up to 90kg and stand 1,2m at the shoulder; lifespan of approximately 15 years; approximately 300 in Kruger

Behaviour: Forest-dwelling browser, feeding during night and day; occur in mixed herds of up to 10 bulls, ewes and calves; young bulls congregate in bachelor herds; often found with impala

Where best to see them in Kruger: Browser; dense bush along permanent water sources; more common in the north although there is a small population along the Sabie River

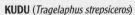

SABLE ANTELOPE (*Hippotragus niger*)

Characteristics: Large antelope with distinctive white and black face and long curved horns; both sexes carry horns which are up to 1,65m long; male weighs up to 270kg and stands 1,6m high. Lifespan up to 15 years; capable of running at 57km/h; approximately 550 in the Park

Behaviour: Grazer of medium grasses; found in groups of two to four, but cows and calves can link up with other clans in herds of up to 30 at times; strict hierarchy with male dominant; males exhibit a variety of threat displays using horns

Where best to see them in Kruger: Grazer; mixed savanna woodlands, most visible around Pretoriuskop and also western mopaneveld near Phalaborwa

ROAN ANTELOPE (*Hippotragus equinus*)

Characteristics: Similar to sable antelope but has smaller body and horns and distinctive white eye and muzzle patches; adult males weigh up to 300kg and are 1,5m high; endangered species that is very rare in Kruger with small population of approximately 70 in the Park

Behaviour: Graze by day and night; found in herds of between two and five; seldom move out of their territory; strict male-dominant hierarchy

Where best to see them in Kruger: Grazer; open grassland pockets within thick woodland; rare in Kruger

BUSHBUCK (*Tragelaphus scriptus*)

Characteristics: Medium-sized antelope with characteristic white patch on throat and white flecks on hindquarters; only rams carry horns; adult rams weigh up to 80kg and are 1m tall; approximately 500 in Kruger

Behaviour: Nocturnal solitary browsers; sometimes form nursery herds; secretive, seldom moving out of bush cover; very good swimmers

Where best to see them in Kruger: Browser; thorn thickets and dense bush close to permanent water, mostly in the south-western foothills and northern sandveld; tame specimens at Letaba Camp

TSESSEBE (*Damaliscus lunatus*)

Characteristics: Fastest antelope, capable of galloping at speeds of over 90km/h; large reddish brown antelope with narrow face and shoulders higher than hindquarters; both sexes have horns; males weigh up to 160kg standing 1,3m high; lifespan up to 15 years; approximately 200 in Kruger

Behaviour: Daytime and nighttime grazer; found in groups of between two and four animals led by a dominant male; frequently use termite mounds as lookout points; can outrun most predators

Where best to see them in Kruger: Grazer; open sweetveld plains of northern Kruger; particularly north of Letaba near the Giriyondo Border Post turn-off, and close to Mopani Camp.

LICHTENSTEIN'S HARTEBEEST (*Sigmoceros lichtensteinii*)

Characteristics: Long, narrow face; both sexes have strongly ringed horns; tawny, yellow coat; shoulder higher than hindquarters; males weigh up to 200kg and stand 1,4m at the shoulder; lifespan 15–20 years; rump, tawny yellow coat; fast runner capable of speeds of up to 70km/h; reintroduced in Kruger during the 1980s; population numbers uncertain

Behaviour: Daytime grazers found in small herds; distinctive habit of rubbing face against flanks; often seen posing on termite hills; very territorial; bulls often bellow loudly during disputes with other males

Where best to see them in Kruger: Watercourses in savanna grassland, mostly in the far north around Punda but also in the Pretoriuskop area

Note that illustrations are not to scale

Kruger's Antelope

Nigel Dennis

Antelopes all have hollow horns and are classified as bovids. Two-thirds of the world's 120 bovid species are antelope – among the remaining third are cattle, sheep and goats. Modern antelope have evolved over the past 24 million years and owe their continued survival to being savanna specialists, each occupying a slightly different yet overlapping ecological niche in grassland and mixed woodland environments. There are 72 antelope species in Africa, of which 21 are found in Kruger. These are:

Eland

Impala

Kudu

Waterbuck

Bushbuck

Nyala

Common Reedbuck

Mountain Reedbuck

Klipspringer

Grey Rhebuck

Suni

Oribi

Steenbok

Sharpe's Grysbok

Common Duiker

Red Duiker

Tsessebe

Lichtenstein's Hartebeest

Blue Wildebeest

Roan Antelope

Sable Antelope

Bushbuck

Browsers

Just as grazers can co-exist on the same grassland, browsers also eat different parts of the same trees.

The top feeders are obviously the giraffe, which can reach leaves that are five metres or more off the ground. They are adaptable browsers which feed on 70% of the tree species in Kruger, but favour acacias and combretum species which make up half their diet.

Giraffe lose condition during winter because these trees drop their leaves, and they are forced to eat less palatable evergreens. These animals like the flatlands of the savanna but can be seen on the rocky slopes of the Lebombo. That's usually a sign of the first spring flush in the acacias and combretums.

Elephants, too, go crazy for new growth, often knocking trees over to get at new leaves. This is often of benefit to smaller browsers as food that is beyond their normal reach becomes available closer to the ground.

Elephants, which weigh up to five tons, stand about three metres off the ground, but can compete with giraffe for the top end of the browsing market because of their trunks, which can be up to two metres long.

Besides giraffe and elephant, the main browsers in Kruger are kudu, duiker, klipspringer, bushbuck, nyala and black rhino.

Kudu in Kruger are found in herds of between six and 20 cows accompanied by a dominant male or two. Most kudu bulls, therefore, live in separate bachelor herds. Kudu migrate extensively through Kruger. In summer, they disperse over wide areas of mixed woodland, while in winter they cluster along rivers and watercourses where trees remain nutritious.

Browsers tend generally to favour the thicker bush in the western parts of Kruger where the grazing is relatively unpalatable but the nutrition held in leaves is very good.

Sleepless in Savanna

A giraffe's height – up to 5,5m – makes it physically difficult for this animal to drink and sleep. Giraffes, therefore, usually sleep standing up, although they do lie down on occasion. They are the ultimate light sleepers, snatching extremely short doses of consistent rest. Some Kruger experts believe that a giraffe sleeps for only about 24 minutes in a 24-hour period! Giraffe have loose social structures and herds can vary in size – even on a daily basis. In Kruger, the average herd size is less than 20. The biggest recorded herd in Kruger numbered 46 animals, smaller than the herds of up to 70 in East Africa. Giraffe herds have a constantly changing leadership of both males and females. They are territorial, ranging over an area of between 20km and 70km, depending on the availability of food. The solitary giraffe one often sees in Kruger are usually rather pungent-smelling old males which can no longer attract females.

Giraffe

Nigel Dennis

Other Animals of Kruger

CHACMA BABOON (*Papio ursinus*)

Characteristics: Social primate living in groups of between 30 and 40 individuals; dominant leader and strict social hierarchy; daytime feeders sleeping in trees, on rock ledges or in caves

Food: Wide diet including insects, fruit, roots, tubers and birds' eggs; occasionally known to hunt young antelope when food is scarce

Where best to see them in Kruger: Throughout Kruger except in very open grassland – there are an estimated 300 troops of baboons living in Kruger

VERVET MONKEY (*Circopithecus pygurythrus*)

Characteristics: Social animals that live mostly in trees in groups of between 15 and 30; often warn other animals of impending danger

Food: Omnivores feeding on fruit, seeds and leaves, insects, nestling birds, eggs

Where best to see them in Kruger: Woodlands close to water, throughout Kruger

SLENDER MONGOOSE (*Galerella sanguinea*)

Characteristics: Most common mongoose in Kruger, lives singly or in pairs, very long tail with conspicuous black tip

Food: Rodents, snakes and reptiles, birds' eggs, insects and sometimes wild fruit

Where best to see them in Kruger: Variety of habitats throughout Kruger

BANDED MONGOOSE (*Mungos mungo*)

Characteristics: Very social, noisy brown-grey animals that live in packs of about 20 individuals; very active during the day, disappearing quickly when alarmed

Food: Mostly insects but also rodents, reptiles, birds, eggs, fruit and berries

Where best to see them in Kruger: Open dry savanna of eastern Kruger

DWARF MONGOOSE (*Helogale parvula*)

Characteristics: Smallest of the African mongooses, very social, diurnal animal living in groups of between 10 and 20 individuals; very curious nature

Food: Mostly insects but also rodents, birds, eggs and small reptiles

Where best to see them in Kruger: Dry savanna and mixed woodlands

SOUTH AFRICAN PORCUPINE (*Hystrix africaeaustralis*)

Characteristics: Largest African rodent; body covered with thick, sharp black-and-white quills, nocturnal animal that sleeps by day often in communal burrows; it does not shoot out quills but charges backwards at aggressors, trying to spike them

Food: Vegetarian diet of bulbs, tubers, tree bark, roots, berries; known to gnaw on bones

Where best to see them in Kruger: Occur in a variety of habitats throughout Kruger, but generally where the landscape is broken and hilly

TREE SQUIRREL (*Paraxerus cepapi*)

Characteristics: Distinctly bushy tails, active during the day, either singly, in pairs or in groups; active in trees and on the ground

Food: Nuts, fruit, roots, grass, birds' eggs and sometimes insects

Where best to see them in Kruger: Woodland savanna throughout Kruger; particularly prevalent in mopaneveld

HONEY BADGER OR RATEL (*Mellivora capensis*)

Characteristics: Distinctive white strip down head and back; shy, nocturnal animals but aggressive when cornered; bear-like claws that are good for digging; thick fur and tough, elastic skin is main defence, especially against bees

Food: Ruthless love of honey and can withstand attacks by swarms of bees; also feeds on small mammals, reptiles, insects, bulbs, roots and fruit

Where best to see them in Kruger: Found in all Kruger habitats, from savanna grassland to dense woodland

AARDWOLF (*Proteles cristatus*)

Characteristics: Hyaena-like nocturnal animal that sleeps by day in burrows; morphologically they appear to be a link between civets and mongooses

Food: Small teeth and narrow jaws limit its diet to insects; feeds mostly on termites but does eat plant material and birds' eggs

Where best to see them in Kruger: Uncommon in Kruger; limited to Pretoriuskop area and the Lebombo flats in the east

AARDVARK (*Orycteropus afer*)

Characteristics: Pig-sized, hairy animal with long snout; walks long distances at night in search of food and sleeps in burrows during the day; tongue is 30cm long

Food: Termites, ants, insect larvae, certain plants

Where best to see them in Kruger: Open savanna grassland, particularly where there are lots of termite mounds and anthills

PANGOLIN OR SCALY ANTBEAR (*Manis temminckii*)

Characteristics: Dinosuar-like scaly body; nocturnal, generally solitary animal about one metre long; small eyes, no visible ears and long, sticky tongue; rolls up into a ball when challenged

Food: Primarily ants and termites which it digs out of the ground

Where best to see them in Kruger: Lightly wooded savanna grassland where there are lots of termite mounds

STRIPED POLECAT (*Ictonyx striatus*)

Characteristics: Nocturnal animals with distinctive white stripes from the nape of the neck to the tail

Food: Rodents, hares, snakes, frogs, birds and insects

Where best to see them in Kruger: Open savanna, drier areas in eastern Kruger

ROCK DASSIE OR CAPE HYRAX (*Procavia capensis*)

Characteristics: Gregarious creatures that live in colonies of up to 50 animals, prominent on rocks where they lie in the sun for hours

Food: Vegetarian diet of grass, leaves, fruit, bark and twigs

Where best to see them in Kruger: Confined to the more mountainous areas of Kruger – the south-western foothills, the Lebombo and the northern sandveld

SPRING HARE (*Pedetes capensis*)

Characteristics: Very powerful hindlegs with short front legs; distinctive ears; mostly nocturnal; lives in communal burrows

Food: Grass, roots, tubers, bulbs

Where best to see them in Kruger: Confined mostly to the northern sandveld

Note that illustrations are not to scale

Martial eagle with leguaan

Nigel Dennis

Kruger's birds

Kruger is one of the great birding spots in South Africa, with more than half of the species found in the country occurring here. Kruger's sheer size – almost 20 000 square kilometres – and variety of habitats, lends itself to a rich and interesting mixture of birdlife. There are approximately 520 recorded species in Kruger, spanning a wonderful variety, from the largest bird in the world – the ostrich – to one of the smallest, the bronze mannikin. Approximately 200 Kruger bird species are summer visitors from Eurasia and elsewhere in Africa.

Kruger straddles the Tropic of Capricorn. Northern Kruger, therefore, forms the southernmost range of many tropical species, while southern Kruger is the northernmost extent of many southern species.

Between these two poles lie a number of other bird-rich habitats, from the luxuriant tangle of the sandveld and the dry and rocky Lebombo, to the low-lying savanna grasslands, acacia thorn thickets and mixed woodlands, as well as the relatively high-rainfall areas of the south-western foothills. Kruger's rivers act as habitat corridors between these different ecosystems and, as a rule, the best birding in Kruger is along the rivers. Probably the only area in Kruger that is not good for birds is the large tract of monotonous mopane shrubveld in the north-east.

Many of Kruger's birds are migrants, flying from Eurasia or other parts of Africa to spend summer in the south. These visitors include the steppe eagle, steppe buzzard, lesser spotted eagle, yellow-billed kite, the European roller, the woodland kingfisher, the southern carmine bee-eater, the white stork and all the cuckoos, including the red-chested cuckoo ("Piet-my-vrou"). The red-footed falcon and lesser

Nigel Dennis

Grey go-away birds

71

Bateleur

Nigel Dennis

kestrel have a migratory range that takes them to Vladivostok in Russia, while black kites ringed in Hong Kong have been found in Kruger.

There are 380 or so species that are resident in the Park all year round. These include the kori bustard – the world's heaviest bird capable of flight, and the remarkable martial eagle which has a wingspan of more than two metres. The vulture species are all resident as is the lilac-breasted roller. All herons and kingfishers (besides the woodland kingfisher) are permanent Kruger species. Among the more distinctive residents are the hornbill family, which are frequently seen dipping in flight over the roads, and the lilac-breasted roller which is found throughout the Park.

Kruger is the best place in South Africa to see the great birds of prey. Fifteen of South Africa's 17 eagles are to be found in the Park where almost 80 raptor species have been recorded.

The aerial king of Kruger is the bateleur – this distinctive, short-tailed eagle is rare outside Kruger but common within the Park. It is one of several species of scavenging raptors that might have disappeared from South Africa had it not been for the proclamation of this game reserve. Kruger has served as a haven for vultures, marabou storks and other birds of prey that were once widespread throughout South Africa but have since vanished in the face of human activity.

Other common eagles in Kruger are the African fish, martial, lesser spotted, tawny and Wahlberg's eagles. Early morning is a good time to see these birds as they often perch on tree trunks waiting for the day to heat up so that they can catch the thermal updraughts to soar and look for prey.

Spotted eagle-owl

In many parts of Africa the owl represents supernatural forces. In traditional Shangaan folklore, the arrival of an owl at one's homestead is considered an evil omen.

Albert Froneman

Birding calendar

Month	Landscape	Bird activity
August	Late winter, dry bush, water scarce, winds indicate spring is on the way	First migrants arrive from Europe and Asia – yellow-billed kites are among the first; weavers begin nest-building; breeding plumage begins appearing
September	First itinerant rains mark arrival of spring, many trees in flower	More migrants arrive in Kruger; weaver nest-building continues; breeding plumage intensifies in colour – particularly noticeable with the violet-backed starling and African paradise-flycatcher; first cuckoos begin calling
October	Start of the rainy season, new leaf growth on trees, grasslands green with new growth	Warblers arrive in great numbers from Eurasia and elsewhere in Africa; appearance of the steppe buzzard; generally bird breeding season is now well under way; black-bellied bustard begin their distinct mating displays; raptors start taking advantage of the thermal updrafts created by the heat
November	Vegetation becomes more lush as rainfall is usually double that of October	The last northern migrants arrive, including thousands of kestrels which fly from their Siberian breeding grounds; this is a good time for insect eaters because the lush grass means there is plenty of food; vultures more visible because of increased carnivore activity on the ground
December	Height of summer; conditions hot and humid with occasional thundershowers; landscape very colourful with summer veld flowers in bloom	Major bird activity as all migrants are in the Park, there is lots of food and summer breeding is at its peak; weavers' nests are now built; many birds are nesting; tinker barbets very visible; lots of raptors over the eastern grasslands; water birds abundant along all major rivers
January	Height of the rainy season, colourful landscape with summer flowers in bloom; marulas begin fruiting	Eggs are hatching and fledglings are learning how to look after themselves; many aggressive hawks – such as Dickinson's kestrel – target the fledglings; this is a good feeding time all round with easy pickings; birding parties common in grasslands and around fruiting trees; this is usually the time when there are most insects in the veld, hence insect eaters are conspicuous
February	Hot and humid conditions, plants are at their most nutritious; vegetation dense and colourful with many summer flowers still in bloom; grasses are easiest to identify because they are all in seed	Prime birding time as all the migrants are settled, the breeding birds are in full plumage and fledglings are beginning to mature; food is abundant with sunbirds particularly prolific in flowering trees; reedbeds are alive with noisy bishops, widowbirds and weavers; raptors are particularly active
March	End of summer with the last major rains; temperatures remain high	The first migrants depart – one of the first to go is the steppe eagle; kestrels begin gathering in their thousands to prepare for their return flights
April	Seasonal shift towards autumn, noticeable drop in temperatures; occasional late summer rains	Most migrants depart for European, Asian and African breeding grounds; many species feed heavily to improve their condition before winter
May	Autumn; many deciduous trees begin dropping their leaves; white syringas in flower; often windy	Pressure on the food chain begins easing because of the departure of migrants; resident species such as lilac-breasted roller and black-collared barbet begin to dominate
June	Winter; cool evenings and warm days; grass cover begins receding; rain is rare	Southern yellow-billed hornbills visible along roadsides; bateleurs dominate the skies; bird numbers are at their lowest in Kruger but water holes can still be rewarding for resident water fowl
July	Winter nights can be cold; mopaneveld changes colour from green to yellow and orange	Fish eagles are vocal in their territorial displays; birdwatching is better in the south where there is a dominance of resident species; birdlife in mopaneveld poor until the first rains come

🐾 Birds at a kill

Vulture at a kill

Nigel Dennis

Bird	Involvement with the kill
Bateleur	Often first at a kill because of its excellent vision and low-altitude flying; vultures often depend on the bateleur's strong beak to break open the carcass
Hooded vulture	Usually moves in to the kill once the mammal predators have had their fill; it is one of the smallest vultures and its share of the carcass is limited to the first and final pickings
Lappet-faced vulture	The largest of the vultures; usually waits to see if the hooded vultures are unmolested by other animals at the carcass before it descends and takes over; it particularly favours the skin
White-backed vulture	Will compete with the lappet-faced – is more adept at getting inside the carcass to tear out the entrails; often has the advantage of sheer numbers
Marabou storks	Dubbed the "undertaker of the veld" the marabou will chase most other birds off the carcass until it has had its fill
Starlings	Will often hang about on the perimeters of the action and pick at tiny scraps overlooked by the bigger birds

Reptiles

The king of the reptiles in Kruger is the crocodile. There are believed to be several thousand crocs in Kruger. They are social animals, found in all seven of the Park's major rivers, and can be seen sunning themselves on sandbanks at the main water holes. Their primary diet is fish, but occasionally they will grab at animals that wander too close to their watery lairs. A large croc – up to four metres – makes a kill every three weeks or so. Crocodiles are ancient animals, having evolved some 60 million years ago. Despite their tiny brains, they are cunning, killing their prey mostly by drowning. They then tear off, and swallow, chunks of flesh. Male crocodiles are more territorial than females – they remain in one place while female crocs migrate to find males to mate with. A crocodile can remain under water for about 15 minutes at a time.

The killer snakes of Kruger

There are 54 species of snakes found in Kruger, only nine of which are deadly poisonous. Although the black mamba is often portrayed as the most dangerous snake in Africa, 90% of bites to humans are actually by the Mozambique spitting cobra and the puff adder. The largest African snake – the python – is fairly common, but difficult to see. It can grow up to five metres in length and kills its prey by wrapping its body around the victim and crushing it. It's very rare to come across snakes in Kruger, even during the guided wilderness walks. Snakes tend to shy away from humans and only attack if they're caught by surprise. Nonetheless, one should be cautious at camps and lookout points. If you come across a snake in a camp, please alert the camp staff immediately.

Croc in action

Michael Poliza

AFRICAN ROCK PYTHON (*Python sebae*)

Characteristics: Largest snake in Africa – up to 5m long; crushes its prey to death; generally nocturnal but seen during the day

Prey: Dassies, hares, cane rats, birds; has been known to take impala and young antelope and warthogs

Habitat: Mixed woodlands near water; very good tree climbers

EGYPTIAN COBRA (*Naja haje*)

Characteristics: Largest cobra, approx 1,5m long; when disturbed it rears up and displays a broad hood; very fast moving striker with toxic venom

Prey: Small mammals, birds and their eggs, frogs

Habitat: Mixed woodlands near water

TWIG SNAKE (*Thelotornis capensis*)

Characteristics: Slender, fast-moving tree snake about 1,3m long; can stay motionless for long periods of time; well camouflaged and very poisonous

Prey: Birds and their nestlings and eggs

Habitat: Mixed woodland near water

BLACK MAMBA (*Dendroaspis polylepis*)

Characteristics: One of the most poisonous snakes in Africa; about 2m long; very fast strikers and can slither at speeds of up to 15km/h

Prey: Birds, rodents, dassies and other small animals

Habitat : Dry lowveld bush; lives in abandoned termite hills, animal holes and among rocks; loves basking in the sun

PUFF ADDER (*Bitis arietans*)

Characteristics: Responsible for more human bites than all other African snakes combined – most attacks are because it is trodden on; front fangs make venom delivery extremely effective; sluggish, fat snake about 1,5m long

Prey: Rodents, birds, other snakes; a puffadder has once been recorded killing a tortoise

Habitat: Very fond of lying in the sun; found in all Kruger habitats – one of the most widely distributed snakes in Africa

MOZAMBIQUE SPITTING COBRA
(*Naja mossambica peters*)

Characteristics: One of the most poisonous snakes in Africa; rears up two-thirds of its body length when disturbed, displays hood and spits venom with amazing accuracy (they can spit venom into the eyes of an aggressor three metres away); average length approximately 1m

Prey: Birds' eggs, small mammals and reptiles

Habitat: Mixed savanna woodland; favours hollow trees and abandoned burrows near water

BOOMSLANG (*Dispholidus typus*)

Characteristics: Highly venomous, greenish tree snake, about 1,5m long

Prey: Birds' eggs, small mammals and reptiles

Habitat: Thick woodlands near water

Note that illustrations are not to scale

Rock monitor

Nigel Dennis

Fish

The seven rivers that cross Kruger support an extremely rich aquatic life. Forty-nine fish species are found in Kruger's rivers, including two of the rarest species in the world – the lungfish and the mosquito-eating killifish. The dominant fish species in Kruger is the common barbel (*Clarias gariepinus*). Its popularity with crocodiles has led to its description as the "impala of the river". Barbel prefer the slower-moving parts of the river unlike stronger swimmers such as the mudfish (*Labeo*), yellowfish (*Barbus marequensis*) and the well-known tigerfish (*Hydrocynus vittatus*).

One of the most extraordinary phenomena in Kruger is the life cycle of the freshwater eel (*Anguilla*). During their feeding stage – also known as the yellow eel stage – they live in Kruger's rivers, preying on fish and crabs. According to natural history scientist Dr Andrew Deacon, this stage can last between three and 20 years. Dr Deacon explains that at some point the eel is ready to breed and makes its way downstream to the Indian Ocean. During this journey the eel undergoes a dramatic metamorphosis from a freshwater creature into a sea fish – the silver eel stage. It changes colour from yellow to silver or white, its eyes become larger and its snout more pointed. On its way to the ocean the eel stops feeding altogether, its digestive system shrivels and its anus may even close. As it gets closer to the ocean its reproductive organs develop and breeding

Other notable reptiles in Kruger are two species of monitor lizards (leguaans), the water and the rock monitors. The water leguaan can be up to two metres long and is found at permanent water sources in Kruger. It feeds mainly on fish, crabs, mussels, small animals and birds. Rock monitors can be found quite far from water in rocky outcrops and crevices. They grow up to 1,5m and feed on small mammals, birds, eggs, other reptiles and insects.

> Amazingly, a Zambezi shark was caught at the confluence of the Limpopo and Luvuvhu Rivers in 1950. Although Zambezi sharks can adapt to freshwater conditions, this was an extraordinary occurance as the 2-metre fish had swum some 400km from its natural habitat in the Indian Ocean.

begins. Amazingly, the eels swim to the other side of Madagascar to lay their eggs and are never seen again. Millions of their eggs are washed back down the African coastline where they hatch among plankton into transparent, leaf-shaped larvae. As they get swept past river mouths they undergo another transformation, triggered by the smell of fresh water in the sea. In what's known as the glass eel stage, they rapidly develop muscles and make their way to the source of the fresh water. As they swim upstream into the lowveld's rivers, they become miniature eels known as elvers. They are able to clamber up waterfalls and rapids until they reach a point in the river conducive to developing into the yellow eel stage. There is a record of an eel that swam over 1 000km up the Zambezi and somehow managed to get up the 100-metre cliffs of the thundering Victoria Falls. It was found in yellow eel stage in a deep pool above the falls. Other sea fish sometimes make their way upstream too – a saltwater bream was caught in the Crocodile River near Crocodile Bridge in 1970.

THE ELEPHANT DILEMMA

The management of elephants is one of the most difficult issues facing Kruger authorities. It is common cause that there are too many elephants in Kruger. Current estimates are that there are approximately 13 000 elephants in the Park, which should support an optimum population of around 8 000. The rapid increase in elephants over the past century has been exacerbated by the provision of too many man-made water holes. Scientists have proved that the number of elephants is having a negative impact on Kruger. During the past 50 years there has been a 60% decline in the number of trees on the eastern Kruger savanna. This has been blamed mostly on elephants, each of which knocks over at least four trees a year. Park authorities have begun closing water holes and are grappling with a number of options, including forced contraception, animal relocation and culling. Culling – the management of excess animals by killing them – has been used on and off by the Kruger Park since 1903, and has always provoked heated public controversy. Initially, many predators were culled in order to boost the numbers of herbivores that had been decimated by the rinderpest and poaching at the end of the 19th century. It seems incredible today that lion, leopard, cheetah, hyaena and wild dogs were shot by rangers as part of Kruger's early management policy. Between 1903 and 1958, almost 2 500 lions were culled – an average of just over 50 animals a year. During the mid-1970s buffalo and zebra were culled to prevent over-grazing. More recently, the focus has been on elephants. Thousands of elephants were killed in the years before the no-cull policy was introduced in 1994, and elephant numbers have risen steadily since then. Kruger elephant expert Dr Ian Whyte says the choice is stark – either Kruger becomes an elephant park at the expense of biodiversity, or biodiversity is maintained and elephant numbers are reduced. This has rekindled the culling debate. Although culling is the easiest solution to implement, it is deeply unpopular in the court of public opinion.

Heinrich van den Berg

Elephant fitted with a radio collar

Warthog
Michael Poliza

PART 2

Exploring Kruger

Ancient animals

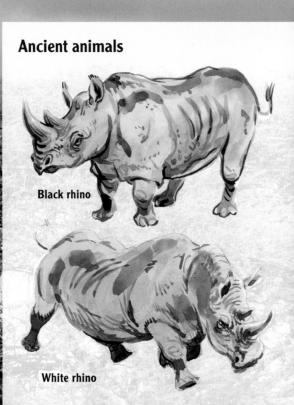

Black rhino

White rhino

Rhinos and crocodiles go back a long time. A common ancestor to the rhinos one sees today has been traced back to 50 million years ago. African rhinos evolved from the Asian lineage approximately 10 million years ago. The black rhino (*Diceros bicornis*) is more primitive than the white rhino (*Ceratotherium simum*), which separated ancestral pathways approximately four to 5 million years ago. Rhinos have passed their evolutionary peak and survive only in protected areas.

The crocodile has a much older ancestry. Its origins lie in the archaesaurs approximately 200 million years ago. Crocodiles, in their present evolutionary state, survived the mass extinction of the dinosaurs 65 million years ago.

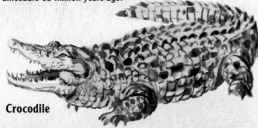

Crocodile

Zebra

Brett Hilton-Barber

South-eastern Kruger

 Habitat pointers

- Thorn thickets along the lower contours of the river valleys
- Open grasslands around Lower Sabie
- Lebombo foothills in the Mpanamana Concession
- Mixed bushwillow and acacia woodlands north of Biyamiti
- Pockets of fine riverine bush along the Sabie River

There's more chance of seeing the Big Five in the south-east of the Park than just about anywhere else in Kruger. Water is available all year round from the two main rivers of southern Kruger – the Sabie and the Crocodile. The basalt underlying the grasslands retains water in pans long after the rains have gone, and supports a sweet grassveld favoured by grazers. There are a variety of habitats in the south-east, including the rugged Lebombo koppies, the open basaltic plains, mixed woodland and thorn thickets along the watercourses. The grasslands around Lower Sabie are usually reliable for large herds of zebra and buffalo, Crocodile Bridge area is good for giraffe and lion while white rhino are invariably seen grazing along the Nhlowa Road. The black rhino is the choice sighting of the south-east, but it is rarely seen, spending most of the day deep in the thorn thickets. The best chance of seeing leopard is to stay at Shishangeni Lodge in the Mpanamana concession, which offers game drives into the hidden kloofs and gorges of the Lebombo. The lowest point in Kruger is where the Sabie River cuts through the Lebombo (120m) range and enters Mozambique. The south-east is hot and dry, with less rainfall (300mm pa) than the Park average (650mm pa). Malaria is a concern during summer.

BEST DRIVE IN THE SOUTH-EAST

Crocodile Bridge to Tshokwane:
Stop off at Duke's and Mlondozi
Water Holes, Nkumbi Viewpoint
and Orpen Dam and end up with
a picnic at Tshokwane. This drive
includes a variety of landscapes –
thorn thickets, savanna grassland,
Lebombo mountains. Allow four-and-
a-half hours including stops.

CAMPS IN THE SOUTH-EAST

Crocodile Bridge
013 735 6012 See page 88

Shishangeni Lodge
031 310 3333 See page 95

Lower Sabie
013 735 6056/7 See page 96

Lukimbi
011 888 3713 See page 106

Biyamiti
013 735 6171 See page 111

CROCODILE BRIDGE GATE EXPLORER OPTIONS

- The Gomondwane Road to Lower Sabie (H4-2);
  34km; 1,5 hours; tar road; thorn thickets give
  way to open grassland around Lower Sabie;
  animal sightings traditionally good;

- The alternative road to Skukuza via Randspruit
  (H4-2; H5, S114); 68km; 3 hours; mostly dust
  road; thorn thickets into mixed woodlands; game
  viewing is a gamble but you may strike it lucky;

- Crocodile River Road to Biyamiti (S25);
  26km; 1 hour; dust road; thorn thickets into
  mixed woodland, good birding and itinerant
  game viewing;

- Nhlowa Road to Lower Sabie (S28); 28km;
  1 hour; dust road; open savanna grassland with
  good views over the Lebombo; usually good for
  grazers and excellent for birding.

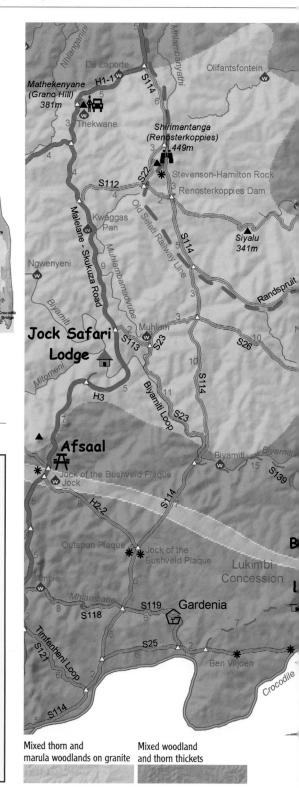

Mixed thorn and
marula woodlands on granite

Mixed woodland
and thorn thickets

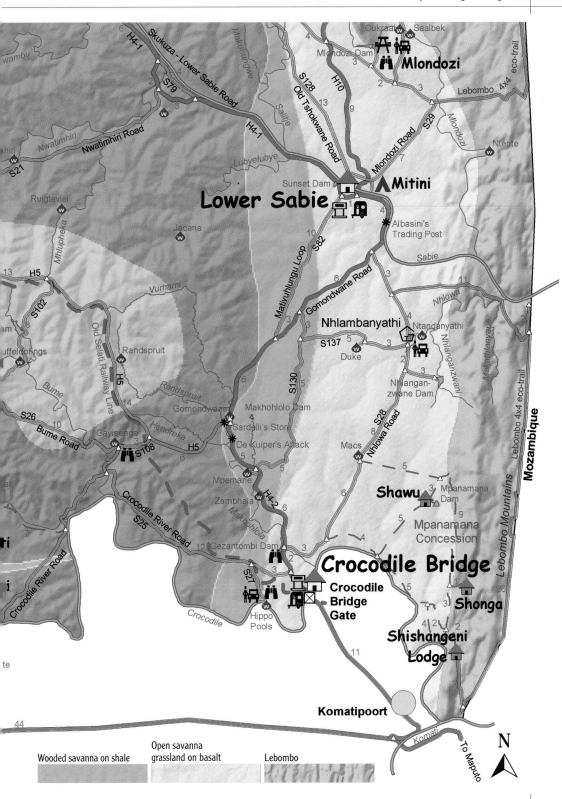

Crocodile River at Hippo Pools

Brett Hilton-Barber

Bronze Medal of the Royal Humane Society for risking his life to dive into the river to rescue a woman and her baby who had been swept off the bank by floodwaters.

The Crocodile River would almost certainly have been the northernmost border with Swaziland had a rather dubious 19th century land deal not been conducted between the Transvaal Land Commissioner, Abel Erasmus, and an unnamed Swazi chief, in which the Swazi border was pushed 80km southwards in exchange for 12 cases of gin.

Crocodile Bridge Gate

Crocodile Bridge cooks. It is one of the hottest places in the country, with summer temperatures often soaring above the 40°C mark. It is the most eastern entrance into Kruger, some 12km from Komatipoort, the closest town to the main border gate between South Africa and Mozambique. The Crocodile Bridge area is a juxtaposition of open grassland and dense thorn thickets. It's one of Kruger's driest areas – receiving about half the average Park rainfall.

The Gate is named after the Crocodile River, which forms the southernmost boundary of the Kruger Park. The river gets its name from the number of crocodiles that it has and would certainly be one of the most dangerous to try to wade across. In 1940, ranger Sinias Nyalunga was awarded the

Crocodile Bridge is the most direct access point to the game-rich south-eastern grasslands of the Park, and sighting opportunities open up very quickly after entering the Park. The game drives here are part of what is known as the "Southern Circle" which has a reputation for good lion-spotting. Several prides operate in this area, each with its own distinct hunting techniques and behaviour patterns. In the past, this has often led to problems of lions crossing the Crocodile River and attacking livestock outside the Park. At one point during the early 1970s, the situation got so bad that 26 escaping lion had to be shot during an 18-month period.

The Crocodile Bridge area also has the highest percentage of Kruger's white rhino population.

CROCODILE BRIDGE AREA SPECIALITIES:

Animals

White rhino

Giraffe

Spotted hyaena

Lion

Cheetah

Birds

Black-bellied bustard

Black-bellied starling

Orange-breasted bush-shrike

Yellow-rumped tinkerbird

Purple-banded sunbird

Crocodile Bridge to Lower Sabie

There are two main routes between Crocodile Bridge and Lower Sabie – the Gomondwane Road (H4-2) and the Nhlowa Road (S28). (See page 85)

THE MAIN ROAD TO LOWER SABIE (H4-2)

The H4-2 – also known as the Gomondwane Road – was the first road built in Kruger. It was laid by ranger CR de Laporte in the early 1920s in what was then the Sabi Game Reserve. Although it was not originally established as a tourist route, it is rated as one of the best game-viewing drives in Kruger. It's one of the few roads in the Park where one has a good chance of seeing lion, hyaena and wild dogs and an outside chance

Brett Hilton-Barber

White rhino at Mpanamana

CROCODILE BRIDGE CAMP

Crocodile Bridge Camp is on the banks of the Crocodile River a few kilometres from the entrance gate. Situated in the sweetgrass knob-thorn, marula savanna, it was once briefly the headquarters of the old Sabie Game Reserve. The camp is an excellent place to stop for a meal when coming either in or out of Crocodile Bridge Gate, and is well-placed for late arrivals and early departures. There is a reasonable restaurant, a convenience store where one can buy snacks and essentials, a gift shop, petrol station, post office and emergency first-aid post. Tragically, the camp's wonderful setting among tall riverine trees and thorn thickets has been compromised by developments across the river. Rather try and get into Lower Sabie and consider Crocodile Bridge only as a last resort if accommodation elsewhere in the south-east is fully booked.

Despite this, Crocodile Bridge is in the heart of good game territory and there are usually a variety of animal sightings close to the camp. Hyaena are often heard outside the camp fence at night, with their unnerving giggles and cries. The proximity of the river ensures that Crocodile Bridge is an excellent birding camp – with many Lebombo and Mozambican birds to be seen. During periods of heavy rainfall, the Crocodile Bridge camp entrance is prone to flooding.

Buffalo drinking

of spotting the rare black rhino. Because of the wealth of game, this is a popular route with visitors and it's best to do it early or late in the day to avoid the traffic.

The first few kilometres from Crocodile Bridge take one through mixed woodland with sweet grazing where a variety of game can be seen all year round. This is a good area for giraffe, which browse on the knob-thorn and other acacia species – and mixed herds of impala and zebra.

There is usually some animal activity at Gezantfombi Dam, 5km from Crocodile Bridge. Gezantfombi, which is siSwati for "the place where the young women bathe", often hosts elephant and is a reliable water source for grazers and browsers.

North of Gezantfombi Water Hole, the H4-2 cuts through dense thorn thickets for much of the route to Lower Sabie. These thickets grow on ecca shales and the spikey, often impenetrable, tangle of various acacia and albizia species is known as Delagoa Thorn Thicket or Gomondwane Bush. These thickets conceal one of Kruger's rarest animals, the black rhino. Also known as the hook-lipped rhinoceros because of the shape of its jaw (which differs from the square jaw of the white rhino), the black rhino has been saved from extinction by conservation efforts in South Africa, which has more than 60% of the world's population of this species. The different jaws of the white and black rhino reflect their eating methods – the black rhino is adapted for browsing while the white rhino is a specialist grazer. White rhinos may also be seen along the H4-2 where the bush is less dense.

The thornveld along the H4-2 opens up from time to time to reveal small localised

Nigel Dennis

The Selati Line

The ill-fated Selati railway line was an expensive folly in terms of human life and hard cash. Intended to link the goldfields of the north-eastern Transvaal with the railway line from Komatipoort to Delagoa Bay, its construction witnessed so many tragedies that each sleeper on the line was said to represent one human life. Work began optimistically enough in 1892 but, two years later, a financial scandal around the funding of the line erupted, the contractors ran out of cash and their company was liquidated. The line was laid only as far as Sabie Bridge (Skukuza), a mere 80km from Komatipoort. During this period, thousands of black and white labourers were employed, truckloads of liquor were consumed and tens of thousands of animals were shot. The line was idle for 15 years – used only by James Stevenson-Hamilton and his rangers who had a handpump-powered trolley which they used to get supplies from Komatipoort – before the project was resuscitated. In 1912, the line reached Tzaneen. For many years the line was in use but the closure of the Selati goldfields cast doubt on its viability. When Kruger was opened to the public in the mid-1920's the line was used for tourist traffic. However, Park authorities decided that the railway line was at odds with nature conservation and decided to close it down. In 1972 the line was used for the last time and was then lifted. The last engine to go through the Park is now a monument at Skukuza and one of the original carriages has been turned into the Selati restaurant at the camp.

Brett Hilton-Barber

Old railway bridge at Skukuza

Zebra

Brett Hilton-Barber

pans and vleis which are excellent birding spots after heavy rains. Gomondwane Dam at the junction of the H5 is an artificially fed water hole that is a popular drinking spot for impala, zebra and wildebeest.

Because of the number of grazers and browsers in the bush, there is also a good chance of seeing predators. Lion and hyaena are particularly prevalent in the dense woodlands and thorn thickets south of the Sabie River. Although they share the same habitat preferences, there is no love lost between lion and hyaena. Hyaena tend to steer clear of lions, although there are cases when hyaena will try and drive lionesses off a kill. Look closely at the concrete culverts on the sides of the H4-2 – hyaenas sometimes use them as dens. Wild dogs are regularly seen along the H4-2, particularly in the early morning.

Part of the H4-2 follows an 18th century footpath that once linked Chief Magashula's

 Male cheetahs are often found in groups, usually consisting of brothers who defend a territory together which may overlap several females' territories.

Heinrich van den Berg

Cheetah

Duke's Water Hole

Brett Hilton-Barber

kraal at Phabeni to the coastal port of Delagoa Bay. One of the first traders in the Kruger area, João Albasini, had a store on this route as did the notorious lowveld gangster, Sardelli the Greek.

The thorn thickets recede as the H4-2 approaches Lower Sabie camp and the landscape opens up dramatically. This is because the underlying geology shifts from shale to basalt, which is associated more with a grassland environment. The Lebombo becomes visible to the east over the reedbeds of the Sabie River – the main koppie one sees to the north-east is Muntshe (435m above sea level). This more open landscape is one of the best places in the Park for seeing cheetah. They prey on impala and other smaller antelope that feed on the sweetveld plains.

Duke's Water Hole – along the S137 – is a recommended stop. It is named after the legendary Tom Duke, Lower Sabie's head ranger for 20 years, from 1903 to 1923. As a boy, Duke survived an attack on his eastern Cape farmhouse during the Frontier Wars. He went on to become a decorated hero during WW1. Like many of the other old guard, he was a respected, reliable, yet hard-drinking ranger. Stevenson-Hamilton said there were many times, during his uphill battle to develop the Park, that Duke felt like the only friend he had: "I always feel well when he is here … [It is] a pleasure to talk to him when he is sober," he wrote. When Duke died in 1934, Stevenson-Hamilton mourned his passing, noting his resilience and ability to deal with problems, even if they had been self-imposed.

Lioness

Heinrich van den Berg

The Battle of Gomondwane

One of the first recorded battles between Europeans and Africans in southern Africa took place in the Kruger Park. Historian Tim Couzens writes in *Battles of South Africa* how a party of 31 Dutchmen set off from Fort Lagoa (Maputo) on 27 June 1725 in search of the rumoured goldfields of the interior. Led by Johannes Monna, and recorded by clerk Frans de Kuiper, the expedition included "a corporal, a drummer, an under-master, an overseer of the pack animals, 20 soldiers and five sailors. There were also eight interpreters and servants. For the transport of the provisions there were 10 pack-animals; for dinner on the hoof there were eight head of cattle". The Dutch party found the going difficult. They were regarded with suspicion and hostility as they progressed through the chiefdoms of Mattolle, Semano and Coupane between the coast and present-day Komatipoort. The local inhabitants had a good hunch that white settlers meant trouble and deliberately tried to undermine the mission with contradictory stories about gold and treasure, exacting payment for this "information". The Dutch suspected they were being deliberately duped and prepared for the worst. Tensions came to a head on 12 July when the party was ambushed by Chief Dawano and his warriors near the present-day site of Gomondwane Water Hole, north of Crocodile Bridge. The Dutch had superior fire-power with their flintlocks – which the Shangaan warriors called *hongo songilo* ("beautiful sticks") – and managed to repulse the first attack, killing six of their assailants. Even though they had lost most of their gunpowder in the Sabie River, the Dutch used their weapons to good effect during their orderly retreat, keeping hundreds of chanting warriors at bay. There were several more skirmishes before they crossed the Komati River and retreated to the more tolerant atmosphere at the coast. They reported to the commanding officer at the fort at Lagoa that they had done their duty but that the expedition had ended in failure and that the famed goldfields of the interior remained as elusive as ever. Gomondwane is the name of one of Chief Dawano's descendants who lived in the Park until the early 20th century.

Duke's has water all year round and is a drawcard for a variety of animals, including lion, which may sometimes be seen at dawn, drinking at the long finger-like waterhole. There are often white rhino along the S137.

Nhlowa Road (S28)

A good alternative to the H4-2 is the Nhlowa Road, which was the original track into the Sabie Game Reserve from Crocodile Bridge at the end of the 19th century. It heads north-eastwards from the entrance gate towards the dry Lebombo Range that forms the border with Mozambique. The landscape, dominated by knob-thorn acacia and marula trees, is generally flat and more featureless than other areas of the south, but it is good for game because of the rich grazing associated with the basalt corridor. *Nhlowa* is the Shangaan word for fresh marula juice, which may be a reference to the harvesting of fruit from the marula trees of the area before the Park was proclaimed.

This is a very open landscape because of the underlying geology of the area, which is basalt. Because basalt is relatively water-impervious, the pans here hold water long after the rains have gone, providing reliable drinking water well into winter. The basalt also supports fertile soils that produce sweet grazing. For these reasons, the S28 has a good reputation for game viewing. There are large herds of impala, zebra and wildebeest

Duke the elephant

One of the largest tuskers in Kruger is a relaxed elephant known as Duke, named after the water hole at which he is frequently seen. Kruger rangers believe he may have the biggest tusks of any living elephant in the world. Besides his huge tusks, Duke can be identified by a square-shaped notch in his right ear. His home range is in the Lower Sabie and Crocodile Bridge areas but he has been seen as far north as Satara.

Brett Hilton-Barber

 MPANAMANA CONCESSION

The Mpanamana Concession is tucked away in the south-eastern corner of Kruger on the edge of the Lebombo overlooking the Crocodile River valley close to Komatipoort and the Mozambique border. The 15 000-hectare private concession has diverse habitats – thorn thickets, flat open grasslands with shrub acacia, dense riverine bush, pockets of marshland along the base of the rugged foothills and a rich variety of woodland trees on the Lebombo itself. It also gets double the amount of rain that Crocodile Bridge gets, even though they are barely 10km apart.

This habitat diversity means one is likely to see a lot of different animals in the concession. The variety of animals attracts all the big carnivores – lion, cheetah, leopard, hyaena and wild dogs. The riverine bush and koppies in the concession are ideal habitat for leopards which are a Mpanamana speciality, particularly in winter. Lodge rangers once witnessed a pack of 13 wild dogs chase a leopard into a tree near Mpanamana Dam. The side-striped jackal, civet and honey badger are regularly seen on night drives.

Mpanamana Dam is the biggest dam in south-eastern Kruger. It was built in 1957 to provide a permanent water source for buffalo and other grazers. During the crippling drought of the sixties Life Magazine ran a series of photographs of two rangers rescuing an impala that had become stuck in the mud at Mpanamana Dam. There are two very large buffalo herds in the area and there are frequent elephant sightings, particularly in summer when the marulas are in fruit. In winter, the elephants move into the Lebombo where they browse on the kiaats.

There are three camps in Mpanamana, the main being Shishangeni Private Lodge which has 20 chalets, each with its own game-viewing deck at tree canopy height looking out over a watercourse that runs into the Crocodile River. The main lodge area has a large lounge and intimate bar and dining area and can take small conferences. Shishangeni caters for children of all ages with childcare facilities and entertainment. Game drives and specialised birding walks can be arranged with the lodge staff.

The concession has two small, secluded bush camps. Shawu is a luxury tented camp with five units overlooking Mpanamana Dam, some five kilometres from the main lodge. There is a wild dog den close to the camp and there are often cheetah sightings in the vicinity. Shonga is the other bush camp – it has five luxury tents.

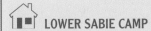

LOWER SABIE CAMP

Lower Sabie is set in magnificent scenery on the banks of the Sabie River. It is the best base from which to explore the game-rich, south-eastern part of Kruger. There are wonderful sycamore figs, marulas and Natal mahoganies in the camp which overlooks Lower Sabie Dam.

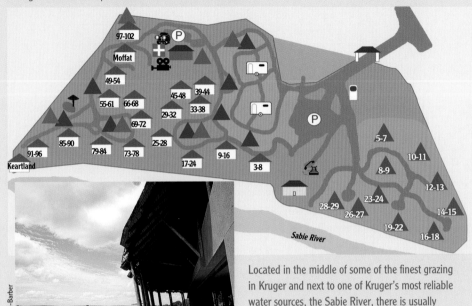

Brett Hilton-Barber

Located in the middle of some of the finest grazing in Kruger and next to one of Kruger's most reliable water sources, the Sabie River, there is usually guaranteed animal activity in the vicinity of the camp all year round. Lower Sabie is built on the site of the original ranger's post. It is a large camp with a variety of accommodation, including permanent luxury tents and more basic camping facilities, and has a restaurant, shop and petrol station. The Old Restaurant has limited satellite TV coverage and is the only place in south-eastern Kruger where one can catch major sports games on TV. The camp is usually booked out months in advance because of its popularity.

The camp has a wonderful viewing deck over the Sabie River where there are huge figs and jackal-berries along the banks, and hippos and crocs in the river bed. Large herds of grazers are usually seen in the grasslands around the camp and lion and leopard sightings are fairly common. This part of the Sabie River has a high population of elephant and waterbuck which can often be seen in the bush across the river from the camp.

There are several good game drives within a short distance of the camp, and the chances are good of seeing the Big Five over a couple of days in this area. Several picturesque water holes are close to the camp. A particularly good one for photography is Sunset Dam (off the H4–1), because one can get close to the water's edge and, despite its name, there is a fairly consistent movement of game throughout the day. Duke's Water Hole (S137) is also a good game-spotting site, where a large pride of lions is often seen, and there are sometimes sightings of cheetah and wild dogs.

The camp offers excellent birding because of the watercourse, riverine bush and the nearby Lebombo. At Nthandanyathi (on the S28) there is a bird hide and a chance to get out of the car while, four kilometres south, there is the large Nhlanganzwani Dam. Because of their proximity to Lower Sabie, these are good water holes to visit either very early in the morning or towards the end of the day if one is staying at the camp. Lower Sabie offers guided bush walks and drives which are highly recommended because of the rich animal life of the lower reaches of the Sabie River. There is a designated day visitor area at Lower Sabie.

in these open grasslands. One also has a better than average chance of seeing cheetah in this area. The S28 is probably the best road in Kruger for white rhino, which are often seen at the S137 turn-off to Duke's Water Hole. (See page 85 and 92 for Duke's Water Hole)

The Nhlowa Road is one of the Kruger's top birding drives because of the proximity of the Crocodile River and the Lebombo range. The plains support big grassland birds like ostriches, bustards and korhaans and there are usually birds of prey circling overhead. Look out for the black-chested snake-eagle from Nthandanyathi Bird Hide and Nhlanganzwani Dam. This raptor circles over the koppies scanning the rocks for reptiles, which are its main diet. It will swoop on a snake and then devour it in mid-air.

Nthandanyathi (Zulu for "the buffalo's water hole") and Nhlanganzwani (derived from the Zulu words for reed beds) are on the faultline between the basaltic grassland and the stone-covered rhyolitic koppies, providing a stark contrast between the different geologies, and a chance to see some of the more arid-orientated vegetation like the euphorbias. In summer, vleis form along the foot of the Lebombo creating a huge marshland that is excellent for birding.

Steinacker's Horse

During the Anglo-Boer War, an irregular commando of men was employed by the British to defend Komatipoort against the Boers. The main motivator behind the force was the colourful Colonel Ludwig Steinacker, dubbed the "Bushveld Bismark". What he lacked in height – he stood just over five foot (1,5m) tall – he made up for in appearance, wearing a brash uniform of his own design with a huge sword and a carefully cultivated, enormous moustache. More of a hindrance than a help to the British, Steinacker's Horse consisted of about 300 English-speaking lowveld residents who were paid 10 shillings a day plus pickles, fresh milk and whisky (which was thought to keep malaria at bay). Based at Sabie Bridge, Steinacker's Horse was tasked with defending the Selati Line but appeared to have spent most of their time hunting and drinking. After the war, Steinacker attempted to keep his unit going, but an unfortunate attempt to take part in the coronation parade in London of King Edward VII led to his being stripped of his command. He briefly returned to Komatipoort before attempting to farm cotton near Pilgrim's Rest. There he lost everything, including his mind. He was arrested by police for planning to murder a former colleague but committed suicide by poisoning himself as he was taken into custody.

Sabie River

The Sabie River's name is derived from the Swazi word *sabisa* which means "to be careful" – apparently in reference to crossing the river because of the slippery rocks and resident population of crocodiles.

Africa Imagery

Sabie River

IN THE LOWER SABIE AREA LOOK OUT FOR:

Animals

White rhino

Hippo

Lion

Waterbuck

Giraffe

Birds

Giant kingfisher

Goliath heron

Brown snake-eagle

African jacana

Burchell's coucal

Lower Sabie to Skukuza

There are two main routes between Lower Sabie and Skukuza – the main road via Nkuhlu picnic site (H4-1) and the Salitje road (S30) (see page 149) which is accessed off the S128.

LOWER SABIE TO SKUKUZA VIA NKUHLU (H4-1)

The Lower Sabie Road (H4-1) to Skukuza is a particularly scenic drive that closely follows the Sabie River through riverine forest and thornveld. This is one of the Park's most popular routes, and the volume of tourist traffic has earned it the nickname of "Piccadilly Circus". Although the distance between the two camps is only 43km, one should allow two-and-a-half hours for the drive because of the number of stops one is likely to make along the way. The fact that the road straddles several ecozones ensures there is an interesting mixture of grazers and browsers, while there are inevitably baboon and vervet monkeys in and under the tamboti and fig trees along the river banks.

North of Lower Sabie are extensive grasslands with sweet grazing. This is one of the best places in Kruger to see the larger herds of zebra and wildebeest. There is an odd geological appearance of Clarens sandstone at the Lubyelubye stream crossing, which is believed to take its name from the Shangaan word *labya* which means "to go through the water wearing one's clothes".

North of the Lubyelubye stream crossing thorn thickets begin to dominate and the bush becomes denser. The road is excellent for birding and one should keep a sharp eye out for leopards as the chance of seeing them along the Sabie is better than almost anywhere else in the Park.

A recommended detour is the three-kilometre N'watimhiri causeway (S79) at the point where the stream of the same name joins the Lower Sabie. There are often

Hippo – one of Africa's most dangerous animals

Hippos account for more deaths in Africa than any other mammal. While they might appear docile, particularly when they seem to yawn lazily, hippos can be incredibly aggressive. The "lazy" yawn is actually the hippo showing its large teeth in a warning display. Their rage can be directed at other hippos infringing on their territory or against any foreign intruder, particularly humans. Several hippo deaths have been recorded in Kruger.

The biggest hippo (*mpfubu* in Shangaan, *imvubu* in siSwati) recorded in Kruger was a bull weighing in at just over two tons. Most male hippos weigh about one-and-a-half tons. Nonetheless, they are surprisingly fast – they can outrun humans, clocking up a top speed of about 30km/h. Hippos eat up to 100kg of grass in a 24-hour period. They feed mostly at night, spending their days in water. It's believed that hippos can remain under water for up to six minutes before surfacing for air, although most submersions are usually not longer than a couple of minutes. Hippos are old Africa. They have been around for 60 million years, having evolved from a pig-like animal during the Palaeocene era.

Hippo

Michael Poliza

99

elephant and buffalo crossing the road to get to the river. *N'watimhiri* means "creek of the puffadders" as these fat, venomous snakes are particularly common in this area, occasionally lying in pathways at sunset to get the last heat of the day.

Shortly before Nkuhlu, the road crosses the N'watin'wambu watercourse which is an elephant route between the woodlands south of Skukuza and the Sabie River. Nkuhlu (the Swazi name for the Natal Mahogany, *Trichilia emetica*) Picnic Spot is about halfway between Lower Sabie and Skukuza. One can do worse than stop for a braai on the slopes overlooking the river, especially if one is a keen birder. There is a shop and fast-food outlet at Nkuhlu. (See page 149 for Nkuhlu to Skukuza)

 ## The Lebombo – rugged hills of the eastern frontier

The Lebombo range is a stony and rugged series of rhyolitic hills that form the border between Kruger and Mozambique. These pink-hued ridges were formed by volcanic eruptions some 200 million years ago. This is one of the lowest rainfall areas in Kruger, and this is reflected in the vegetation types – the drought-resistant bushwillow species and the succulent euphorbias are common on the ridges where there are concentrations of Lebombo ironwood. Between the koppies are deep gorges that have their own ecosystems. The dark clay drainage lines support round-leaved bloodwood, marula and knob-thorn acacias. The Lebombo extends south beyond Kruger and forms the border of Swaziland and Mozambique and then Swaziland and South Africa. In the extreme southern Lebombo is Border Cave which is the oldest known burial site in the world, dating back some 80 000 years. It was here that the world's oldest known mathematical instrument – the 37 000-year-old Lebombo bone – was found in the 1970s. The bone – a baboon fibula – has 29 distinct notches on it and may have been used as a lunar phase counter as it resembles the calendar sticks used by the San in Namibia. Approximately 100 million years ago the Indian Ocean extended to the foot of the Lebombo.

Africa Imagery

Lebombo mountains

Lower Sabie to Tshokwane

The main road between Lower Sabie
and Tshokwane (H10) has a number of
interesting detours and drives that allow
one to explore the eastern grasslands and
the southern Lebombo.

LOWER SABIE TO TSHOKWANE (H10)

One of Kruger's most gratifying drives
– from a perspective of scenery and game
viewing – is the road north from Lower
Sabie to Tshokwane (H10). The road winds
gently through knob-thorn and marula
savanna, and the open grassland enables
one to see animals several kilometres away.
Shortly after the low-level bridge near
Lower Sabie camp – which is an excellent
birding spot – there is a 14-km detour off
the H10 that skirts the southern Lebombo
and rejoins the H10 near Muntshe Hill.
This is the Mlondozi Dam road (S29). The
other alternative is the old main road to
Tshokwane (S128). (See page 149)

The H10 provides some of the best
views in Kruger. Mlondozi Dam picnic site
provides stunning vistas over the plains and
the Lebombo, as well as a combination of
bird and animal life at the water's edge and
in the surrounding countryside. The dam is
on the Mlondozi watercourse, which carves
a wetland path around the base of Muntshe
Hill (435m), a dramatic granophyre ridge that
juts out of the lowveld floor, signalling the
transition zone between the eastern plains
and the Lebombo koppies.

This is a good place to see marabou and
yellow-billed storks, kudu, hippo and elephant.
Herds of zebra, buffalo and wildebeest can
often be seen across the surrounding plains.
In siSwati, *mlondozi* means "perennial
stream", an apt description as the stream
above the dam transforms into a long, vibrant
vlei during the rainy season, with a series of
interesting water holes – Mafotini, Loskop,

Giraffe have seven vertebrae in their long
necks, which is the same number of neck
bones that humans have.

Nigel Dennis

Giraffe

Hillside, Muntshe and Rietpan. This is a productive birding area during late summer; there are often unusual sightings for Kruger here, such as the black coucal, which appears in years of good rainfall. Large herds of buffalo, zebra and wildebeest often congregate in the plains around Mlondozi and Muntshe in autumn and early winter.

According to Kruger researcher and writer Hans Bornman, the Mlondozi creek was the northern base of the Swazi Inyatsi regiment during the mid-1800s. The warriors who were stationed here were known as the Balondolozi who were involved in several skirmishes with Shangaan groupings over control of the area.

There is a 12-km circular road (S122) around Muntshe Hill, which is particularly pretty during the wet season because of the wild flowers in bloom. There are usually kudu, zebra, wildebeest and occasionally cheetah on this road.

North of Muntshe, the H10 crosses the broad eastern grassland plains where most trees struggle to transcend shrub form – except along the drainage lines which are marked by leadwoods and marulas. There is less game in these grasslands compared to the area north of Lower Sabie, but there is something quite extraordinary about the depth of space of this open savanna. If one is lucky during times of season change, one may see large herds of zebra and wildebeest on the plains below. The H10 approaches the Lebombo and then ascends into the range to Nkumbe, one of the best look-out spots in the whole of Kruger.

Nkumbe is the highest point in the Lebombo south of the N'waswitsontso. The views over the vast grassland plains and the Shilolweni woodlands from the thatched shelter at the get-out point are spectacular and will remain etched in one's mind forever. Absorb the soul of the savanna by spending half-an-hour at Nkumbe with a pair of binoculars and a refreshment of one's choice, studying the lightly wooded grasslands below.

Nkumbe

Wild dog pups

Albert Froneman

From Nkumbe, the H10 winds down out of the Lebombo into the thorn thickets and mixed woodland valleys of the Tshokwane area. Orpen Dam, nestled in the Lebombo between Nkumbe and N'wamuriwa koppies, is on the N'waswitsontso River. There is a

Brett Hilton-Barber

small thatched shelter, well positioned on the edge of the Lebombo, that provides a fine view over the surrounding koppies and the sandbanks below. There is a resident group of crocodiles, often hippo in the vicinity, good views and excellent birding.

Vervet monkeys are found throughout Kruger. Watch how they groom each other. There is a theory that mutual grooming by early primates evolved into what we call love.

Brett Hilton-Barber

Vervet monkeys grooming

103

Impala

Nigel Dennis

How a barroom discussion led to the world's biggest game reserve

One could say it all started over a beer on the stoep of Hanneman's Hotel in Komatipoort one hot summer's day in the early 1900s. Major James Stevenson-Hamilton was reflecting on the first five years of his stewardship of what was then the Sabi Game Reserve. He was also having his ear bent by the local innkeeper who put up a convincing argument as to why the warden would soon be out of a job. The innkeeper's argument was simple – there was no sustainable business model to keep the concept of a wildlife reserve afloat, particularly in the face of hostile public opinion led by the pro-hunting lobby.

Stevenson-Hamilton's thinking shifted profoundly after that beer. He formulated a plan to turn the reserve into a national park, modelled along the lines of the Yosemite Park in the United States. He put this to the colonial authorities in 1912. He found support from his former Boer War enemy, Denys Reitz, who constructed the legal framework for his vision. Yet it took another 14 years to overcome hostile public, mining and agricultural opposition to the idea before the Hertzog Party was voted into power in 1924. The new Minister of Land Affairs, Piet Grobler, put his personal enthusiasm into steering through Parliament an Act that consolidated the Sabi and Shingwedzi Game Reserves into a single common national park controlled by trustees on behalf of the nation. Former Kruger head Tol Pienaar invoked a neat turn of phrase when he once described Stevenson-Hamilton, Reitz and Grobler as "the Word, the Deed and the Law". Their collective vision survived the political turmoil and transformation of 20th-century South Africa to become one of the world's top wildlife destinations.

It also prevented numerous attempts by big business to exploit the rich natural resources that lie beneath the Kruger, stripping away mining rights between the Olifants and Letaba Rivers in the 1920s and halting an attempt in the 1960s to mine for coal on the banks of the Luvuvhu River. Equal to their task was the late entrepreneur Anton Rupert who pioneered the Peace Parks concept which has taken Kruger to another level – incorporation into a transfrontier park linking South Africa, Mozambique and Zimbabwe in what will eventually be the world's largest game reserve. Not a bad outcome to a 100-year-old pub argument!

Crocodile Bridge to Malelane

There are several routes between Crocodile Bridge and Malelane. The most direct route is the Crocodile River Road (S25), while the longer route is via the Bume or Randspruit roads via Biyamiti weir. (See page 85)

CROCODILE RIVER ROAD (S25)

The Crocodile River Road (S25) heads westward into fairly dense thorn thickets and grassland where one has the option of either heading into the central part of the southern Park – along the Bume Road (S26) into the Biyamiti Loop (S23), or to carry on following the Crocodile River towards Malelane.

Generally, the further west one travels in the south of the Park, the more dense the vegetation becomes. This is particularly true during late summer when the bush is at its thickest, which makes it harder to see game.

There is a get-out point along this road is at Hippo Pools (S27), eight kilometres from the entrance gate. There is a guard on duty at Hippo Pools who can show one the remains of San art on the rocks overlooking the river. Unfortunately, most of the artwork disappeared in 2000 when floods washed away many rocks from this part of the river. The area is unshaded and can get extremely hot in summer. There's a good chance of seeing hippos and crocs from Hippo Pools and there are often buffalo along the broad river bank.

One unusual incident reported from the Croc River Road dates back to 1960's when former ranger Thys Mostert saw a fight to the death here between two male giraffe. The road passes the site of the site where General Ben Viljoen destroyed his artillery pieces at the end of the Anglo-Boer war.

LWAKAHLE CONCESSION

Lwakahle Concession is a 15 000-hectare private reserve in the Crocodile thorn thickets midway between Biyamiti and the Crocodile River. Lwakahle, which is derived from the siSwati word for "they fight well", is steeped in history as there are several Iron-Age sites here dating from the 16th and 17th centuries as well as a section of the old Delagoa Bay transport road. There are three distinct habitat zones in the concession – the bushwillow and raisin bush scrubland in the south, the gabbro sweetveld in the middle and knob-thorn, marula savanna in the north.

Lukimbi Lodge is the luxury camp in the Lwakahle. It has 16 luxury suites, each with its own private lounge and deck overlooking a woodland valley and stream. The camp has an excellent spa which offers beauty treatments and reflexology. It also has a well-stocked library, conference centre, gym and pool. There is a computer station available for sending and receiving e-mails. The camp has a chapel – just in case the flush of bushveld romance necessitates a sudden (or planned) exchange of wedding vows.

One of Kruger's more unusual kills took place at Lukimbi soon after its launch in 2002 – a leopard pursued an impala into the dining area of the lodge sometime after midnight and slaughtered it near the buffet table. It was probably a good thing that all guests were asleep – by the time they arrived for breakfast, staff had cleaned up the grisly remains of the kill. The woodlands around Lukimbi have both white and black rhino and elephants are frequent visitors to the camp.

Brett Hilton-Barber

Crocodile Bridge to Skukuza

There are two main routes to Skukuza from Crocodile Bridge – the tar road via Lower Sabie (see page 85) or along one of the dust roads through the mixed woodlands of the broad Biyamiti catchment area. These are the Randspruit (H5) and Bume River (S26) roads which eventually join the dirt road between Malelane and Skukuza (S114).

RANDSPRUIT ROAD (H5)

The Randspruit Road (H5) heads west from the main Crocodile Bridge, Lower Sabie tar road (H4-2) at Gomondwane Water Hole. At this junction, a few century-old bluegums mark the site of a trading store run by the infamous lowveld hustler Sardelli the Greek. In *Lost Trails of the Lowveld*, TV Bulpin describes Sardelli as "tough and brutal and cunning as a crocodile". Sardelli sold a brutally harsh form of liquor that he brewed himself. He also ran a gang of brigands who specialised in robbing mineworkers returning to Mozambique from the Witwatersrand. Sardelli is suspected of having murdered and robbed another lowveld storekeeper, Charlie Woodlands, while the two of them were on a trip to Delagoa Bay. Sardelli served in Steinacker's Horse during the Anglo-Boer War, manning an outpost in northern Kruger. After the war, he set himself up selling the guns he'd confiscated from the Shangaans and the Sotho communities under his jurisdiction. His mental and material circumstances deteriorated rapidly. According to Bulpin, he took a job as a cattle herder at Mica "for three pounds a month and a sack of mealiemeal. He eventually died in a lunatic asylum".

The Randspruit Road follows the track of the old Selati railway line which ran along the top of the Randspruit watershed, linking Skukuza to Komatipoort. The rails have since been removed. In 1923, before the Park was officially opened to tourism, South African

 Giraffe males have gained some notoriety as being homosexually orientated. This is because sparring and mock-fights between males often lead to expressions of lust. The long gestation periods of females (fourteen-and-a-half months) may have something to do with this.

Railways offered a tourist service called "Round in Nine" – a nine-day scenic trip around the country. The most popular part of the trip was the journey along the Selati line which included stops for bush walks and an evening bushveld braai.

The area is characterised by low, rolling hills with rather coarse sandy soils on the hilltops where the grass is either sparse or a mixture of sweet and sourveld. The sweet grass generally grows on the darker clay soils

Nigel Dennis

Burchell's coucal

The Marula –
medicine tree of the Lowveld

The marula (*Sclerocarya birrea*) is the "medicine tree" of the lowveld and is regarded as sacred by some communities. This deciduous tree is found throughout Kruger and grows to about 18m in height. It's easy to recognise from its rounded canopy and grey-brown bark which peels off in round patches to reveal a paler under-surface. Marula male and female trees are distinctive and, for this reason, muthi from the tree has played an important part in marriage and fertility rituals. It is said that concoctions from male and female trees can influence whether a parent-to-be will have a son or a daughter. The marula is prized for its nutritionus fruit which is rich in Vitimin C. For centuries, lowveld communities have brewed a strong alcoholic beverage from the fruit, which is also used to make jam. The seed kernels are roasted as a delicacy. Bark from the tree has been used traditionally to treat malaria; leaves are used in a treatment for burns. The inner bark is apparently an effective antihistamine used to treat insect bites and stings. The marula fruit, which appears in summer, is coveted by many different animals, particularly elephant. There is no truth to the myth that the marula fruit ferments in the elephant's stomach, causing the animal to become drunk. Other browsers that feed on the marula include impala, kudu, baboons and monkeys.

Brett Hilton-Barber

Marula tree

on the lower slopes, so look out for game along the drainage lines that feed into the seasonal streams and rivers.

Knob-thorn acacias, bushwillows and marulas dominate this environment, which favours browsers rather than grazers. The more common browsers here are giraffe, kudu, and duiker, while impala – which are both browsers and grazers – are always around. Klipspringer can often be seen on the occasional rocky outcrops, and there are often elephants in the riverine areas where there are wonderful specimens of leadwood, jackal-berries, sycamore figs and sausage trees. The herd size of grazers in this environment is generally smaller than on the open plains.

The Randspruit Road is one of the better places in the Park for spotting the rare black rhino. Black rhinos were reintroduced into Kruger after the original populations were shot out at the end of the 19th century. The reintroduced black rhino have gone for the same habitat as the original populations – the N'watimhiri and Gomondwane thickets north of Crocodile Bridge and south of the Sabie River. The Randspruit road goes through the woodlands inhabited by another rarely seen animal – the sable antelope which has been known to kill lions with its long, graceful and deadly horns.

The S102 between the Randspruit and Bume Roads is a recommended detour. The road dips through the thorn thickets and gallery forests of the Bume valley woodlands past Mpondo Dam, a reasonably large water hole where there are often animals drinking. There are often kudu around Buffeldornsings Water Hole further along the S102.

The Randspruit Road (H5) joins the Malelane Skukuza dirt road (S114) 5km south of Shirimantanga, where the ashes of James Stevenson-Hamilton were scattered after his death in 1957.

Black rhino

Nigel Dennis

THE BUME ROAD (S26)

The Bume Road winds through the mixed knob-thorn and marula woodlands on the southern western face of the Bume watercourse. The Bume is a seasonal stream that feeds the Crocodile River. A good birding stop is at the Bume River weir. Sightings along this road are itinerant – the habitat suits browsers, particularly giraffe, elephant and kudu, while there are almost always small herds of impala along the roadside.

Magic guarri trees are prominent in this area, particularly on the lower slopes. Other significant trees in this area are the bushwillow species, leadwoods along the drainage lines, Y-thorned torchwood (*Balanites*) and apple-leaf.

N'WATIMHIRI ROAD (S21)

The N'watimhiri Road (S21) follows the river of the same name past the distinctive Siyalo koppie (341m), and on to two pans – the Nhlotini, the N'watimhiri – through

the Sabie Crocodile thorn thickets on granite/gneiss. The bush on either side of the road is fairly dense so it's best to drive slowly in order to see game. Look out for both the black and white rhino in this area. There is a particularly good three-kilometre loop road off the Lower Sabie Road (H4-1), the N'watimhiri Causeway (S79) which takes one through beautiful riverine bush at the confluence of the N'watimhiri and Sabie Rivers. Birders should keep an eye out for the African hawk-eagle in the tree canopies or circling above the road.

 An elephant's teeth are used for grinding vegetation. Over an elephant's lifetime, six sets of molars are developed, but are used only one at a time. Arising from the back of the jaw, the teeth move forward and push out molars that are worn out or broken. When the last molar moves forward, at the age of 40 to 45 years, it must last the rest of the elephant's life (elephants live up to 70 years). If the tooth wears down completely, the animal can no longer chew effectively and will starve.

Biyamiti River

Brett Hilton-Barber

The Biyamiti area

The Biyamiti catchment area is the heart of central southern Kruger. The river has its source near the Shitlhave Water Hole near Pretoriuskop and is an avian highway for birds crossing east and west across the Park. The river supports beautiful tracts of riverine woodland, which can best be experienced at Jock's Safari Lodge or Biyamiti Camp that both overlook the river. The vegetation of the central south is mixed bushwillow and acacia woodland, lots of magic guarris, marulas with leadwoods and jackal-berries along the watercourses. There is both sweetveld and sourveld grazing.

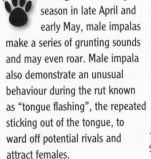

During the breeding season in late April and early May, male impalas make a series of grunting sounds and may even roar. Male impala also demonstrate an unusual behaviour during the rut known as "tongue flashing", the repeated sticking out of the tongue, to ward off potential rivals and attract females.

Impala rams locking horns

Nigel Dennis

In the Biyamiti area look out for:

Animals

White rhino

Duiker

Giraffe

Buffalo

Hyaena

Birds

Violet-backed starling (in summer)

Green wood-hoopoe

Swainson's spurfowl

Woodland kingfisher (in summer)

Jacobin cuckoo (in summer)

Biyamiti Road (S139)

One of Biyamiti's main drawcards is the road leading to the camp – the S139 – which follows the river through the mixed woodland. Only residents are allowed on this drive that dips over a number of watercourses that run into the Biyamiti. There are wonderful trees along the route – leadwoods, marulas and weeping boer-beans, which often grow on top of termite mounds. There is a white-headed vulture nest near Blinkwater lookout point, which offers a good view of the Biyamiti, a few kilometres upstream of the camp. The area around the Biyamiti Water Hole windmill is usually the centre of a lot of birding and animal activity. There are often elephant and buffalo on the banks of the Biyamiti.

BIYAMITI CAMP

Biyamiti Camp is an intimate, no-frills bush camp in the mixed woodlands on the Biyamiti River, four kilometres upstream from its confluence with the Crocodile River.

It is built close to the site of a fortified settlement that was occupied several hundred years ago by some of the first Shangaan settlers moving east from Mozambique. According to

Albert Froneman

the *Dictionary of Kruger Park Place Names*, the name Biyamiti has its roots in the Shangaan *ku biya* (to make a barricade) and *miti* (huts). This refers to the fact that the Shangaan migrants had to erect defence systems around their kraals to protect themselves from the Swazi who had traditionally occupied the area.

Unlike many other SANParks camps, the chalets are not set in a laager-like ring but in a loose line overlooking the river and surrounding bush. There are 15 self-catering cottages, equipped with electricity, stoves, fridges and freezers. There is no shop or petrol station at Biyamiti. Firewood is on sale at reception.

The Biyamiti is a seasonal river and is, therefore, usually dry, but that does not diminish the prolific birdlife. Biyamiti Camp is a good year-round birding spot, but it really comes alive in summer.

Biyamiti is renowned for its cuckoos, which are very active along the watercourse in late summer before departing for their African or European breeding grounds in March.

Kruger's rarer antelope

Roan antelope

Lichtenstein's hartebeest

Sable antelope

The botanically rich, high-rainfall mountainveld of the south-west provides habitat niches for some of Kruger's rarest antelope. This is the only part of Kruger where the the grey rhebok is found. Other uncommon sightings here include eland – first recorded around Shabeni Hill in 1883 by the transport rider JG Basson; sable – the first animal to attack a tourist in Kruger in the 1930s; and Lichtenstein's hartebeest, successfully reintroduced into Kruger from Malawi after local populations became extinct. Other rare antelope in the south-west include red duiker, roan antelope and mountain reedbuck.

Klipspringer

Brett Hilton-Barber

South-western Kruger

> ### 🍃 Habitat pointers
> - Malelane mountain veld around Berg-en-Dal
> - Pretoriuskop sourveld in the Numbi Pretoriuskop areas
> - Finger of sweetveld grazing from Afsaal along Voortrekker Road to Phabeni
> - Mixed bushwillow and acacia woodlands between Jock's and Skukuza

The south-west is the most mountainous part of Kruger and gets more rainfall than anywhere else in the Park. The granite foothills can be divided into two main habitats – the Malelane mountain veld in the south around Berg-en-Dal and the Pretoriuskop sourveld to the west around Numbi and Pretoriuskop. Because of the rain and higher altitudes, there are a variety of microhabitats within the foothills that support rare plants not found elsewhere in Kruger. In between the hills are mixed knob-thorn and marula woodlands which undulate eastwards across the rolling catchment areas of the Sabie and Crocodile Rivers. The best game viewing in the south-west is probably around Berg-en-Dal where the mixed grazing attracts herds of buffalo and zebra, and the lions that hunt them. The area around Afsaal usually has some animal activity because of the sweet grass. There are often lion and hyaena sightings here. Look out for rhino on the Voortrekker and Napi roads. Closer to Skukuza most of the granite outcrops have resident klipspringers. The Voortrekker Road often has rhino. Rarer antelope to look out for in the south-west include the mountain reedbuck, Lichtenstein's hartebeest, the oribi and the grey rhebok. Pretoriuskop is better known for its scenic drives than the number of animals one is likely to see. However, it is an ideal summer camp because it is much cooler than the rest of the Park. Most rock art in Kruger is found in the south-western foothills.

BEST DRIVE IN THE SOUTH-WEST

Malelane to Skukuza:
Superb drive through rolling plains and granite koppies; stop off for refreshments at Afsaal where there is usually a concentration of game, drive slowly through the woodlands past Jock's, take in Shirimantanga koppies or Mathekenyane hill (Granokop) for good views over the surrounding woodlands. Allow three-and-a-half hours, including stops.

🏠 CAMPS IN THE SOUTH-WEST

Malelane
 013 735 6152 See page 117

Berg-en-Dal
 013 735 6106/7 See page 119

Jock's Safari Lodge
 013 735 5200 See page 126

Pretoriuskop
 013 735 5128/32 See page 137

🔭 MALELANE GATE EXPLORER OPTIONS

- Matjulu Loop (S110); 23km back to main road; (1,5 hours) tar and dust road into the heart of the southern biome, mixed woodlands and mountains with reputation for good sightings;

- Crocodile River Road (S114, S25) to Crocodile Bridge; 141km, 5,5 hours; dust road; thorn thickets and riverine bush; good for cheetah;

- Main Road to Skukuza (H3); 64km; 2,5 hours; beautiful drive through rolling hills of mixed woodlands, interesting sightings around Afsaal;

- Afsaal to Pretoriuskop (H2-2); 34km; 1,5 hours; historic drive along the old transport riders' route; past Ship Mountain into the south-western foothills; often good for rhino, eland and hyaena.

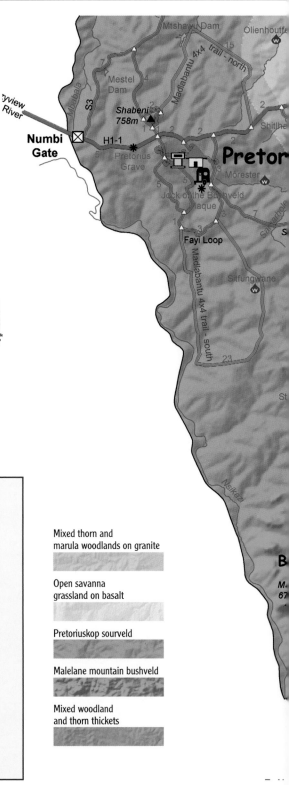

Mixed thorn and marula woodlands on granite

Open savanna grassland on basalt

Pretoriuskop sourveld

Malelane mountain bushveld

Mixed woodland and thorn thickets

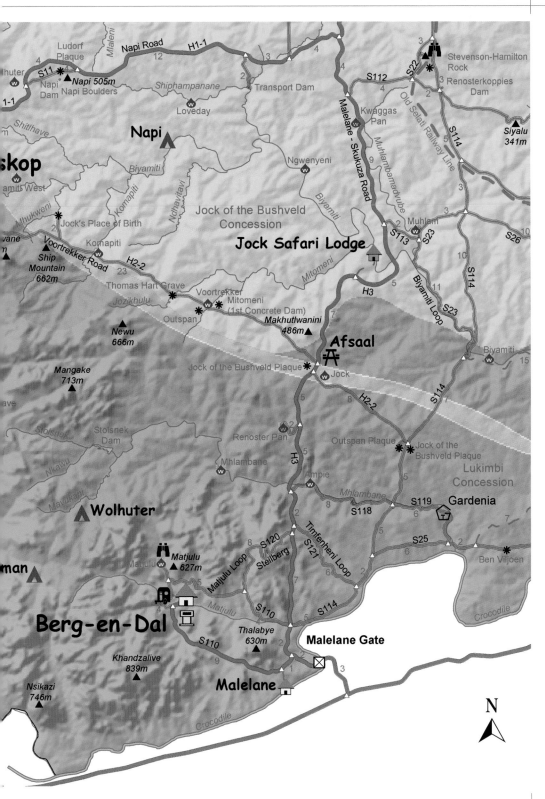

Malelane Gate

Entering Kruger through Malelane Gate is like taking a trip back in time. Behind one lies the pumping heart of South Africa's subtropical export industry based on the growing and processing of citrus, sugar, avocados, bananas, mangoes, litchis, nuts and vegetables. Before one is the pristine environment as it existed before the economic development of the lowveld. The granite koppies adorned with large-leaved rock figs and bushwillows, and the valleys graced by jackal-berries, magic guarries and tambotis, lie in stark contrast to the agribusiness that has taken root on the other side of the Crocodile River.

Malelane Gate is on the Crocodile River, about 50km upstream from Crocodile Bridge. Be warned, it is one of Kruger's busiest gates and there are often long queues of cars waiting to get into the Park at weekends and during school holidays.

The Malelane area has long been an area of human habitation. Just south of the entrance gate is the ancient ochre mining site of Dumaneni. Kruger historians JJ Kloppers and Hans Bornman believe that over 100 000 tons of red ochre were mined at Dumaneni between 46 000 and 28 000 years ago. The San appeared to have been the first miners, using ochre for artistic and medicinal purposes. Iron-Age smelters found at Dumaneni indicate that the mine was operative during the Iron Age, which began in southern Africa approximately 2 000 years ago. Red ochre has long been associated with power. In Siswati it is known as *ludumane* which means "power four times the sound of thunder". In Swazi culture only chiefs and sangomas were allowed to wear ochre, which was mixed with animal fat and smeared on their bodies.

Malelane has been a river crossing for hundreds of years and takes its name from

Malelane mountain bushveld

Brett Hilton-Barber

the Malelane Regiment of King Mswati II of Swaziland which was stationed here in the 1850s when the area was under Swazi control. Mswati's regiments conducted regular forays into present-day Kruger during the mid-19th century and, at points, his influence extended as far as southern Zimbabwe and central Mozambique. Many of the names in southern Kruger are Swazi in origin, while Shangaan names dominate further to the north.

The game density in the south-western part of Kruger is not as high as that of the south-east where the grazing is more nutritious. However, compared to what the situation was like 100 years ago, there is an abundance of wildlife. Most of the animals in the lowveld were shot out by the late 1800s by hunters – or sportsmen – as they called themselves. Among them were Cornwallis Harris, FC Selous and Pieter Jacobs who alone shot 500 bull elephants and over 100 lions during his hunting expeditions across the subcontinent.

It was this wholesale, unregulated slaughter that prompted President Paul Kruger – himself once an ardent lion hunter – to proclaim the Sabi Game Reserve in 1898. Driving through Malelane Gate is to enter the heart of this original reserve, where the Park's first warder, Colonel James Stevenson-Hamilton was tasked in 1902 with the challenging job of establishing a game sanctuary in the face of conflicting human interests.

It may seem odd, but in those early days of Kruger lion and other carnivores were regarded as vermin and hunted as they were seen as a threat to building up the Park's antelope populations.

Although the Malelane area has the potential for good sightings of lion and sometimes hyaena and leopard, the real treasure of the region is the wild dog.

 The African wild dog is one of the most endangered animals in the world. There are only an estimated 5 000 wild dogs in Africa, of which just on 400 are found in Kruger.

Nigel Dennis

Wild dogs

 MALELANE CAMP

Malelane is a small camp on the banks of the Crocodile River just over three kilometres from Malelane Gate. In 2003, ranger Bruce Leslie was attacked by a leopard in the bush near the camp staff quarters. The quick-thinking ranger survived by thrusting his hand *into* the leopard's mouth to prevent it from biting his throat. He then managed to shoot the animal as it tried to pin him down. Afterwards he discovered the leopard had a broken jaw and had not eaten for days, hence it's decision to go for a human "soft target". Malelane camp has five small huts with a communal dining area and ablution facilities, and a small camp site set among tall trees. The development on the other side of the river does compromise the bush experience, and Malelane should be treated as a transit point in or out of the Park rather than a destination. No day visitors are allowed. The nearest shop is at Berg-en-Dal, six kilometres away. Malelane offers early-morning and evening game drives and guided walks.

Malelane to Berg-en-Dal

There are two ways to get to Berg-en-Dal from Malelane. The most direct way is via the tar road section of the S110, while the longer route is is to take the dirt road section of the S110 via Matjulu Loop. (See page 115)

MALELANE GATE TO BERG-EN-DAL (S110)

The S110 between Malelane Gate and Berg-en-Dal takes one into the Malelane mountain bushveld of south-western Kruger. There is a high diversity of plant and animal species to be seen along this road because of the number of different habitats that co-exist within a confined geographical area that enjoys some of the highest rainfall in the Park. The road goes along a ridge into the Matjulu River valley, which is surrounded by granite mountains. Among these are Kruger's highest peak Khandzalive (839m), as well as Tlhalabye (630m), and Matjulu (627m).

Although game viewing in the south-west can be unpredictable, the S110 usually has some animal activity. This is one of the few parts of western Kruger where the grazers of the eastern lowveld are regularly seen. They generally stick to the lower contours where the grasses are more nutritious and there are often herds of buffalo, wildebeest, zebra and impala which appear to migrate towards this area seasonally. Kudu and duiker are the browsers most likely to be seen in the Malelane Mountain Bushveld, which also has established populations of white rhino. Among the rarer Kruger animals to be seen in this area are the common reedbuck and sable antelope. The main predators that operate here are hyaena and wild dogs, although lion are also frequently seen.

The higher altitudes of this area support different species from the valley woodlands. Mountain reedbuck may be seen rarely in the upper pockets of grassland. They are not found anywhere else in Kruger. Klipspringer are obvious but hard to see as they stand dead still on prominent outcrops.

The dominant trees are the bushwillows and magic guarris, but the woodlands include a number of trees uncommon elsewhere in Kruger – the Zulu milkberry (*Manilkara concolor*), Cape chestnut (*Calodendrum capense*) and white pear (*Apodytes dimidiata*). Large-leaved rock figs (*Ficus abutilifolia*) are common among the boulders and mountain kirkia (*Kirkia wilmsii*) – which is associated more with the northern sandveld – is also common on the upper slopes.

Buffalo

Nigel Dennis

BERG-EN-DAL CAMP

Brett Hilton-Barber

Berg-en-Dal is a large camp built on the Matjulu River within the protective ring of the Malelane mountains. The harsh face-brick design of the buildings may not be to everyone's liking, but the relatively undisturbed woodland environment within the camp is an adequate compensation. The camp has fine views over Matjulu Dam and thick bush towards the steep granite foothills that encircle the wooded valley floor.

Berg-en-Dal is a large camp that also caters for conferences and school holiday programmes. It has all the facilities of the major camps – restaurant, gift shop, petrol station, laundry, swimming pool and Internet café. Wildlife documentaries are screened regularly. Berg-en-Dal is a good stopover for day visitors to do a short walk and a swim. There is a very attractive walk around the perimeter of the camp from the causeway past the dam up the river, along a dry river bed and through the woodlands behind the camp accommodation. The walk is wheelchair-friendly and incorporates a Braille trail.

The Berg-en-Dal area is rich with remnants of the Late Stone Age and Iron Age. When construction work began on the camp in the early 1980s, potsherds and bones were found dating back several hundred years. The artifacts are housed in a display at the camp.

The south-western foothills of Kruger and the neighbouring Bongani Private Reserve have a high concentration of rock art. Well over 100 rock-art sites have been discovered in these hills and there are believed to be many others that are yet to be found. None of the sites is accessible without a guide. The best way to view rock art in Kruger is to do the three-day Bushman Trail, although one needs to book months in advance for the experience.

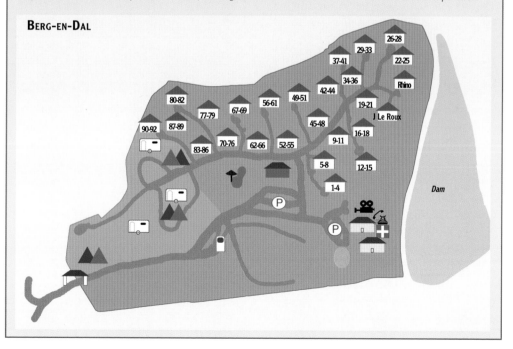

BERG-EN-DAL

IN THE BERG-EN-DAL AREA LOOK OUT FOR

Animals

White rhino

Mountain reedbuck

Wild dog

Klipspringer

Buffalo

Birds

African hawk-eagle

Scarlet-chested sunbird

Pied kingfisher

White-browed robin-chat

Mocking cliff-chat

MATJULU LOOP (S110)

The S110 from Berg-en-Dal is a dusty loop road through the upper catchment area of the Matjulu watercourse. *Matjulu* in Shangaan is a colloquial description for the "place of the Zulus", and got its name during the Swazi occupation of the lowveld in the 19th century (siSwati and isiZulu share the same linguistic roots).

The key to enjoying the south-western mountain terrain is not to look for game so much as to experience the landscape, which is infinitely more layered and complex than the rest of the lowveld. Classified as Malelane mountain bushveld, the foundation of this particular ecosystem is granite and gneiss. Because granite does not easily weather, there are lots of rocky outcrops with shallow, stony soil on the upper slopes and relatively fertile clay soils in the valleys and drainage lines. These conditions favour trees rather than grasses, and, because granite is not a very mineral-rich base, what grass cover there is does not have the same nutritional value as that found on basalt.

Nombolo Mdluli

Nombolo Mdluli is one of the ranger legends of Kruger. He was an oral custodian of the Park's history during his 52-year career in the bush. He began working as an assistant ranger in 1919 at an outpost called Rolle 55km north of Skukuza. In 1921 he was posted to Malelane to work with the inexperienced new ranger SH Trollope. Mdluli accompanied Trollope on his first hunt during which they came across four lion. Trollope shot three of them and wounded a lioness. Then, ignoring Mdluli's impassioned advice that this was madness, Trollope pursued the injured animal into thick bush. The lioness ambushed Trollope and grabbed him by the thigh. Mdluli shot it dead. Several years later, Mdluli had another near-death experience with a lion. Based then at Shingwedzi, he was attacked by a lion that had earlier killed a young boy in a corn field. As the lion charged Mdluli, he stood his ground and shot it dead with a .303. It may seem incredible today that his reward was a Singer sewing machine and a hat made out of the lion's skin, five pounds and permission to kill any other troublesome lion. Mdluli donated his rifle to the Skukuza Museum, where it is on display. Before his retirement in 1971, Mdluli helped Park staff relocate Rolle, which had been abandoned in the early years of the Park.

From a game-viewing perspective, one is more likely to see browsers like kudu, giraffe, impala or duiker along the Matjulu Loop than grazers such as zebra, buffalo and wildebeest. The thick vegetation also makes game viewing difficult, and, if one's expectations for seeing animals are low, one may be pleasantly surprised.

Along this road (S110), beneath Matjulu Hill (627m) is a water hole where white rhino often drink, while kudu and giraffe are sometimes seen. Wild dogs are sometimes seen around Matjulu Water Hole which is a kilometre off the Matjulu Loop. Hyaena are rarer and occur more towards Afsaal and Pretoriuskop. This is not ideal lion habitat although they are in the area. There are many leopard lairs in the koppies on the Matjulu Loop although these elusive hunters are not often seen.

There have been only a handful of human fatalities caused by leopards in Kruger. One incident occurred close to Matjulu Water Hole in 1998. An old, emaciated female leopard brazenly attacked and killed junior ranger Charles Aldridge Swart who had got out of his vehicle on the Matsulwane Bridge during a night drive. Leopards are usually shy of humans but this creature had been driven crazy by hunger and broke the bounds of normal leopard behaviour.

Former head ranger Bruce Bryden described what happened: "While the tourists were stretching their legs, Charles strode to the southern end of the bridge and perched on the railing with the rifle in his lap. He was still sitting there listening to the night sounds and pulling at his cigarette when the leopard crept up behind him and crushed his neck, killing him

The Malelane Mountain bushveld is the only place in Kruger where the grey rhebok and the mountain reedbuck are found.

instantly." When news of his death reached Berg-en-Dal, Cpl Albert Makuleke followed the leopard spoor in the dark, caught up with it and shot it dead with his R1 service rifle. It was found to have had severe bovine tuberculosis. A devastated Bryden remarked afterwards: "It could have happened to any of the guides; it just happened to be Charles who was unfortunate enough to be the one in the wrong place at the wrong time."

The Steilberg Road (S120) connects Matjulu Loop with the Malelane Skukuza road (H3). It winds through the broken landscape of the Malelane mountain bushveld before descending into the mixed bushwillow woodlands of the Mhlambane catchment area. The road has some inspiring and unusual Kruger landscapes, but is not noted for good animal sightings.

Nigel Dennis

Caracal

Rock art in the Kruger Park

Although Kruger rock art has its own stylistic personality, it is part of a much broader legacy of rock painting in southern Africa where there are literally tens of thousands of rock art sites scattered across the subcontinent. Most of the rock art found in Kruger is in the south-western foothills but recent research suggests that shelter paintings are prolific throughout the Park. A SANParks rock art survey done in 2007 by Conraad de Rosner revealed an additional 57 sites in addition to the 120 known sites, identified mostly by Mike English, who pioneered rock art research in Kruger.

Conraad de Rosner

De Rosner believes there is much more. Almost all of Kruger's rock art appears to have been made by San hunter-gatherers of the Late Stone Age, although former Kruger head Dr Salomon Joubert reported there were several sites in the far north of the Park that are of a completely different and more recent style. These geometric finger paintings are believed to have been made by Khoi pastoralists who inhabited the Limpopo valley from the beginning of the first milennium. Most of the San rock art in Kruger is much older – with dates of between 1 500 years and 3 000 years old. Most researchers agree San art is deeply spiritual, reflecting upon the rituals and spirit-world experiences of their ritual specialists: the !gi:xa, or shamans. However, Kruger rock art also appears to incorporate naturalistic elements – several sites depicting hunters with bows and arrows that appear to reflect the reality of hunting. There are also many depictions of trance states and a strong regional theme is the occurence of strange, other-wordly 'vapour trail' figures – humans with long, streamer-like protrusions. These have been found at no fewer than 12 different locations. Other common themes are the depiction of three-legged animals, hollow-bodied figures with patterning within them, and armless human figures. Animals most represented in Kruger rock art are the eland and mountain reedbuck. Depictions of giraffe, buffalo, sable, roan, impala and elephant have also been recorded, while dots and dotted lines

regularly occur, which some researchers believe are indicators of potency. One of the most beautiful images, according to de Rosner, is that of a zebra found in a shelter near Bushman Wilderness Camp – only the white stripes are painted with the dark rock suggesting the rest of the animal. Materials used to paint the images include various plant saps, ochre, ash and blood – possibly to add potency. The best way to see the rock art is to either do the Bushman Walking Trail near Berg-en-Dal (see page 299) which is close to several interesting sites, or to book into the neighbouring Bongani Reserve which may have the highest concentration of rock art in Mpumulanga, with 180 sites identified so far by de Rosner.

Pictures (top): a human skull found near southern Kruger during the 2007 rock art survey;
(right) SANParks rock art guide examining a painting;
(main picture on opposite page) vapour trail figures that are a regional characteristic of Kruger rock art;
tracing of klipspringer and mythical figure

SANParks

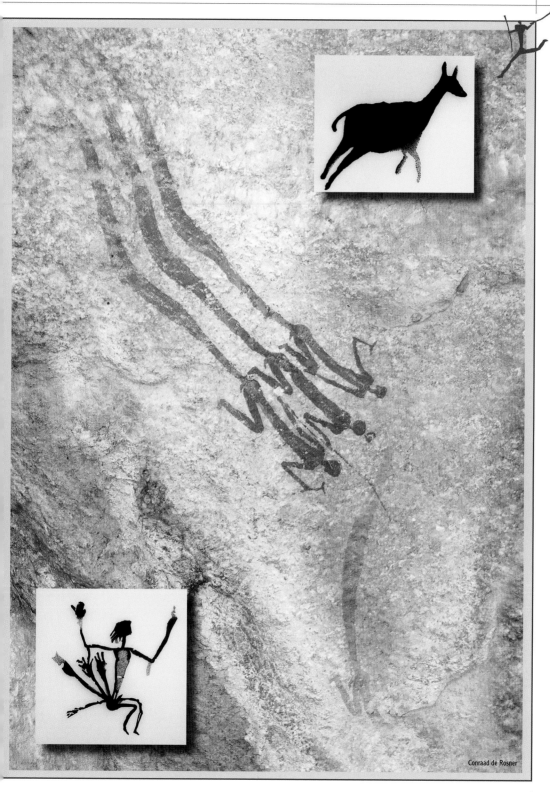

Conraad de Rosner

Malelane to Skukuza

The two main options of getting from Malelane to Skukuza are on the tar road (H3) via Afsaal or along the dust road (S114) via Biyamiti Weir and Renosterkoppies (see page115). Both routes have interesting loop roads and are recommended for both birding and game viewing.

MALELANE TO SKUKUZA VIA AFSAAL (H3)

The tar road from Malelane to Afsaal (H3) passes the landmark Tlhalabye Hill (630m), crosses the Matjulu River and climbs through the edge of the south-western foothills into the rolling woodlands of south-central Kruger. The first part of the drive is especially good for raptors. The road drops from the Malelane mountain bushveld into the mixed knob-thorn and bushwillow woodlands of the Mhlambane catchment area where the landscape opens up.

The white rhino is an H3 speciality, although they are more likely to be seen in the woodlands along the road than at Renoster Pan off the H3 along the Mhlambane creek.

AFSAAL

The old transport riders who originally used Afsaal as their regular camp on the road to Delagoa Bay were shrewd observers of the bush. They would have noticed that it sits strategically next to a strip of sweet grazing that attracts a variety of antelope all the year round, providing some of the best hunting on the road to Crocodile Bridge. The old leadwoods around the nearby Josekhulu Drift still bear the marks of their target practice (see pages 115 and 137 for the Voortrekker Road).

There is a geological reason why the hunters of the 19th-century found such a reliable supply of venison for their pots here. Afsaal sits on a great horn of gabbro which curves across south-western Kruger from Lukimbi Concession along the Voortrekker Road past Ship Mountain into the upper Biyamiti catchment area and then almost to Phabeni. Unlike the granite around it, the gabbro supports nutritious grazing.

This sweetveld finger into the sourveld ensures there is almost always some animal activity around Afsaal at its junction with

 The diminutive dassie or hyrax is among the elephant's closest living relatives. The relationship stems from a remote ancestor common to hyraxes, sea cows (dugongs and manatees) and elephants. There are hyraxes from the fossil record that are almost the size of a rhinoceros and these large, now extinct relatives, may help to explain why the dassie still possesses an unusually long gestation period (approximately eight months) for such a small animal.

Dassie

Mike Myers

the Voortrekker Road (H2-2). There are almost guaranteed sightings around here of zebra, wildebeest and impala and there are often hyaena and wild dog in the vicinity. Among the more unusual animals to look out for here are Lichtenstein's hartebeest, the southern reedbuck and caracal.

Afsaal is a convenient day-time stop-off. It has a shaded picnic spot with a well-stocked shop, fast-food outlet and braai facility. Keep an eye out on the bush while you're braaing – in early 2007 a group of tourists at Afsaal got the fright of their lives when a leopard leapt out of the bush, snatched a large steak off their braai, and disappeared into the bush alongside the stream bed.

Thick clusters of red ivory (*Berchemia zeyheri*) around the picnic site are dwarfed by an enormous jackal-berry tree astride an ancient termite mound, which is home to a tame colony of dwarf mongooses. According to mammal expert Heike Schutze, mongooses have a close association with hornbills, which act as sentries for the little mammals, calling if there is danger. She has noticed that mongooses are often reluctant to leave their burrows in the morning until hornbills arrive.

The red ivory has an attractive red flower that attracts lots of birds during summer. The berries are a local delicacy. Traditional healers say a good cure for a headache is to smoke the roots of red ivory after crushing them into a powder.

AFSAAL TO SKUKUZA (H3)

The area around Afsaal is one of the best places in southern Kruger to see lions. Scan the flatter boulders of the Makhoutlwanini Koppies just north of the picnic site on the tar road to Skukuza (H3). Lions are sometimes seen standing on the boulders studying the surrounding savanna, or resting in the shady, long grass beneath the trees of this broken woodland.

Hornbill

Nigel Dennis

North of Afsaal, the road descends into the woodlands of the Biyamiti basin, winding through dense riverine woodland in the flood plains near Jock's Camp. During the dry season animal life becomes more concentrated along the watercourse, whereas in wetter times the game disperses more widely over the veld. In summer, there are often active feeding parties of hornbills within the clusters of magic guarri in the mixed bushwillow woodlands. They are most active around the guarris when small purple berries are produced in summer.

JOCK SAFARI LODGE

Jock's Camp is a private camp located on the edge of an attractive flood plain between the Biyamiti River and the Mitomeni watercourse. The 6 000-ha concession straddles the Biyamiti watercourse, which is a magnet for animals and birds so there is usually good game viewing all year round.

Named after the legendary terrier, Jock in *Jock of the Bushveld*, the luxury private camp has 12 units, each with its own *tsala* (private deck) and plunge pool, overlooking the river beds.

There is a statue near reception of Jock fighting a sable antelope. A number of the original 19th-century transport wagons are parked under the groves of tall jackal-berries, weeping boer-beans, Cape ash and Natal mahoganies. A huge old jackal-berry dominates the main entertainment area of Jock's. The outside deck and bar are designed around the tree, which appears to be over 400 years old. From the deck, there is a good lookout over the river, grasslands and knob-thorn woodlands mixed with magic guarri and black monkey orange (*Strychnos madagascariensis*) trees. Although the black monkey orange can be poisonous to humans, it is readily eaten by browsers such as kudu, elephant, baboons and even eland. Rhinos can sometimes be seen from the entertainment area. There are lots of magic gaurris and combretum species here and, in summer, the landscape is punctuated by the flowering of the distinctive pink Swazi lily.

A prominent cluster of boulders can be seen across the Biyamiti stream bed from the entertainment deck – at its base is an ancient rock art site that appears to have been a nomadic hunting camp occupied over a long period of time. The lodge offers a guided walk to the koppie which, according to San beliefs, has potent spiritual energy. The San were the last Stone-Age people, living in small nomadic groups following migrating animal herds. Their hunter-gatherer ways remained virtually unchanged for over 10 000 years until the arrival of Bantu-speaking pastoralists from the north. There is a curious plate-sized hole in the boulders near Jock's camp which is believed to have been ground out by successive generations of San. The hole appears to have been fashioned over hundreds – if not thousands – of years, possibly by shamans connecting to the spirit world. Among the artifacts found here are pottery shards, remains of red ochre and white ash (created by burning the shells of giant land snails).

Jock's Safari Lodge

North of the Biyamiti valley, the landscape opens up into stretches of grassland savanna which are a favourite grazing ground for zebra. Mahlambdube Water Hole – zebra pan – was probably used as a campsite by Carolus Trichardt who opened up the Delagoa Bay route in 1845. Look out for waterbuck along the Kwaggaspan wetland before the Renosterkoppies turn-off.

Just north of the Renosterkoppies turn-off (S112) the H3 joins the Napi Road (H1-1), the main road between Skukuza and Pretoriuskop. From here northwards, thorn thickets replace the mixed woodlands. The giant granite dome of Mathekenyane, just off the H1-1, is one of a series of inselbergs that run from west to east across the lowveld floor. It is a perfect vantage point for the whole of southern Kruger and is particularly dramatic in spring when the knob-thorn woodlands below are in full yellow flower.

To the west are the clearly identifiable koppies of Legogote, Ship Mountain and Pretoriuskop, with the escarpment rising behind them; to the south-east lies the prominent huddle of the Malelane mountains, while the clearly visible Lebombo ridge marks the eastern horizon and the border with Mozambique.

The thorn thickets become very dense along the H1-1 as one gets closer to Skukuza, which means that game viewing in summer can be frustrating because of poor visibility through the bush. Tree size increases and the animal life gets busier the closer one is to the water.

Kiaat

Most of the woodcarvings and wooden bowls one sees on sale as one drives into southern Kruger are made out of kiaat, or wild teak (*Pterocarpus angolensis*). This tree is limited mostly to the Pretoriuskop area where it is quite dominant. It does favour other areas where there is a deep and sandy soil, but is not common throughout the Park. It is a slow grower, and is loved by kudu and elephant. It is commonly

Wooden carving
SANParks

used for furniture as it works easily and polishes well. The kiaat is recognisable in the wild by its distinct roundish pods, which ripen in late summer and are eaten by baboons, vervet monkeys and yellow-footed squirrels. It has small, golden-yellow flowers which emerge in spring. The kiaat has many medicinal properties. According to tree experts Fanie and Julye-Ann Venter, the gummy, red sap can be applied to the human eye to treat cataracts, while the ashes from burnt ripe seeds can be rubbed in the mouth to cure bleeding gums. Infusions made from the bark are used to relieve stomach pains, headaches, earaches and ulcers, while the roots are burned to make a medicine to treat asthma and tuberculosis.

MALELANE TO SKUKUZA VIA BIYAMITI WEIR (S114)

An alternative to the H3 tar road between Malelane and Skukuza is the S114, a dust road that also crosses the game migration route near Biyamiti weir and has a number of interesting detours along the Biyamiti and Bume watercourses. The road can get dusty during the dry winter, but it generally has less traffic and allows one more privacy to watch game. The first few kilometres of the S114 follows the Crocodile River between Malelane Gate and the Timfenheni Loop (S121) turn-off. There are often impala, feeding in the company of baboons, along this stretch of the road before it leaves the river and enters the mixed bushwillow and marula woodlands of the Mhlambane drainage area.

There are several sideroads branching off from the S114 that are worth a random drive. One attractive detour is to Gardenia Water Hole, a smallish pan on the Mhlambane

Male baboon

Michael Poliza

Mathekenyane

Brett Hilton-Barber

Loop (S118), close to the junction of the Mhlambane and Crocodile Rivers. There is a bird hide at the water hole which is named after the attractive copse of thick, old Transvaal gardenia (*Gardenia volkensii spatulifolia*) trees at the water hole. Look out for the croc that's often lurking in the shallows. A good time to visit the hide is in late spring or early summer when the gardenia briefly flowers – sunbirds go crazy for the nectar in its fragrant, waxy white-and-yellow flowers. The S118 also has two good viewpoints across the Mhlambane River where there are sometimes elephant and buffalo in the dry river bed and woodland trees.

Upstream from the Mhlambane creek is Stolsnek, a rocky saddle that separates the Stolsnek stream from the Bukweneni Creek. This is where famed lowveld hunter Gert Frederik Coenraad Stols was buried in 1886 (see page 135).

Back on the S114, there is usually a fair amount of activity on the road to Skukuza between the Afsaal turn-off and the Biyamiti River crossing. This is where the road crosses the gabbro strip of sweetveld grazing that runs between the shallow valleys of the Biyamiti and Mhlambane river systems.

Biyamiti Loop (S23) is a recommended detour along this road. The 16-km road follows the river before rejoining the S114 via the S23 at Muhlambamadvube Water Hole. Cheetah are sometimes seen along this road, which has good views across the river into the grassland, woodlands and thorn thickets.

Between Biyamiti Loop and the Shirimantanga Koppies are rolling mixed bushwillow woodlands. Here the S114 is joined by the Bume River Road (S26) and Randspruit Roads (H5) (see page 85).

An alternative, longer detour to Skukuza is the N'watimhiri Road (S21) which passes

Kudu does

Brett Hilton-Barber

A bull elephant can weigh up to seven tons and elephants have the largest brains of any land animal.

Colin Bell

Elephant

Siyalo Hill (347m) and a series of pans on the N'watimhiri Stream which joins up with the Lower Sabie road south of Nkuhlu.

The bush shifts from mixed woodland to thorn thicket the closer one gets to Skukuza. Shirimantanga Koppies and Renosterkoppies Water Hole are recommended stopping points. (See page 85)

Afsaal to Pretoriuskop (H2-2)

The Voortrekker Road is one of Kruger's most interesting drives with several historical points of interest along the way. The road loosely follows a stretch of the 19th-century wagon track between Lydenburg and Delagoa Bay. It was along this road, near Ship Mountain, that Jock of the Bushveld is believed to have been born. (See page 294 for a detailed guide to the Voortrekker Road and page 141 for Jock of the Bushveld)

Malelane to Crocodile Bridge

The most direct route from Malelane to Crocodile Bridge is via the Crocodile River Road (S114, S25). A lengthier detour is via the H3 towards Skukuza, turning off either on the Bume (S26) or Randspruit roads (H5). (See page 85)

Crocodile River Route (S25)

There are usually lots of impala along the Crocodile River Road (S25) and therefore a chance of seeing cheetah and other predators which prey on this small antelope. Cheetah use the cover of the thicker bush along the drainage lines to stalk their prey, they then flush them into the more open veld, where their speed is an advantage. The road takes one through several different ecosystems – Malelane mountain bushveld, bushwillow woodlands, thorn thickets and pockets of riverine trees.

The Crocodile River Road is better than average for game viewing, but developments across the river detract from the wilderness experience. The road passes the old 19th-century crossing point on the Crocodile River which was also the site of a trading store run by Alf Roberts in the late 1800s, known as Tsengemanti ("the place to buy water" in Shangaan). It's not known whether this referred to one of the more popular products sold by Roberts – Nellmapius's Transvaal Gin, a colourless brandy with an exceptionally high alcohol content. (See page 105 for Crocodile Bridge to Malelane)

Mhlambane Loop (S118) and Gardenia bird hide may be worthwhile detours. Access to the Lwakahle Concession is off the Crocodile River road. (See page 85)

Numbi Gate

The first visitors to Kruger came through Numbi a year after the Park was opened to tourists in 1926. A grand total of three cars was recorded in 1927, each being charged a one-pound entrance fee. At that time, Pretoriuskop was the only overnight facility for tourists in the Park. Two years later, when the initial road network had been established, a few more camps were built and it was possible to travel as far as Olifants River, 850 cars entered Kruger. Although this is minuscule compared to the current annual visitor figures of more than 1 million people, the authorities at the time were taken aback by Kruger's popularity.

The Park's first warden, Colonel James Stevenson-Hamilton, recalls that there was not sufficient tourist accommodation

Numbi Gate area

Brett Hilton-Barber

Changing landscapes

The animal life around Pretoriuskop has undergone a radical change in the last century. Up until 1924, the area was used for winter grazing by livestock farmers who burned the veld each year. This kept tree growth to a minimum and attracted grazers such as zebra, wildebeest and sable antelope. When the Kruger National Park was proclaimed that year, the winter grazing rights fell away and the bush began to revert to its natural state – within a few decades, thick terminalia kiaat woodland replaced the grasslands around Pretoriuskop attracting browsers such as kudu, and encouraging the grazers to head into the eastern sweetveld plains.

IN THE NUMBI/PRETORIUSKOP AREA LOOK OUT FOR:

Animals

Sable antelope

Lichtenstein's hartebeest

Black rhino

Kudu

Leopard

Birds

Brown-headed parrot

African cuckoo hawk

Arrow-marked babbler

Gorgeous bush-shrike

Crested barbet

to cater for the demand, and that rangers frequently had to surrender their own quarters to tourists and sleep outside. He quotes one ranger remarking: "I did not mind so much their using my soap, towels, plates, knives and forks, but I do wish they had not used my toothbrush."

Numbi is one of the most dramatic entrances to the Kruger Park because its higher altitude gives one a sweeping vista over the lowveld to the east and the granite foothills to the north and south. The contrast between the densely populated rural communities outside the Park and the pristine wilderness inside is also striking. The entrance gate gets its name from the Siswati word for the small fruit of the Transvaal milkplum (*Englerophytum magalismontanum*). The milkplum, which has a sweetish taste and is high in Vitamin C, was used by the Voortrekkers to make a form of brandy known as *mampoer*. In traditional African medicine, ground milkplum bark is used to treat rheumatism.

NUMBI GATE EXPLORER OPTIONS

- Albasini Road to Phabeni Crossroads (S3) 17km (45 minutes); dust road, scenic drive through kiaat terminalia woodlands with good lowveld views;

- Napi Road to Skukuza (H1-1) 54km, (2,5 hours) tar road; descends from foothills into low, rolling hills of mixed woodland; excellent birding route; game more regularly seen from Napi Boulders;

- Drives around Pretoriuskop (variable distances, 1 to 2 hours); dust road; beautiful granite koppies in mixed woodlands; kudu and white rhino; interesting birding;

- Voortrekker Road to Afsaal (H2-2) 44km; (2 hours); dust road; historic transport route descending from foothills into sweet thornveld and mixed woodlands; usually good for a variety of game.

 The only place in Kruger where the South African hedgehog is found is in the Pretoriuskop foothills. These little animals are hard to see as they shelter in thick bush, living in rock crevices and changing their sleeping spots daily. When under threat they roll into a little spikey ball.

Like the Malelane/Berg-en-Dal area, the Numbi foothills enjoy some of the highest rainfall in the Park and, therefore, have a high diversity of plant and animal species. However, the vegetation, which is defined as Pretoriuskop sourveld, is thick and game is not easily spotted. The terrain is more favourable to selective browsers such as kudu, which is the first animal one is likely to encounter after arriving at Numbi.

Other animals that enjoy the sourveld grass are white rhino and sable antelope. Sable herds in Kruger are small, averaging between two and four animals, but herds of up to 10 individuals are found in the area between Pretoriuskop and Malelane, led by dominant bulls.

The underlying geology of Pretoriuskop sourveld, like most of the south-western part of the Park, is granite with intrusions of gneiss. The higher altitudes are almost all bare granite outcrops and, where there is soil, it is coarse and reddish and relatively infertile. The soil on the mid- and lower slopes is clay-like and richer in nutrients, the predominant trees here being kiaat, silver cluster-leaf and a variety of acacias. Tambotis and figs are common on the drainage lines.

Pretoriuskop Area
PRETORIUSKOP TO ALBASINI ROAD (S7)

One of the dominant features on this road (S7) is Shabeni Mountain (759m), the biggest undisturbed rock face in the Park. One of the most dramatic drives in Kruger is the loop around Shabeni (H1-1– S7) which includes the Mestel watering hole on the Albasini Road. Look out for baboons and klipspringer on the promontories and bateleurs soaring above the rocks. Although they are not often seen around Shabeni,

The Magic Guarri

The magic guarri (*Euclea divinorum*) acts as an early warning beacon to other trees in times of impending drought. Distributed throughout the Park, this slow-growing, dense evergreen shrub produces a pheromone when it becomes stressed. This triggers the release of tannin in the leaves of surrounding trees which makes them unpalatable to browsers such as kudu. The increase in tannin content is a self-protection mechanism that prevents the bush from being eaten out. The guarri itself is not favoured by animals, although birds like its fruit. Alcoholic beverages have been made from the fruit, while twigs broken off from the tree were used as toothbrushes in the old days because of the fibrous texture.

Brett Hilton-Barber

Nigel Dennis

Serval

Ship Mountain

there are lion in the area. Ranger Harry Wolhuter once came across a curious sight during a patrol here in 1938. At the foot of Shabeni was a car with a flat tyre. A tourist was busy trying to change the wheel and had not noticed a lion in the grass four metres away, watching him curiously. Wolhuter yelled at the man to get back into his car and, as he did so, the lion pounced — but it was after the bedroll that the spare wheel had been resting on, and not the tourist. The bedroll was found the next day in the grass nearby, completely shredded.

One can either take the loop back to Pretoriuskop or continue on the Albasini Road through the beautiful granite koppie landscape towards Phabeni. Along this road is the site of one of the world's longest-

running experiments into the effects of burning. Begun in 1954, the study investigates the interaction between fire and rainfall on tree and grass growth.

Originally, Pretoriuskop was a stopover on the route from Lydenburg to Delagoa Bay (Maputo) by the transport riders of the 1800s. It gets its name from the Voortrekker Willem Pretorius, who died here in 1845 and was buried by João Albasini. His grave can be seen soon after entering the Park on the main Skukuza road (H1-1).

To the south of Pretoriuskop camp is the distinctive mountain Manungu (689m), named after a local chief of the same name who ran a trading store and livestock camp between 1845 and 1853. Manungu was part of Albasini's retail network, which serviced

Brett Hilton-Barber

Ship mountain and the saddlebags of gold

It is rumoured that a stash of 19th-century gold coins is buried somewhere at the foot of Ship Mountain. Chief Matafini – a former Swazi military commander who fell out with his king Mbandeni – took refuge in the Crocodile River valley in the 1880s. He apparently buried his substantial wealth – a couple of saddlebags of gold coins – in the vicinity of Ship Mountain to avoid paying tax to the Transvaal Government. While on the run from tax collectors, he was murdered by bandits and apparently took the secret of his treasure's whereabouts to his grave.

transport riders and other travellers moving between the mining towns of the interior and Delagoa Bay.

Fayi Loop (S14) is one of the better places in the vicinity for seeing lion. In 1886 a hunting party led by veteran hunter Gert Stols was camping near Fayi Creek, when they were attacked by two lions. Several oxen were killed before the lions were driven off into the night. Stols set up an ambush the next day using one of the dead animals as a lure. The lions walked into his trap and he shot one dead and wounded the other. The hunters pursued the wounded cat into the Fayi Creek gully where they in turn were ambushed. The injured lion leapt out of the thick grass, savaging one of the hunters before turning on Stols. Stols shot it dead. Ironically he survived the lion encounter only to die that night of a heart attack. He was buried near what is today known as Stolsnek (see page 129).

Pretoriuskop to Malelane

The most direct way from Pretoriuskop to Malelane is via the Voortrekker Road (H2-2). The longer route is to take the Napi Road (H1-1) (see page 115) to the main Skukuza Malelane road (H3) (see page 124) and head south. Both routes include Afsaal picnic site. (See page 124)

THE VOORTREKKER ROAD (H2-2)

The Voortrekker Road (H2-2) south-east from Pretoriuskop follows the 1849 track blazed by Carolus Trichardt, son of the Voortrekker Louis Trichardt. He was commissioned by the then Transvaal Government to open up a regular route between the northern interior and Delagoa Bay and, against the odds, managed to do this.

Albasini's caravans were the main users of this road. Over the years, his porters ferried thousands of kilograms of goods from the coast and carried back huge loads of ivory. The trader Fernandes das Neves accompanied one of Albasini's caravans in 1860 and reported that it took 24 days to complete the 250-mile (402km) journey between the coast and Pretoriuskop. One hundred and fifty Shangaans each carried 40lbs (18kg) of trade goods, 68 porters carried food and camping equipment and 17 elephant-hunters kept guard.

The Voortrekker road was improved in 1896 by the trader Alois Nelmapius to facilitate the transport of supplies to Lydenburg and Mac Mac, where gold had just been discovered. The road was then used extensively by transport riders on their way to what was then Portuguese East Africa (Mozambique).

The road descends from the mountainous Pretoriuskop sourveld into the rolling hills

The shy oribi

The area between Pretoriuskop and Phabeni is one of the few places in the Park where one may glimpse the oribi, the largest of the pygmy antelope family, and one of Kruger's rarest antelope. A curious fact about the oribi is that they rarely drink fresh water, getting almost all their moisture requirements from browsing. There is some uncertainty as to the status of oribi in Kruger. There have been two attempts to reintroduce these high-altitude browsers into Kruger. In 1962, 29 oribi from Badplaas were released near the Fayi Loop near Pretoriuskop, and 10 years later another 98 were brought in. However, these attempts do not appear to have resulted in any sustainable population and oribi sightings are rare. Stevenson-Hamilton recorded his surprise at coming across an oribi at the foot of the Lebombo in the vicinity of Muntshe, almost 100km from its more familiar habitat in the lightly wooded Pretoriuskop foothills.

Oribi

SANParks

🏠 PRETORIUSKOP CAMP

PRETORIUSKOP

Pretoriuskop is a large camp set in the mixed terminalia and kiaat woodlands in Kruger's south-western foothills. It's the oldest camp in Kruger and was opened in 1928 shortly after tourists were first allowed in the Park. In 1947, the British royal family stayed at Pretoriuskop during their South African visit.

Pretoriuskop's attraction to the early travellers making their way to Delagoa Bay was its altitude. Situated high above the malaria- and tsetse fly-ridden lowveld, it was deemed a safe resting spot from which to prepare for the hellishly hot journey across the plains to Komatipoort and then on to the sea. The same principle still operates – the relative coolness of Pretoriuskop makes it a good place to stay during the hot summer months, from October to March. It is a child-friendly camp with a large swimming pool set among granite boulders.

The Sable Trail that winds through the camp is educational from a natural and human history point of view.

Pretoriuskop is the only camp in Kruger where non-indigenous trees have been allowed to grow. The colourful bougainvillaea and red flamboyants were planted by Harry Wolhuter, the first ranger in the Park, who used the camp as his base in the late 1920s. He used to hold staff meetings under an old Natal mahogany tree – the *indaba* tree – which still stands today and is popular with birds. These exotics provide a colourful counterpoint to the indigenous knob-thorns, figs and marulas in the camp.

The best birding spot in Pretoriuskop Camp is the mini forest around the swimming pool which is set in among flat granite boulders. This is a particularly busy area and usually a good variety of birds can be seen within a half-hour amble.

Brett Hilton-Barber

Leopards are first found in the fossil record of Africa just over 3 million years ago.

Brett Hilton-Barber

Leopard

of mixed bushwillow woodland past a number of distinctive geological features, and is a good drive for accessing the game-rich plains south of Skukuza.

It was on this road that the little terrier Jock – of *Jock of the Bushveld* fame – was born. Jock's story is told by Sir Percy Fitzpatrick, a former transport rider who went on to become an influential politician and businessman in the early 20th century.

On the Voortrekker road close to Pretoriuskop is where the first white rhino were reintroduced to Kruger. One can see the remains of the structure where two bulls and two cows were let loose in October 1961 (having been shot out of the area by 1896). During the 1960s, a total of 320 white rhino were reintroduced into the southern Park from the Umfolozi Game Reserve in KwaZulu-Natal, and a further 12 were released in the north. The

Pretoriuskop area is one of the best places to view these animals.

The Voortrekker road is one of the better roads in the south-west for game viewing because it follows a belt of sweetveld that intrudes into the western sourveld. The sweetveld begins close to the foot of the distinctive Ship Mountain (662m) – apparently named because it resembles the hull of an upturned ship – which was used as a navigational aid by these early pioneers. Ship Mountain, with its weird lichen-covered boulders, was literally dumped onto the landscape by ancient volcanoes. It is the remnants of a geological upheaval some 200 million years ago during which the gabbro and basalts of eastern Kruger were spewed onto the lowveld floor.

It is geologically distinctive from the surrounding granite-supported countryside in that it consists of gabbro, a hardier

Zebra

Michael Poliza

Albert Froneman

Lion encounter

Being drunk in the bush is an invitation to danger. However, to every rule there is an exception. In *Wild Life in South Africa*, James Stevenson-Hamilton recounted the experience of a ranger called Sakubona in the early days of Kruger's history. Late one night an inebriated Sakubona returned home from a party at a nearby kraal when he literally walked into a lion along a narrow bush path.

"According to his own account, he felt indignant, and after inquiring of the lion what it meant by blocking his road in this manner, poked it on the nose with his stick, on which it growled, bit him in the leg, and then ran away". The next morning a ranger examined the footprints and tracks and confirmed there had been some sort of incident involving man and lion.

"Of course no-one, not even Sakubona himself," wrote Stevenson-Hamilton "knows what exactly did happen but he assuredly did have a single-handed and unarmed encounter with a lion in the dark, and came off best. Personally, I think had he been sober the result might have been unfortunate for him, but he was just in that condition when it is impossible to know fear. He had arrived at just that stage of spiritual elevation when a man feels there is nothing in the world of which he is not capable. Also of course, there are lions and lions!"

When the Park opened to tourism Sakubona supplemented his income as a gate guard by rolling up his trousers and showing his scars to tourists for a small fee.

139

White rhino are fast food grazers par excellence. They are capable of taking more than one mouthful per second when the grass is fresh and green. They tend to feed in the early morning and late afternoon and either rest in shade or wallow in shallow pools during the heat of the day. During these rest periods, they often depend on the warning calls of oxpecker birds to alert them to impending danger.

Wilderness Safaris

White rhino

relative of basalt that supports more palatable grazing than the surrounding granite. There are often grazing animals around the foot of Ship Mountain, particularly zebra and wildebeest as well as warthog, giraffe and kudu.

Oral history has it that Ship Mountain was a stronghold used by Sotho-speakers in the 18th century to protect themselves and their cattle against Swazi raiders coming from the south. Sotho warriors used to hide their women, children and cattle in caves on the top of Ship Mountain and then use the natural armoury of rocks to beat off attempts by the Swazi to get to the summit.

About halfway between Ship Mountain and Afsaal is Josekhulu Drift where there are often birding parties among the tall trees near the water. Josekhulu was named after Albasini's induna, or headman, a large Zulu man known as "Big Josef" who was in charge of the area. Close to Josekhulu is the site of a trading store set up by Thomas Hart during the 1870s to sell supplies to the porters who used to carry supplies from the coast to Pretoriuskop. Hart staved off the loneliness of his isolated existence by having a host of unusual pets including a cheetah, honey badger, jackals, parrots, monkeys and a couple of snakes. He was murdered by bandits in 1876 and buried next to the road by sympathetic Swazi warriors.

Further down, the road crosses the Mitomeni Spruit – the place of the jackal-berry trees – which was a favoured outspan point used by transport riders. One can still see the bullet holes in the leadwood tree that they used for target practice. The small, fleshy berries of the jackal-berry are used in many parts of Africa to make beer, while traditional healers say that inhaling smoke from the bark of the jackal-berry is an effective cure for a cough.

Even though there are not a lot of animals in this part of the Park, there are considerably larger numbers than there were a century ago. By the 1900s, almost all the game had been shot out of this area by early hunters – so much so that, when Stevenson-Hamilton first surveyed this area in 1902, the only wild animal he saw between Ship Mountain and Skukuza was a single reedbuck. At the time, the entire animal population of the Park was believed to be fewer than 100 000 animals. Today, there are more than 100 000 impala in Kruger, not counting any of the other animals.

Numbi Gate to Skukuza

The most direct route from Numbi to Skukuza is along the Napi Road (H1-1). A slightly longer route is via the Albasini Road (S3) (see page 149) and Doispane Road (S1) (see page 149). If one has a whole day at one's disposal, an interesting choice is to take the Voortrekker Road (H2-2) (see page 115) to Afsaal (see page 124) and then north along the Malelane Skukuza Road (H3) (see page 115).

Dung beetles

These insects were among the most important religious symbols of ancient Egypt. There are almost 2 000 species of dung beetles, many of which are found in Kruger. They break up animal droppings into little balls, roll these away and bury them. Inside the ball, they lay a single egg, and the dung will act as food for the beetle larva when it hatches.

THE NAPI ROAD TO SKUKUZA (H1-1)

The main road from Numbi to Skukuza is the Napi Road (H1-1) which cuts past Pretoriuskop and descends from the granite foothills into the rolling hills of mixed bushwillow woodlands south of Skukuza. Although the bush is initially quite thick and game is difficult to see, there are often rarer antelope here such as sable and eland.

Shitlhave Water Hole is a good place to stop on this road. Named after Sgt Jafuta Shitlhave, the first ranger appointed by Stevenson-Hamilton, it is the source of the Mbiyamiti River, and situated on the same belt of gabbro from which Ship Mountain protrudes. Look out for southern reedbuck and waterbuck in the tall grass around the water hole. The Napi Road takes one along the crest of the watershed that divides the two major catchment areas of southern Kruger – the Sabie and the Crocodile.

By the time one reaches the Napi Boulders (505m), the bush starts thinning out and game viewing becomes easier. The Napi Road winds past Mlaleni Hill (492m). Stop at Transport (Vervoer) Dam

Jock of the Bushveld

One of South Africa's classic books is Sir Percy Fitzpatrick's biography of his dog, Jock, told in *Jock of the Bushveld*, published in 1907. Fitzpatrick, an Irish transport rider who used to take supplies between Lydenburg, Barberton and Delagoa Bay, knew the lowveld intimately. Jock, his terrier, was his hunting companion during his trips in the bush. The plucky dog developed his own hunting style, which was to try and trip the animals he was chasing, pull them down and then grab them by the snout while Fitzpatrick took aim and shot. Jock's adventures included encounters with crocodiles and baboons, buffalo and kudu. There is a turn-off from Voortrekker Road before Ship Mountain which leads to the site where Jock is believed to have been born.

Lilac-breasted roller

Michael Poliza

The sorry story of Adolf Soltke

In the late 19th century, transport riders on the Voortrekker Road came across a young German carrying an umbrella and wearing a suit and a bowler hat in the blazing lowveld sun. Adolf Soltke was on his way to the goldfields on the escarpment to seek his fortune. The transport riders felt sorry for him and gave him a lift. While they were encamped in the vicinity of Ship Mountain, Soltke apparently saw a lilac-breasted roller that he wanted to collect. Unfortunately, as he jumped off the wagon his shotgun went off, shattering his right leg. One of the transport riders rode 100km to try to get help and returned two days later with a drunken chemist named Doc Munroe who was unable to do much. Two days later, a doctor arrived from Mac Mac and amputated Soltke's leg. However, Soltke succumbed to gangrene and died the next day. He was buried under a tree at the same place where Jock of the Bushveld is believed to have been born several months later.

which marks the start of the sweetveld. There are inevitably grazers like zebra and buffalo around Transport Dam and it is also a favourite drinking spot for elephants. Large herds of waterbuck gather here, too.

Early in the day, there are often lion in the vicinity of the dam, which got its name from the Department of Transport which donated funds for its construction. The small granite koppies in the area around

 Kudu have the same nine-month gestation period as humans. Kudu ewes will give birth to their calves – which weigh 15kg on average – in dense bush and will keep them hidden for up to 30 days. Weaning takes place at about six months, but calves will remain with the mother for up to two years.

Kudu

Nigel Dennis

Nigel Dennis

Klipspringer

 Shitlhave Water Hole

Brett Hilton-Barber

Transport Dam usually have klipspringer. They like to be on the sunny side of the rocks in the morning and in the shade in the afternoon. If they are disturbed they leap away from boulder to boulder (*klipspringer* is Afrikaans for rock jumper) with incredible agility, and have been seen bounding up steep slopes that humans would find difficult to clamber up. Their main predators are leopards and caracals.

There are two main routes to Skukuza from Transport Dam – either the shorter route, eastward along the tarred Napi Road (H1-1), or northwards along the N'waswitshaka dirt road (S65).

The Napi Road joins the main Malelane-Skukuza road near a group of granite koppies. There is a good lookout spot at Mathekenyane (Grano Hill) as the road descends into the thorn thickets of the upper Sabie valley.

The N'waswitshaka Road (S65) dips gently through woodlands of varying intensity. There are always impala along this road, which is a good place to look out for cheetah.

Bee aware

Honey bees are one of the most important pollinators of plants in Kruger. Kruger scientists are concerned that the appearance in 2000 of the exotic bee mite (*Varroa destructor*) may have a significant impact on Kruger's plant life. A study in the Pretoriuskop area showed that within two years the mites were found in all colonies of honey bees. Conservationists are concerned as to what the broader impact could be on Kruger if the local honey bee population is adversely affected .

The deadly horns of the sable

The first tourist to be hurt by an animal in Kruger was a man gored by a sable antelope in the early 1930s. The tourist apparently got out of his car near Pretoriuskop to take a photograph of a sable behind a tree. When he was about six metres from the object of his photographic intentions, it suddenly charged at him, impaling his thigh with one of its metre-long horns. The snorting bull made several attempts to slash at the man with its horns as he lay wriggling around, bleeding in the dust. The tourist's life was saved by his screaming wife who leapt from the car and drove the animal off with sticks and stones. It was later ascertained that the sable bull that attacked the man had been driven mad by injuries inflicted during a fight with another sable male. Sable can be extremely aggressive, particularly when challenging other males or predators. Even lions treat a sable with caution and respect. There have been several reports from Kruger over the years of lion being killed by sable. *Mhalamhala*, as the sable is known in Shangaan, has a fine repertoire of horned aggression displays. These include symbolic butting – a form of vigorous head nodding – head tossing, horning the ground and sideways slashing.

Nigel Dennis

Sable antelope

145

Leopard and prey

Leopard

Impala

Waterbuck

Common duiker

The Sabie River bush between Skukuza and Lower Sabie has one of the highest concentrations of leopard in the world. These elegant cats are not easy to see because they hunt mostly by night and spend the day lying low. Leopards will eat just about anything from insects and snakes to medium-sized antelope, but seem to prefer prey less than 80kg in weight. In Kruger the leopard's most consistent prey is the impala. Kruger mammal writer Heike Schutze believes that leopards prefer bushbuck, reedbuck and waterbuck over impala. It's no coincidence that these are the buck that occupy the same riverine bush habitat as the leopard does.

Giraffe

Skukuza and surrounds

Habitat pointers

- Thorn thickets along the Sabie River valley
- Mixed woodlands with granite koppies south of Skukuza
- Established riverine forest along the Sabie River banks
- Mixed marula, bushwillow and acacia woodlands between Skukuza and Tshokwane

The Skukuza area is dominated by the Sabie and Sand river systems, which support an abundance of wildlife. Because the Sabie usually flows all year round it is the most dependable source of water for the animals of southern Kruger. The area consists mostly of acacia thorn thickets along the lower contours of the landscape, and mixed marula, knob-thorn and bushwillow woodlands on the upper slopes. In summer the lush vegetation can get very thick, and game spotting can be difficult. Some of the finest riverine forest in Kruger is to be found along the banks of the Sabie, which has a high leopard population. The riverine bush to the west of Skukuza – in the Tinga concession – is much thicker than the bush along the river to the east. Bushbuck and even nyala are found in the thicker bush. The Sabie and Sand River loops to the east of Skukuza camp are among the best places for seeing lion and hyaena in Kruger. Buffalo and elephant are regularly seen from the camp itself. South of Skukuza there are a series of granite inselbergs stretching across the veld. Look out for klipspringer on these rocks and rhino and giraffe in the surrounding woodlands. The area is excellent for bird-watching, particularly in Skukuza camp (beneath the large trees along the river walkway), the nearby Lake Panic bird hide and Skukuza nursery.

Nigel Dennis

BEST DRIVE AROUND SKUKUZA
Skukuza to Lower Sabie:

Drive slowly along the Sabie River which is prime lion and leopard territory, stop off for a meal at Nkuhlu and bird-watching at Sunset Dam. The drive includes riverine bush, thorn thickets and open grassland. This road has a wide variety of animals that are constantly coming to the river to drink. Allow for three-and-a-half hours, including stops.

 CAMPS AROUND SKUKUZA

Tinga Safari Lodges
013 735 8400 See page 156

Skukuza
013 735 4000 See page 158

Rhino Post
011 467 4707 See page 169

Wooded savanna on shale

Lebombo

Mixed woodland with sweet grazing

Mixed thorn and marula woodlands on granite

Open savanna grassland on basalt

Pretoriuskop sourveld

Mixed woodland and thorn thickets

 PHABENI GATE EXPLORER OPTIONS

- Sabie River Road to Skukuza (S3) 46km (2 hours): dust and tar, thickly wooded riverine forest and then into Sabie River thorn thickets; avoid during heavy rains;

- Albasini Road to Pretoriuskop (S3) 25km (1 hour); dust road, scenic drive through kiaat terminalia woodlands with good lowveld views;

- Doispane Road to Skukuza (S1); 38km (1,5 hours) tar; descend from higher woodlands into Sabie thorn thickets and woodland savanna; usually good game sightings.

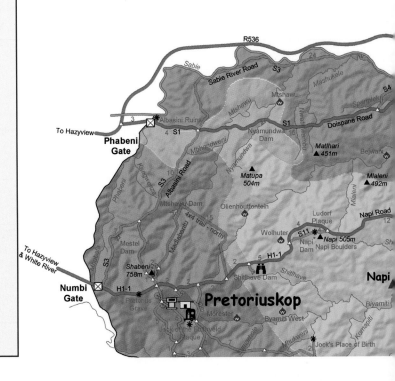

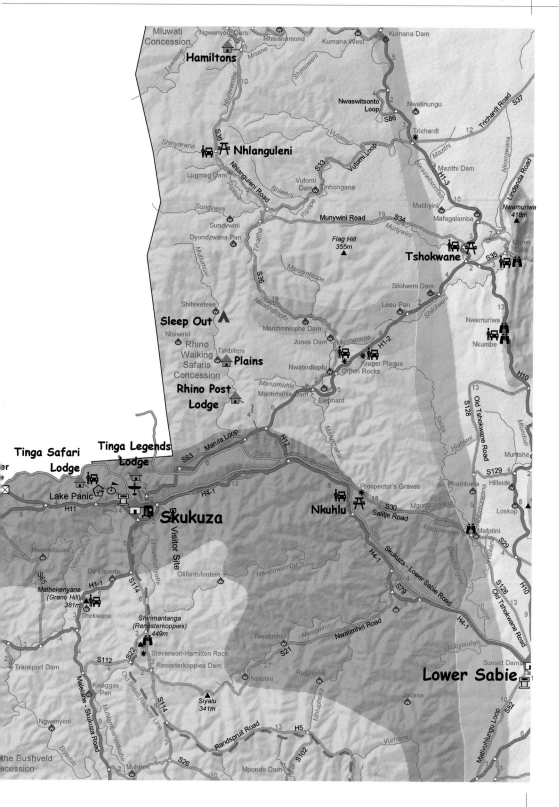

Giraffe are a favourite prey of lion, but they can put up a tremendous fight by kicking vigorously with their strong back legs, and have been known to ward off attacks – and even kill predators – in this manner.

Wilderness Safaris

Giraffe

Skukuza and surrounds

Skukuza is most easily reached from Gauteng via Numbi Gate (see page 131), Phabeni Gate (see below) or Paul Kruger Gate (see page 154).

Phabeni Gate

Phabeni Gate was built in 2002 to ease access to the Park for people travelling from Johannesburg or Pretoria via Hazyview. Its contemporary African architectural style embodies the spirit of the new South Africa and the three indigenously themed rondavels at the gate are an interesting contrast to the traditional thatch-and-brick aesthetic of most buildings in the Park.

Phabeni, "shelter" in Sotho, is also the name of the stream one crosses shortly after entering the gate. There is often good game viewing in the immediate vicinity of Phabeni because it is a geological island of basalt-like gabbro set among the granite koppies. The dark clay soils found on gabbro support a sweeter grass than the sourveld associated with the granite. This attracts both grazers and browsers and the vegetation is sparser, allowing one to see further than one normally can in the thickets. Impala or kudu are usually the first animals to see when entering through Phabeni. The dominant trees here are knob-thorn acacias, marulas and bushwillows.

Within 100 metres of the entrance, one finds the Albasini ruins, the humble brick remains of João Albasini's home and trading store which he set up in 1846, having bought the land from Chief Magashula for 22 cows. This is a good place to get out of the car, stretch one's legs and get a sense of the surrounding bush. The modest display gives one an insight into Albasini's rough-and-ready life and the kind of comforts one sought in such a remote location as it was in the late 1800s.

Phabeni Gate

Brett Hilton-Barber

João Albasini – lowveld pioneer

João Albasini (1813–1888) was a legendary ivory trader who set up a supply network across the lowveld in the 19th century. A Portuguese Italian by birth, Juwawa, as he became known, arrived in Delagoa Bay in the early 1800s to seek his fortune. He soon acquired the reputation of being a good elephant hunter and set himself up as a trader. He established a number of stores in the lowveld, the most famous being the site on Phabeni Creek where a small museum exists today. Albasini met the Voortrekker parties headed by Louis Trichardt and Hendrik Potgieter when they arrived in Delagoa Bay and assisted them with transporting supplies to their encampments inland. Albasini moved from Delagoa Bay to Phabeni Creek in 1845 after buying the land from Chief Magashula of the Sotho-speaking Kutswe tribe and appointed two headmen – Manungu and Jozikuhlu (Big Josef) – to run trading outposts near Pretoriuskop and at the base of Ship Mountain. In 1847, Albasini moved to Ohrigstad and then later to Lydenburg where he married Gertina Maria Petronella Janse van Rensburg, the daughter of a prominent Voortrekker. However, he was a restless individual, and soon moved northwards to the Soutspansberg before buying a farm near the Luvhuvhu River north of Punda Maria. He organised his own private army of Sotho-speakers who assisted him with protecting his trade networks and in hunting elephant. In 1858, he was appointed Portuguese vice-consul to the Transvaal and, a year later, was appointed by the Transvaal government as the superintendent of "native tribes" with the primary duty of collecting taxes from them. This resulted in something of a backlash against him and he was involved in several skirmishes with reluctant tax payers. Albasini died in 1888 and was buried on Goedewensch Farm near the Luvuvhu River where the Albasini Dam was named after him.

Brett Hilton-Barber

Albasini ruins

Phabeni to Pretoriuskop

The most direct way from Phabeni to Pretoriuskop is via the Albasini Road (S3) which offers a variety of loops through the foothills incorporating either Mestel Dam or Shabeni Rock.

THE ALBASINI ROAD (S3)

The Albasini road is a beautiful drive linking Phabeni Gate to Pretoriuskop and Numbi Gate. It winds through the domed granite foothills through kiaat and terminalia forests. It has wonderful views over the lowveld, but is not a very productive game drive. (See page 149)

Phabeni to Skukuza

The two main options are to take the upper Sabie River Road (S3), a dirt road that tracks the Sabie River to Paul Kruger Gate, or the main tar road, the Doispane Road (S1). (See page 152)

Acrobat of the Skies

Bateleur

Michael Poliza

The bateleur eagle is one of Kruger's most distinctive birds of prey. Recognisable by its red facial skin and bulky black and tawny body, the bateleur has a different design from other raptors. Its head protrudes relatively far in front of its wings and it has almost no tail, which gives it greater manoeuvrability (its name is derived from the French word for acrobat). The bateleur cruises at low altitudes and so is often the first bird of prey to arrive at a carcass, often beating vultures to the scene of a kill. It has a sharper beak than vultures and therefore often plays a useful role for other scavenging birds by slicing through the thick hide of the carcass to open the body up. In indigenous cultures the bateleur is a bird of omen. The Zulu refer to it as the "warrior bird" because the sound of its wings are reminiscent of warriors beating their spears against their shields. In Xhosa folklore, to kill a bateleur is to invite trouble or war, and a phrase to commemorate the passing away of a great man is to say, "The bateleur is dead".

Upper Sabie River Road (S3)

The S3 tracks the border of Kruger along the Sabie River, upstream from Paul Kruger Gate. Most of the drive is through riverine bush and thick woodland, crossing a number of streams that feed into the Sabie. There are only two spots where the road gets to the river's edge, allowing one views over the sandbanks and streamlets of the Sabie River. Historically, this road was tipped as a good white rhino route, but development on the other side of the river appears to have driven these grazers away. The riverine bush supports a number of browsers such as giraffe and kudu, and there are sometimes sightings of the nyala here, even though they generally prefer the habitat in the extreme north of the Park. There are wonderful thickets of tamboti as well as magnificent sycamore figs and leadwoods rich with birdlife. However, one cannot escape the sense of human encroachment across the Sabie, which compromises the taste of wild Kruger. Although the road is partly tarred, it is best to avoid this route after heavy rains. At the Kruger Gate one joins the main road to Skukuza.

Doispane Road (S1)

The Doispane Road (S1), named after the influential ranger Doispane Mongwe, is the main road from Phabeni Gate to Skukuza. It descends into the Sabie River catchment area with the Nyamundwa stream marking the divide between the western sourveld and the eastern sweetveld. Game viewing usually improves to the east of the stream crossing, because the grazing is more palatable.

The Nyamundwa Water Hole is worth a stop to check out whether the resident hippo and crocs are in. There are often buffalo and other grazers at the water hole, particularly around mid-morning.

The landscape opens up as one gets closer to Skukuza. Knob-thorns and marulas dominate the upper and middle slopes while figs, tambotis and sausage trees prefer the lower, more-watered contours. A series of picturesque koppies marks the favoured "Doispane" outspan of ranger Harry Wolhuter (near the turn-off to the dust road (S4) to Paul Kruger Gate) who used to camp here regularly in the early 20th century. Wolhuter once caught a lion cub here after shooting its mother during a hunt. "Elizabeth", as the cub was known, became quite tame and played blissfully with the ranger's dogs. When she became too big to manage, Elizabeth was presented to Land Minister Piet Grobler who in turn handed her over to the Johannesburg Zoo. Wolhuter recalled that several years later on a visit to the zoo, his son called the lioness by her name and she came bounding over, clearly recognising his voice.

The Doispane koppies mark a change in the landscape. Eastwards, the climate is drier, leadwoods and magic guarri trees become common, impala herds are bigger, and the savanna opens up. This part of the Park is an overlapping area in the territory of the bigger predator species, with the possibility of seeing lion, cheetah, leopard, hyaena and wild dogs.

Because of the proximity of the Sabie River and the mixed woodlands and open grassveld, there is a varied choice on the menu for hunters of all kinds.

Leopard come from the Sabie River forests to hunt in this woodland, which is also the western habitat range limit for cheetah from the eastern grasslands. Packs of wild dogs are sometimes seen on the tar road in the vicinity of the S65 turn-off. Lion and hyaena are more common eastwards towards Skukuza. On a lucky day, one may see all the Big Five along this road.

An interesting detour to Skukuza is to turn right on the S65, which crosses the N'waswitshaka River and joins up with the Napi Road from Pretoriuskop. There is a beautiful bushveld forest along the N'waswitshaka River. There are often cheetah sightings along this road. Lion sometimes drink at dawn at the waterhole along this road and klipspringer may be seen on Sihehleni Koppie (388m).

Cheetah with cub

Brett Hilton-Barber

Ngulube the little tusker
Warthogs use their tusks for digging and defence. The top tusks – which grow up to 60cm – are used to dig out roots, tubers and bulbs, while the shorter, sharper lower tusks (15cm) are used to fight off enemies. The lower tusks are kept sharp by the way they rub against the upper tusks. Warthogs go into their burrows backwards so that they can use their tusks against any predator foolish enough to enter their holes.

The easiest way to tell the difference between male and female giraffes is to look at their "horns" – which are not really horns but knob-like protrusions from the skull. A male giraffe's "horns" are bald, while those of a female are covered with hair.

Paul Kruger Gate

Paul Kruger Gate is the closest entrance to Skukuza and the quickest way to get in and out of the Park from Kruger's "capital". One is confronted by the large, somewhat controversial bust of Paul Kruger by sculptor Coert Steynberg as one crosses the Sabie. Oom Paul scowls over the Sabie River, having survived the politics of the new South Africa and attempts to have the bust removed in the interests of political correctness. The former president of the Transvaal Republic was a fervent Afrikaner nationalist and racist to boot – but he was also an anti-colonialist who had environmental foresight and a love for the bush. Whatever one's view may be, his name has become synonymous with the South African wildlife experience, and tourism authorities are understandably loath to tamper with the destination branding.

The gate is on the Sabie River which is the dominant watercourse in southern Kruger. The Sabie is known for its hippos and crocodiles which lie log-like on the sandy river banks, or cruise the mid-stream with just their eyes poking above the water. The Kruger Gate bridge is a good birding spot with the rare Pel's fishing-owl recorded along this stretch of the Sabie at sunset.

Imagine the severity of the floods of 2000, when Paul Kruger Bridge was actually under water! The floods had their lighter moments. Bruce Bryden recalls the incredulous sight of a shrieking baboon clinging surfer-style to a log that was swept down the river – the log hit the bridge and the baboon escaped onto dry land.

Paul Kruger statue at Paul Kruger Gate

Brett Hilton-Barber

Crocodile drama on the Sabie

One of Kruger's most fearsome battles between man and beast took place between Paul Kruger Gate and Skukuza one hot summer's day in November 1976. Two Skukuza rangers – Tom Yssel and Louis Olivier – went fishing at a water hole on the Sabie River near the staff village. The two were wading thigh-deep in the river when the water suddenly erupted around them as a five-metre crocodile shot out of the reeds and grabbed Yssel by the leg. Olivier desperately tried to save his friend and lunged at the reptile as it headed for deeper water. He managed to get astride it and, thrashing about in the shallows, desperately tried to prise the crocodile's jaws open. The struggle lasted for what seemed like ages, before Kruger helicopter pilot Hans Kolver, who had been enjoying a cold beer on a sandbank nearby, rushed over to help. Kolver dug his fingernails into the crocodile's eyes, but it maintained its deadly grip, shaking Yssel from time to time to improve its grip. Yssel was in agony and losing blood fast as the men tried in vain to pull him free. Neither side would give in. The croc then surprised everyone by letting go of Yssel and grabbing Kolver by the wrist, pulling him under water. By this time, Olivier had managed to get a knife and rushed back over, stabbing the crocodile in its eye sockets. Only then did the crocodile release Kolver, and sink back under water. Olivier and Kolver, terrified that other crocodiles would be attracted by the blood, hauled Yssel out of the river and rushed him to hospital. Miraculously, he survived. The crocodile was shot the next day by another ranger, as it was badly wounded. Olivier and Kolver were awarded the Wolraad Woltemade Decoration for Conspicuous Bravery in 1978.

Crocodile

Nigel Dennis

PAUL KRUGER GATE TO SKUKUZA (H11)

If one is going to get caught speeding in the Kruger Park, it is likely to occur between Skukuza and Paul Kruger Gate. Travel slowly along this road, which often has interesting sightings as the big predators hunt in the thorn thickets along the Sabie River watercourse. There are two noteworthy birding spots just off the H11, Lake Panic and Skukuza Nursery (see page 156). Further on this road is the unfenced Skukuza Village, which is off-bounds to tourists. Wild animals freely roam through the staff village but generally give humans a wide berth. However, as lowveld author Hennie van Deventer recounts, two fatal leopard attacks have rocked the close-knit Skukuza community. In March 2001, a young schoolboy, Binkie Nobela, noticed a leopard prowling around the staff village. He alerted rangers who searched for the animal without success. An hour later popular Skukuza resident Kotie de Beer was jogging near Skukuza Nursery when she was killed by the leopard which then disappeared into the bush. In a strange but tragic twist of fate, two years later Binkie Nobela was killed by an old leopard in broad daylight close to his home. Rangers tracked the culprit and shot it dead. It is not known whether it was the same leopard responsible for de Beer's death.

TINGA PRIVATE GAME LODGES

The two Tinga lodges are the most accessible luxury experience in Kruger. They are in Jackalsbessie Concession just north of Skukuza. Tinga Narina is 13km from Paul Kruger Gate, and Tinga Legends is 18km from the gate and six kilometres from Skukuza. The concession has rights to 35km of Sabie River frontage, including the confluence of the Sand River. This is the equivalent of having ringside seats to the bushveld drama of life and death – among the sightings reported by Tinga guides are that of a martial eagle seizing a baby impala, and a tawny eagle attacking a juvenile baboon in the thorn thickets that line the Sabie River. The two lodges each consist of nine luxury units with their own private viewing decks and plunge pools. Legends has a great wooden walkway between the chalets which are surrounded by leadwoods, black monkey thorn and sycamore figs. Narina is built on stilts in the riverine bush, and is named after the Narina trogon, a shy and secretive, brightly coloured forest bird which inhabits the denser pockets of riverine bush along the Sabie. The bird was first named by explorer Francois Levaillant after Narina, a beautiful Khoikhoi woman who accompanied him on his 1807 expedition.

Both lodges offer game drives and guided bush walks, and the area is renowned as big cat territory with frequent sightings of lion and leopard.

Brett Hilton-Barber

IN THE SKUKUZA AREA LOOK OUT FOR

Animals

Lions

Hyaenas

Thick-tailed bushbaby

Warthog

White rhino

Birds

Purple-crested turaco

African green-pigeon

Hamerkop

African fish-eagle

Black cuckoo-shrike

Lake Panic and Skukuza Nursery

Lake Panic and Skukuza Nursery are both accessed from the main road between Skukuza and Paul Kruger Gate (H11).

Lake Panic apparently got its name from its status as the emergency reservoir for Skukuza Camp. Early Skukuza staff used to say there was no need to panic about water supplies because of the reliability of the dam, and somehow the name stuck.

 SKUKUZA EXPLORER OPTIONS

- Visit Lake Panic and Skukuza Nursery (H11; S42) 6km (half-an-hour to 1,5 hours): thorn thickets, riverine bush, good birding and plant shopping;
- Rhino Koppies Route (H1-1; S112; S22; S114;) 31km; (1,5 to 2,5 hours); scenic drive through thorn thickets, mixed woodland and rugged koppie landscape; historic route with good get-out points;
- Sabie Sand Loop (H4-1; H12 and H1-2) 31km (1,5 hours); river drive through mixed woodland; very good game road and best chance of spotting lions around Skukuza.

The mystery of the missing Kruger Millions

For more than 100 years, there has been a persistent rumour that the President of the Transvaal Republic, Paul Kruger, buried a great deal of the Republic's treasure in the Kruger Park area when he was toppled from power. These were the so-called Kruger Millions. The rumours were particularly prevalent in the 1920s when expeditions would regularly arrive seeking permission to dig at a spot where a reliable informant had sworn the gold was buried. They always left empty-handed. If there is such treasure, it has never been found.

There is a resident croc in the dam that feeds off the fat barbel that scavenge in the water below the hide. This is one of the few places in Kruger where osprey are seen. Skukuza nursery is a good place to stretch the legs, admire the sunbirds and buy some indigenous plants to take home.

The game around here is quite used to the presence of humans, and wild animals often wander through the streets of the nearby Skukuza staff village.

Skukuza Nursery has become a prime birding spot since the construction in 2006 of a wooden walkway through the reedbeds and woodlands around the nursery. It is also a place to get interesting indigenous plants at cheap prices. (See page 149)

RHINO KOPPIES ROUTE

The acacia thorn thickets and mixed woodlands south of Kruger are a favourite habitat of the white rhino, and are also generally good for game. In summer, the vegetation can be very thick, which limits sightings, but that is not to say there is a lack of animal activity in the surrounding bush. The well-watered catchment area of the Sabie River consists of a series of gently rolling hills with knob-thorns, marulas and bushwillows on the upper slopes; magic guarri, sickle-bush and acacias on the lower slopes and leadwoods, sausage trees and sycamore figs along the watercourses.

A number of granite koppies protrude sharply from the gently undulating

Brett Hilton-Barber

Lake Panic

SKUKUZA CAMP

Skukuza is the "capital" of Kruger and an excellent camp for the first-time visitor to get acquainted with the history of the Park and the scope of activities on offer. It is the Park's largest camp, bustling with activity, and the centre of administration and scientific research.

The site where Skukuza stands today was originally known as Sabi Crossing because it was the best place to cross the dangerous river. The first Kruger Park ranger appointed – Barberton policeman Paul Bester – took up his position here in 1898 when the Sabi Reserve was proclaimed. That year, he built the first rondavel at Skukuza. The wildebeest skin he used as a door was regularly torn off by hyaenas at night.

During the Anglo-Boer War, Sabi Crossing was occupied by Steinacker's Horse (see page 97). The regiment built a small blockhouse on the banks of the river. It was, in the words of lowveld historian TV Bulpin, "a sunbaked little place whose garrison of desperadoes had gambled and quarrelled their days away while the officers had kept discipline by a periodic resort to their fists".

Brett Hilton-Barber

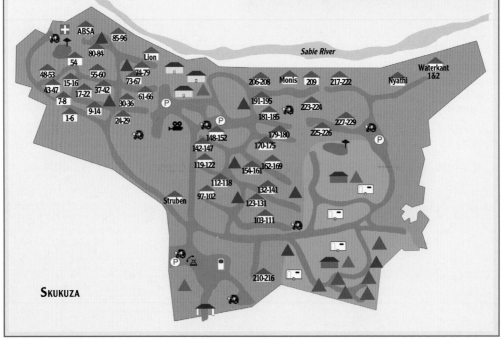

Sabi Bridge then became a siding on the ill-fated Selati railway line. The disused railway bridge lies upstream from the camp as a monument to the intriguing relationship between human folly and get-rich-quick schemes in the lowveld.

It was renamed Skukuza when James Stevenson-Hamilton moved his operational headquarters there, having consolidated his political control over the Park. *Skukuza* was his nickname, the Shangaan word for "he who turns everything upside down", which was a somewhat bitter reference to his enthusiasm for ridding the Park of its human inhabitants as he transformed Kruger from an over-hunted, disease-ridden outback into one of the world's top game reserves.

The camp is situated close to the confluence of the Sabie, N'waswitshaka and Sand Rivers and is in a particularly game-rich part of Kruger. The thorn thickets and mixed woodlands around the camp usually host animal activity all year round as the Sabie is a major source of water in the southern Park. A survey done in 1970 revealed that 25 leopards lived in a five-kilometre radius of Skukuza camp.

Skukuza offers all the facilities of an established village, including restaurants, police, medical and emergency vehicle repair services. It has the best shopping in the Park and there are a range of activities to keep one entertained during the day while the animals are resting. (See Tired of Driving, page 160)

A relaxing way to acclimatise to Skukuza is to spend half-an-hour ambling along the tree-lined walkway along the edge of the camp overlooking the reedbeds and sandbanks of the Sabie River. There is often game flitting through the mixed riverine woodland on the banks, and elephant and buffalo regularly come down to the river to drink in front of the camp. Guests at Skukuza on Christmas Day in 1971 received an interesting present from the Park. A leopard brazenly killed a waterbuck on the river sandbank right in front of the camp restaurant.

A day-visitor's area near the main camp has a swimming pool and braai facilities.

 Spotted hyaena females are considerably larger than the males. Females are also masculinised due to having more testosterone in their bodies than most male hyaenas. As a result, females dominate the social hierarchy, are more aggressive, and have a penis-like clitoris. Also, their vulva is fused to look like a pseudo scrotum and testes, making it extremely difficult to determine the sex of a hyaena.

Wilderness Safaris
Spotted hyaena

landscape – these are a series of inselbergs that run in an east-to-west direction across central southern Kruger. One of these is Mathekenyane Koppie (385m) (also known as Granokop), which offers wonderful views of the escarpment to the west and the landmarks of Ship Mountain, Legogote and Pretoriuskop. To the south, the Malelane mountains are visible, while on a clear day one can see the Lebombo over the game-rich grasslands to the east.

A short distance away, on the S112, is Shirimantanga Hill where Stevenson-Hamilton and his wife, Hilda, requested their ashes to be scattered. Stevenson-Hamilton died in 1957 at the age of 90, 11 years after his retirement in 1946. Although his vision of Kruger was secure when he stepped down, he worried that it would become "a glorified zoo and botanical garden, dotted with scientific experimental stations of every kind, hotels and public recreation grounds, which are all

TIRED OF DRIVING?

One of the downsides of the Kruger experience can be the amount of time one has to spend in one's vehicle. If one is tired of driving, Skukuza is an ideal place to spend a morning or afternoon because the camp features:

- The best shopping in Kruger for essentials, clothing, craft and curios;
- Photograph processing and development facilities;
- An open-air amphitheatre where wildlife movies are shown every night except Sundays;
- Restaurants and fast-food outlets;
- Plenty of space to walk around – including a walk along the banks of the Sabie River;
- ATMs
- Post office;
- Internet facilities;

- Car hire, car wash and vehicle repair facilities;
- A resident doctor and pharmacy;
- The Stevenson-Hamilton Memorial Library, which is more of a museum than a library, stocking a wealth of memorabilia used by rangers, as well as stone tools and other exhibits;
- The Campbell 1929 Hut Museum which preserves the oldest hut in Skukuza (S1) to show tourist accommodation in the old days;
- A swimming pool; and
- Activities for children, including touch displays and organised outings.

There is also the Skukuza nursery a few kilometres from the camp that stocks a wide variety of indigenous plants, and a pleasant hour can be spent at the bird hide at Lake Panic.

SANParks

Skukuza library

Shirimantanga

Africa Imagery

preliminaries to the liquidation of the last vestige of wildlife".

Shirimantanga is part of a picturesque collection of huge boulders, collectively known as "Rhino Koppies", where these animals are often seen. This is a good drive to do at sunset.

Sabie Sand Loop

A highly recommended drive around Skukuza is the loop around the confluence of the Sabie and the Sand Rivers (H1-2, H12 and H4-1) which combines riverine forest with open grasslands and thorn thickets. Although there is usually heavy tourist traffic on this road, it

Red bushwillow – staple diet for browsers

One of the staple diets of browsers is the red bushwillow (*Combretum apiculatum*). Found throughout the Park but dominant in the south, this smallish deciduous tree is the second-most common tree after mopane and the leaves are eaten by elephant, giraffe, kudu, bushbuck, impala, eland, klipspringer and steenbok. Traditional healers make a concoction from the leaves to treat stomach disorders. While its leaves are palatable, animals avoid its seeds which are mildly poisonous and can cause prolonged hiccupping. The red bushwillow supports a lot of insect life which makes it a popular tree for insect-eating birds. It gets its name from the fact that its leaves turn reddish brown in winter. Its drought-resistance ensures that it is a food source for browsers even in the driest of times. It is recognisable by the small, four-winged clusters of fruit that ripen in late summer and autumn.

P. Van Wyk

161

🐾 Insects – the unseen animals of Kruger

Insects play a vital role in the veld, providing food for mammals (like the aardvark and certain bat species) birds, lizards, snakes and frogs. Research by Leo Braack suggests that there are approximately 2,4 metric tons of canopy-dwelling insects per square kilometre around Skukuza during the rainy season. If one had to include termites, grasshoppers and water-dwelling insects, this figure would probably rise to over seven tons per square kilometre. According to scientist P Viljoen, the estimated biomass per square kilometre for large mammalian herbivores (impala and bigger) is about 2,4 tons, the same as that of canopy-dwelling insects.

Lions are first found in the fossil record of Africa between 2,5 and 3 million years ago.

Albert Froneman

is probably the best chance the visitor has of seeing lion and a variety of other game in the shortest space of time. There are several stopping points overlooking both rivers and a number of loop roads that take one into the thorn thickets.

Many lion prides hunt in this area without competing because there is plenty of game to go around. The degree of potential prey is evident from the number of game trails that traverse the roads from the grasslands to the water's edge where there are big marulas, knob-thorns, weeping boer-beans, sycamore figs, jackal-berries and matumis.

This is a good road to do early in the morning because of the chances of coming across a kill from the night before. Mid- to late afternoon is the other good time to do this drive, as this is when the big carnivores become active. Vultures often arrive in the afternoon at quiet pools on the Sand River for a bath. Despite their reputation as bloody scavengers, they are actually quite clean birds, using water and sand to wash off parasites on a daily basis.

There is a good get-out spot at the Mutlumuvi looking over reed beds and thick riverine forest on the other side.

Maroela Loop off the H1-2 takes one away from the river into the thorn thickets. Although visibility through the bush is limited in summer because of the dense vegetation, this can be a productive drive for game viewing and birding.

Colonel James Stevenson-Hamilton

The success of Kruger as one of the world's leading game reserves is due mainly to the man who actually made it happen. Scottish-born James Stevenson-Hamilton (1867–1957) was the man tasked with transforming Paul Kruger's vision of an African Eden into a viable game reserve.

This tough and doughty soldier and adventurer took up his post in 1902 shortly after the Anglo-Boer War, and was instructed to preserve what little wildlife there was in what was then the Sabi Game Reserve. He took on the challenge with grit and enthusiasm, with one of his first jobs being to persuade tribespeople living in the Park to move out in exchange for not paying tax for one year. He also took on the vested interests of settler farmers and landowners who regarded the Park either as winter grazing or hunting grounds.

SANParks

The major was also given responsibility for policing the Shingwedzi Reserve which was seen as a lost cause because of hunting and lawlessness However, his persistence paid off and his efforts were rewarded with the consolidation in 1926 of the Sabi and Shingwedzi reserves into a single Park.

Known for his perseverance and obstinacy, Stevenson-Hamilton devoted his life to Kruger, deciding only to get married at the age of 63 once his obligations as a game ranger had been met. He and his wife, Hilda, had three children. He died peacefully at the age of 90 and his ashes were scattered at one of his favourite places in the Park – Shirimantanga Hill just south of Skukuza.

Skukuza to Lower Sabie

There are two main routes between Skukuza and Lower Sabie. These are the Sabie River Road via Nkuhlu Picnic site (H4-1) – which can get very busy during weekends and school holidays, and the less travelled dusty alternative, the Salitje Road (S30). (See pages 149 and 167)

THE MAIN SABIE RIVER ROAD (H4-1)

The Sabie River Road from Skukuza to Lower Sabie (H4-1) tracks the Sabie River through mixed thornveld into the open grasslands of the south-east. It is both a beautiful drive and a good game route as the riverine bush, nutritious thornveld browsing and sweetveld grazing attract a wide variety of herbivores which, in turn, attract the predators. The chances of seeing lions, leopards, hyaenas and their kills are as good on the H4-1 as anywhere else in Kruger. The Sabie riverine forest supports a large population of leopards, probably because of the high density of impala in the area. Studies by Michael Mills and Paul Funston indicate there are almost 100 impala per square kilometre in this part of the Park.

The H4-1 can be something of a mixed blessing, however. On the one hand, the area teems with wildlife because of the sweet grazing and permanent water, but, on the other, it is probably the busiest road in the Park and good sightings quickly attract a lot of vehicles, which can compromise the quality of the game viewing.

The first 12km from Skukuza offers many vantage points over the Sabie River, which has undergone a radical change because of the 2000 floods. The raging

Sabie River near Skukuza

Africa Imagery

floodwaters washed away many of the big old sycamore fig trees that lined the river, and the course of the central river channel shifted, changing the location of sandbanks and reedbeds. Some scientists argue that these floods brought about the most rapid changes to an ecosystem since the Park's inception.

Stop on one of the river loops overlooking the Sabie and consider this: during the average dry season, the Sabie flows at a rate of between three and five cubic metres a second, which increases to 15 to 20 cubic metres a second for the average wet season. Before the February 2000 floods, there were four times that the Sabie burst its banks and registered a flow of between 600 and 700 cubic metres a second. The February 2000 floods were 10 times more intense than any of these floods with the flow measured at 6 000 cubic metres a second at Skukuza and 7 450 cubic metres a second at Lower Sabie! The last time a flood of such magnitude was experienced was in

1925. At the other end of the scale, during the drought of 1992 the Sabie stopped flowing altogether!

One of the consequences of the flood has been a change in the birdlife along the river. The sycamore figs were an important source of food for many bird species and there has been a noticeable short-term decline in birding activity along this stretch of the Sabie. Nonetheless, there are still many raptors cruising the Sabie. Look out in particular for Wahlberg's eagle (which nests along the river), the martial eagle and the bateleur. The high-level bridge over the Sabie River just east of its confluence with the Sand is a good birding spot.

The Lower Sabie Road to Nkuhlu has some of the most beautiful trees in southern Kruger. There are several places along this road that invite one to stop and watch. Nkuhlu Picnic Site is a good braai or refreshment halt with terraced views over the river. There is a gift and convenience shop and fast-food outlet at Nkuhlu.

Kruger's birds of prey

The Kruger Park is renowned for its raptors, many of which can be seen in the Skukuza area. Among the birds of prey associated with Skukuza and the Sabie River are Wahlberg's eagle which nests along the river, the conspicuous African fish-eagle, the tawny eagle, a quiet bird that likes more open habitats, and that carrion scout, the bateleur. The martial eagle hunts along the Sabie for its favourite food, the leguaan, while the African harrier-hawk (gymnogene) busies itself in the forest canopy looking for nests to raid. The shikra (little banded goshawk) is one of the most prominent smaller raptors found along the Sabie.

Wahlberg's eagle

Tawny eagle

African fish-eagle

Bateleur

Shikra

Martial eagle

African harrier-hawk

Leopard

Heinrich van den Berg

South of Nkuhlu, the thorn thickets are gradually replaced by lightly wooded grassland with good views over the river and the surrounding plains. (See pages 98 and 293 for Nkuhlu to Lower Sabie)

THE SALITJE ROAD (S30)

An excellent early-morning drive is the Salitje Road (S30), accessed off the H12 just north of the low-level bridge over the Sabie. There are often hyaena and lion sightings on this road, which was named after a Shangaan chief who ruled the area before the Park was proclaimed. The S30 skirts the northern banks of the Sabie River before rolling through mixed woodlands into the eastern grassland plains. There are fewer vantage points over the Sabie River than there are on the H4-1 but, along the way, there are some wonderful quiet pools surrounded by tall riverine trees. Kudu and duiker browse along the forest fringes and impala feed in the more open grassland.

Mafotini Water Hole is on the edge of the eastern grasslands. The water hole takes its name from a nearby footpath used by refugees and illegal immigrants from Mozambique. The path was often used during the 1970s and 1980s by people fleeing the civil war in Mozambique. Rangers frequently patrolled the path and arrested many Mozambicans who had decided to brave the Kruger bush in a bid to get a better life in South Africa. *Mafotini* was Shangaan slang for "Fourteen", referring to the law which provided for 14 days of detention for illegal immigrants before they were sent back across the border. The path was primarily used at night to avoid detection, and many refugees lost their lives in lion attacks during this time.

East of Mafotini Water Hole the landscape opens up into the basalt grasslands. The long ridge of Muntshe mountain stands above the grasslands. From Mafotini one has a number of options.

Nigel Dennis

Wildebeest

Knob-thorn – sweetveld indicator

The third-most common tree in the Park after the mopane and red bushwillow is the knob-thorn (*Acacia nigrescens*). Its presence indicates that the surrounding grasslands are sweetveld and it is usually found in association with marula trees. The knob-thorn is a medium to large tree with a spreading crown, growing up to 16m tall. It is most easily recognisable in spring when its bright yellow flowers liven up the landscape. It has thorn-tipped knobs which are more conspicuous on younger trees. In winter, its narrow pods become black

Knob-thorn acacia in flower

Africa Imagery

(hence the name *nigrescens* – Latin for "becoming black"). It is a heavy wood that contains lots of tannin, grows slowly and is both drought-resistant and sensitive to frost. It is eaten by a range of browsers, particularly giraffe, elephant and kudu. Studies in Kruger show that giraffe are important pollination agents for the knob-thorn – they collect pollen on their heads and necks while feeding, and distribute it to other flowering trees.

To the north the Old Tshokwane Road (S128) takes one through the open grasslands to Nkumbe lookout point in the Lebombo. This drive is recommended for the big herds of grazers one is likely to see along the road as well as the dramatic views from Nkumbe over the plains. (See page 102)

The S129 east of Mafotini is an excellent birding drive, taking one to the vleis at the foot of Muntshe hill and Mlondozi Dam on the edge of the Lebombo. (See page 101)

South of Mafotini the S128 takes one through the sweet grasslands to Lower Sabie. This was one of the first roads to be built in the old Sabi Game Reserve and was the main road between Lower Sabie and Tshokwane. This is a good game drive, particularly in late summer when the veld still has water in the numerous pans that form along the basalt.

There are usually large herds of zebra in the grasslands around Lower Sabie. Zebras may look harmless but they are impressively

aggressive under the right circumstances. They are known for their fearsome ability to kick – a trait that lions are apparently wary of, but their most dangerous weapon, according to legendary Kruger ranger Harry Wolhuter, is their teeth. Zebra are not purely passive creatures. Wolhuter personally witnessed a herd of zebras attacking a pack of wild dogs in the 1920s. The zebras surprised the wild dogs that had been stalking them by turning on them and charging with their teeth bared. The wild dogs sensibly beat a hasty retreat. (See pages 96 and 293)

Skukuza to Satara

There are two main roads between Skukuza and Satara in the central grasslands. These are the main tar road via Tshokwane (H1-2) and the Nhlanguleni dust road (S36) which leaves the main road at the elephant drinking holes midway between Skukuza and Tshokwane.

Skukuza to Tshokwane (H1-2)

The road from Skukuza to Tshokwane (H1-2) climbs out of the thorn thickets of the Sabie River system into woodlands of bushwillows, terminalia and wild teak. Gradually, these woodlands give way to the more open savanna of the central grasslands where large herds of grazing animals and their predators are to be found.

There are several good water holes on this road – the first being the cluster of Manzimanhle, Elephant's Drinking Hole and N'watindlopfu some 15km from Skukuza. Elephants may have favoured this area for thousands of years as there is a striking panel of ancient San rock art in a nearby granite hill that depicts four elephants. This is significant in that, of the 109 rock art shelters found in Kruger and studied by ranger Don English, only three depict elephants. The painting was discovered in 1987 by Ranger Sam Fourie and Kruger information officer Gert Erasmus. Fourie was subsequently trampled to death by an elephant a few years later in the Stolsnek area near the base camp of the Wolhuter hiking trail. Kruger elephant expert Ian Whyte has made a convincing case that elephants were not in abundance in Kruger before the proclamation of the Park and that human intervention is one of the direct causes of elephant over-population.

RHINO POST SAFARI LODGE

Rhino Post Safari Lodge is in the pristine 12 000-ha Mutlumuvi private concession just north of Skukuza. The concession specialises in bush trails run by Rhino Walking Safaris through the mixed knob-thorn and marula woodlands of the Sand River catchment area. The concession is named after the Mutlumuvi stream, which is a tributary of the Sand. According to the Dictionary of Kruger Park Names, *Mutlumuvi* is the Shangaan derivative of the Tswana *motla o mobe*, the literal translation of which is "dangerous when it comes down in flood".

This area has one of the highest populations of white rhino in Kruger so there is a good chance of seeing these animals during a walk. Hikers on walks in the concession have reported seeing elephant, giraffe, zebra and other big game during their outings, including lion. Two armed guards and a guide accompany each hiking party, which is limited to a maximum of eight people.

The upmarket Rhino Post Safari Lodge has eight luxury thatched chalets, each with a private deck overlooking the thick Mutlumuvi River bush. When the lodge was being built in 2000, workers reported that a leopard regularly strolled to the edge of the building site and watched the construction with interest. It has hung about the camp ever since. Plains Camp is the current base for the walking safaris. It is an eight-bed, luxury tented camp near Timbiteni Water Hole, which is the site of an old Iron-Age settlement. Potsherds were found here when the borehole was sunk. The real gem at Rhino Post, however, is the Sleepout Deck where there are wooden platforms in the trees near the Shiteveteve spring, a regular game drinking spot. Guests sleep out under the stars, guarded by two rangers who will also do the cooking.

Brett Hilton-Barber

N'watindlopfu is a good game photography site, especially during winter and spring when water is scarce and lots of animals congregate here. The light is particularly good for photography in the early mornings.

There are two get-out points on the Skukuza-Tshokwane Road (H1-2), both set among the granite boulders spilled by geological upheaval across the lowveld floor. These are the Eileen Orpen Plaque and the Kruger Tablets, which are convenient spots to stretch the legs and admire the granite koppies.

Further along the H1-2 are two of the Park's top water holes for game photography – Leeupan and Silolweni. Leeupan, which is surrounded by sweetveld grazing, marks the start of the eastern grasslands. There are good views in all directions and, true to its name, the pan is frequented by lion, especially early in the morning. During the day, a variety of grazers come to the water to drink and, occasionally, vultures are seen bathing.

Young baboons

Nigel Dennis

Rhinos may look slow and cumbersome, but the black rhino can charge at speeds of up to 50km/h while the white rhino can manage 45km/h at full tilt.

Mike Myers

Rhino

Silolweni is a more expansive water hole with two dead trees with big red-billed buffalo-weaver nests in them. This is a regular drinking spot for buffalo, wildebeest and zebra and there are often giraffe in the surrounding acacia woodland. During the rainy season, the grasslands surrounding Silolweni are transformed into vleis (*Silolweni* is Siswati for "swampy during the rainy season") which attract a wide variety of bird species. (See page 173 for Tshokwane) (See page 175 for Tshokwane to Satara)

NHLANGULENI ROAD (S36)

The Nhlanguleni Road is a less-trafficked alternative into the central grasslands than the main Satara Road from Skukuza because it bypasses Tshokwane. There is often a lot of animal activity between the turn-off to the S36 up until the Manzimhlope Dam as there is a large patch of sweetveld grazing here. The road passes through mixed broadleaf woodland on quite coarse, sandy soils through three secondary river systems – the Ripape, N'waswitsontso and Sweni catchment areas. These watercourses are usually rich in game and patrolled by predators but, for the most part, the S36 is not the most reliable road to see lots of animals. That is not to say it has no surprises. Lugmag Dam, on the Ripape River, is a recommended stop on this road as it is a major water hole in the Kruger's mid-west and is frequented by buffalo and other grazers that feed in the surrounding mixed thornveld and woodland.

Just north of Lugmag Dam is Nhlanguleni picnic site, where one can buy cold drinks and firewood – there are braai facilities available. *Nhlanguleni* in Shangaan means "the place of the magic guarri tree" (see page 133 for more details on the magic guarri). From Nhlanguleni northwards, the size of the woodland

Impala – fast food for predators

Impala (*mhala* in Shangaan) is the one guaranteed sighting in Kruger. They are the most common antelope in the Park, with a relatively stable population of about 100 000 at any given time. They are the staple diet of many predators, and during calving in early summer even martial eagles and baboons may try and hunt new-born impalas.

By the end of summer one of the male impalas in the herd will have become the dominant male and the other male impalas will form bachelor herds during the winter. They often hang around on the fringes of the dominant male's harem and will occasionally try and challenge his authority. The dominant male can fertilise up to 50 ewes. During calving, bachelor herds become integrated back into the main herd for added protection.

Impala ewes are believed to be able to hold back on calving for up to a month in order to wait for new grazing or water for their young. New-born impala are hidden by their mothers in long grass or bush thickets for their first few days of life until they are strong enough to keep up with the herd. Impalas have a good sense of hearing and smell. They are quite social animals, co-existing with other animals in grazing parties. They also have a natural association with baboons, often eating fruit and leaves dropped by the primates in the trees above them.

Nigel Dennis

Impala

The nocturnal tree-living bushbaby can jump five metres between branches – which is 33 times its body length. It can make a variety of sounds including a mournful scream that sounds like a human baby, which is how it got its name. There are two kinds of bushbabies found in Kruger – the lesser (pictured below) and the thick-tailed bushbaby.

SANParks

Bushbaby

trees begins shrinking and the vegetation becomes scrub-like and stunted. Ngwenyeni Water Hole, just before the turn-off to the N'waswitsontso River road, is a favourite bathing place for vultures. They take their baths from lunch time to late afternoon and are quite happy to share their ablutions with other vulture species – up to four different kinds of vulture will share a water hole with considerably more elegance than they do a carcass. *Ngwenyeni* means "place of the crocodiles" in Shangaan as these reptiles are often seen sunning themselves on the sandbanks next to the water.

Crocodiles feature prominently in African folklore and are the source of many

Bat-eared fox

Nigel Dennis

proverbs associated with powerful men. In Shangaan culture if a man is described as a "crocodile" it means he is wealthy but quiet. The Shangaan expression "a crocodile does not grow thin" refers to the fact that powerful men can do what they like.

Shortly before Muzandzeni Picnic Spot the road crosses the Sweni River which is noted for the dense pockets of ilala palms that grow on the river banks. Look out in this area for Africa's fastest antelope – the tsessebe. The palms indicate the proximity of the tropics. There is more game along the S36 north of the Sweni River as the grazing is sweeter – the good grazing begins when the woodlands become noticeably more stunted and there are increasing pockets of thornveld.

Around Tshokwane

Stevenson-Hamilton set up Tshokwane as a ranger's post in 1928. He used it as a jumping board for inspecting the northern areas of the old Sabi Reserve, which had the Letaba River as its northern border. As he said, "It was an easy day's ride from my headquarters, and held more game and lion than any other square mile in the reserve". Its status as a game-rich area remains true today. Tshokwane was the name of an old Shangaan chief who lived there until his death in 1915. He was a mine of information about the tribal history of the area, and regaled Stevenson-Hamilton with stories about Swazi and Zulu raids into the area half-a-century before.

Nhutlwa the Giraffe

The giraffe (*nhutlwa* in Shangaan) is the tallest animal in the world, with the male measuring up to 5,5 metres from hoof to head and weighing almost two tons. A newborn calf weighs about 100 kilograms and can stand within an hour of birth. Giraffe are found mostly in southern Kruger with the highest concentrations in the central grasslands. They usually occur in groups of three with nursery herds of cows and calves averaging around 12 individuals. According to Kruger mammal expert Heike Schutze, their core territories are approximately 80 square kilometres, but in the course of a year they can wander over a 650 square-kilometre range. Giraffe browse over 40 kinds of trees, their favourite being acacias, bushwillows and terminalias. An individual giraffe can consume up to 80kg of food a day and although they drink when water is available, they have been known to go for a month without water. They are sociable animals, often found with herds of zebra and impala. Stevenson-Hamilton once came across a female giraffe suckling a zebra foal that had lost its mother. Wildlife artist Charles Asterley Maberley recorded a fight between male giraffes in which the sparring parties swung their necks to head-butt each other with the apparent aim of breaking the opponent's neck.

Giraffe

Nigel Dennis

Aardvarks

Aardvarks (*Xomboni* in Shangaan) are pig-sized nocturnal insect-eaters found throughout Kruger where there are swathes of termite mounds. Their burrowing claws and 30-cm tongue are perfectly adapted to their food needs of ants, termites and other insects. They roam up to 15km a night looking for food and hole up in burrows during the day. Former Kruger Information Officer and author, PF Fourie says aardvarks don't come out of their holes easily. He had the "very rare privilege of watching a 130-kg man, well known for his strength, trying to pull an aardvark out of its burrow when it was not more than half-way in. Needless to say, he made no impression on the aardvark".

Aardvark

Nigel Dennis

Juvenile bateleur

Mike Myers

Tshokwane, a major stop on the savanna highway between north and south, has a picnic area, provision store and gift shop as well as a fast-food outlet, which makes it a good spot for breakfast, lunch or refreshments. The picnic area is dominated by a giant sausage tree (*Kigelia africana*) which protrudes from a thatched shelter. Former Tshokwane ranger Ampie Espag once broke all the Park rules by secretly raising two lion cubs at home after he'd been forced to shoot their mother at Leeupan. He fed them on condensed milk, meat and water and said he loved them like his own children. However, word soon got out and Espag was ordered to put his cubs down. When he refused, Harry Wolhuter was ordered to do the job for him. This almost destroyed their friendship.

Tshokwane to Satara

There are three main routes between Tshokwane and Satara – the main tar road (H1-3), the Lindanda (S35) and Trichardt Roads (S37) via N'wanetsi and the Nhlanguleni Road (S36).

The main Satara Road (H1-3)

The H1-3 crosses 44km of open veld past a series of pans into the central grasslands. A number of watercourses make their way past Tshokwane, although the lack of reliable water has prevented its development into an overnight camp. Tshokwane marks the beginning of the lion territory associated with Satara and the central Park. Just north of Tshokwane is the Vutomi Loop (S34) which follows the Munywini River to the west before joining up with the Vutomi Road (S33), which follows the Ripape River back to the main Satara Road. This road is renowned for its lion sightings and the Vutomi Water Hole is often a good giraffe viewing spot. The area around Tshokwane is also associated with sightings of "white" animals – the most recent being a white lion and a white kudu seen during the mid-1980s.

The Ripape area was an important winter grazing ground for thousands of zebra and wildebeest that used to migrate westwards in summer into what is now the greater Sabi Sand Reserve. According to Kruger historians Kloppers and Bornman, the erection of Kruger's western fence in 1961 disrupted this east-west migration path, causing the death of thousands of animals. Zebra and wildebeest died en masse in 1962 along the fence line, trying to get back into Kruger. The tragedy was exacerbated by a fire that year that destroyed most of the grassland between Nhlanguleni and the Sand River, causing the death of many of the grazers inside the Park. This migration instinct disappeared during the three decades the fence remained up. It was taken down in the 1990s, allowing a free flow of animals between southern central Kruger and the private reserves, but time will tell whether the centuries-old migration pattern will re-emerge. The Ripape and Vutomi areas remain important winter grazing areas but zebra and wildebeest appear to move to the south-east of Kruger for their summer grazing.

The earth-shaking roar of a lion can be heard over five kilometres away; the lion's roar is the loudest vocal sound created by any felid.

Michael Poliza

Lion roaring

Nungu the Porcupine

Porcupines are the largest African rodents, weighing up to 27kg. Although they are common in Kruger, they are rarely seen because of their nocturnal habits. By day they hide in their burrows and emerge after dusk to forage, sometimes wandering up to 15km, seeking a variety of foods, including roots, bulbs, bark and wild fruit. Their sharp black-and-white quills, which can be up to 50cm long, are their main form of protection. They don't shoot their quills at attackers as is often claimed. Instead, porcupines will approach an aggressor backwards or

Porcupine

Nigel Dennis

sideways, spiking their attacker with their quills which detach very easily. Lion are known to have died from quills stuck in their faces after botched attempts to eat a porcupine. Their other main enemies include leopard, hyaena, large raptors and pythons. According to Kruger mammal expert Heike Shutze, there is at least one pride of lions in Kruger that specialises in hunting porcupines. Early Portuguese records from southern Africa show that porcupine quils – which are hollow – were used to carry alluvial gold dust in treks accross the bush.

The H1-3 follows the N'waswitsontso watercourse for 20km from Tshokwane through prime lion territory. This is generally a good game drive because the grazing in this part of Kruger is particularly nutritious due to the underlying gabbro and basalt. In summer the pans along the watercourse fill up quickly after the rains. Late morning is a good time to stop off at Mazithi and other water holes as this is the time grazers like to drink. A few kilometres north is N'watinungu, "creek of the porcupines" in Shangaan.

The four-kilometre N'waswitsontso Loop (S86) is a highly recommended detour off the main road as there are often predators lurking in the riverine bush. Further north on the H1-3 is the southernmost baobab in Kruger. Baobabs are common north of the Tropic of Capricorn, but their range does not extend much further south. Another indicator of northern vegetation is the predominance of palm trees along the Sweni watercourse shortly before Satara.

THE LINDANDA ROAD (S35)

The Lindanda Road edges past the N'wamuriwa Hill on the edge of the Lebombo, and crosses the eastern grasslands until it joins up with the Trichardt Road (S37) which heads north to N'wanetsi Picnic Site. The Metsi-Metsi Wilderness walking trail base camp is on the eastern side of N'wamuriwa, which has one of the most beautiful views over the central grasslands and Lebombo. The hill often attracts lightning strikes, which are a natural cause of veld fires. After a thunderstorm, rangers regularly use the top of the hill to check the area for fires.

Lindanda was the Swazi nickname of ranger Harry Wolhuter, and referred to the cloth wrap he used to wear around his waist. It was on this road, close to the confluence of the Metsi-Metsi and Banyini streams, that Wolhuter had his near-death experience with a lion. It is fascinating to see the stone cairns that mark the distance he was dragged by the lion that knocked him off his horse, before he managed to kill it and free himself.

Harry Wolhuter and the night of the lions

One of the most famous stories of the Park is the 1904 saga of ranger Harry Wolhuter, one of the Park's first rangers. Wolhuter was riding on horseback along what is today the Lindanda Road (S35), when he was attacked by two lions shortly after nightfall.

Toppled from his horse, he was seized by a male lion and dragged by his shoulder for almost 100m into the bush. At this point, the semi-conscious ranger managed to retrieve his sheath knife from his belt and stab the lion vigorously. The mortally wounded lion then dropped Wolhuter, who managed to climb into a tree before the second lion came after him.

Wolhuter believes he was saved by his dog Bull, who kept barking at the second lion and distracting it before ranger assistants arrived and carried him back to camp. After resting a day, Wolhuter was carried in a litter by four of his subordinates to get medical help. They arrived at Komatipoort four days later. Wolhuter was patched up by a doctor and then sent by train to Barberton hospital where he lay at death's door for several weeks before recovering.

Wolhuter's knife and the skin of the lion he killed are on display in the Stevenson-Hamilton Library at Skukuza.

THE TRICHARDT ROAD TO N'WANETSI (S37)

The Lindanda Road (S35) joins the Trichardt Road (S37) which follows the path taken by the ill-fated voortrekker expedition of Louis Trichardt, who led a breakaway group of 53 voortrekkers from the interior plateau on a mission to reach the coast to establish ties with the colonial authorities in Portuguese East Africa. From a game perspective, the S37 can be rewarding as it takes one through the flattish, stunted knob-thorn and marula grasslands favoured by the large herds of grazers. However, on a bad day one may see virtually nothing but grass, scrub and sky. (See page 149)

Tshokwane to Lower Sabie

There is one main route between Tshokwane and Lower Sabie which is the H10. There are many interesting deviations and viewpoints along the route, which is one of the finest drives in Kruger.

Flight of the falcons

A good time to visit Nkumbe is in late summer when falcons and kestrels gather in huge flocks to build condition before they fly off on their long northern migration to eastern Asia. Most of these are amur (eastern red-footed kestrel) and lesser kestrels. The exact migration route of the amur remains a mystery – while they are well documented passing over northern India at the start of their journey southwards, they are not seen in this area on the return trip, prompting speculation that they cross the Indian Ocean and then head over the Himalayas back to their Siberian breeding grounds.

Amur falcon

Lesser kestrel

Madness and Malaria

The Trichardt voortrekker party began their tortuous route through the escarpment in early December 1837. As anyone who has spent a rainy summer in the northern Drakensberg will attest, this is a particularly bad time to attempt such an undertaking. The weather was terrible – storms and incessant rain made the descent through the thick bush of the escarpment gorges a misery. They clambered, slithered, quarrelled and prayed their way down through the slippery mud and impenetrable bush between the granite outcrops. Their pace was painfully slow and they found themselves stuck for days at a time.

Christmas was the Christmas from Hell. They woke up to find that three of the teenage boys had deserted in the middle of the night, taking guns, food and ammunition. Not only did this deplete valuable supplies, but it reduced the amount of muscle-power available to lower the cumbersome wagons, stock and equipment down the mountain. Four days later, the three boys sheepishly returned, after realising their chances of survival were significantly enhanced by staying with the group. They paid a price – one of the elders, Tannie Scheepers, made it her personal duty to sjambok all three with every ounce of strength her body could muster. It took Trichardt's party two months and 10 days to lower their nine wagons down the escarpment to the lowveld, which they reached at the end of January 1838. Louis Trichardt wrote in his diary that the day they reached the sycamore fig at the foot of the mountain was the happiest day of his life.

However, his troubles were only beginning. Little did Trichardt know that his journey through the lowveld and coastal flatlands held a deadly surprise. He thought his main threat would be hostility from the Sekororo – the local community made up of a number of disparate clans that had settled in the area after the upheavals of Zulu expansionism in the early 19th century. To neutralise this threat, he took a Middle-Eastern type of gamble and kidnapped a small group of Shangaan men and women. He promised to release his hostages once he got to the Lebombo. Either the hostage strategy worked, or the spirit of ubuntu prevailed, or they were kept safe by the rumour that white men brought nothing but bad luck and the sooner one saw the back of them, the better. At all the homesteads they encountered, they were treated courteously and presented with a good deal of marula beer. The hostages were freed at the Lebombo and Trichardt's party crossed into present-day Mozambique through the N'wasitsontso gorge. They were enthusiastically received by the governor of Portuguese East Africa when they reached Delagoa Bay on April 13, 1838 but he nonetheless deemed it prudent to confiscate their weapons. Their joy at reaching the coast soon turned to grief as they realised that their main enemy had not been the Sekororo but the anopheles mosquito. Half the party had contracted malaria and, within months, 27 of them died, including Louis Trichardt himself. As the historian TV Bulpin remarked rather gloomily of the expedition, "Like many another human tale, hope marked its beginning – tears marked its end".

Ox wagon

Brett Hilton-Barber

TSHOKWANE TO LOWER SABIE (H10)

The road from Tshokwane to Lower Sabie is a wonderfully scenic drive through the Lebombo hills and down into the south-eastern grasslands. The drive should include a detour to Orpen Dam (4km west, off the S32) with stopoffs at Nkumbe Lookout Point, Mlondozi Dam and Muntshe Hill.

Orpen is a water hole on the N'waswitsontso River on the edge of the Lebombo with a fine view over the koppies and thick woodlands. In Shangaan, *n'waswitsontso* means either to "drip intermittently" or "the river that runs under the sand", alluding to the sporadic nature of the river's flow. For most of the year, the N'waswitsontso is a dry stream bed, but this appears deceptive as there seems to be a perennial underground stream beneath the sandbanks.

Elephants often dig drinking holes in the river during the dry season to get to the

Elephant herds are usually made up of closely related females and their babies, generally led by the oldest female, the matriarch. Elephant bulls may travel in smaller bachelor herds or wander singly during must.

underground water. The river, which winds for more than 100km through Kruger from Talamati Camp across the south central woodlands, was first referred to in writing by the earliest Dutch visitor to Kruger, Francois de Kuiper. He noted it in his diary in 1725 as the Matindonde River.

Beyond Nkumbe, the road drops out of the Lebombo and crosses the eastern savanna plains towards Lower Sabie. There are several excellent birding spots on the road, including the vleis at the foot of Muntshe Hill, Mlondozi Dam and the Sabie River crossing just below the camp. (See page 101 for Lower Sabie to Tshokwane)

Brett Hilton-Barber

Nkumbe landscape

Predators' choice

Buffalo

Black-backed jackal

Lioness with cubs

Studies by mammal expert Gus Mills show that Kruger lions eat more buffalo during drier years, while their taste shifts to zebra during periods of higher rainfall. This may be due to buffalo being prone to rapid loss of condition during droughts. There also appears to be a difference in favoured prey between lions and lionesses. Lions are prone to hunt buffalo, whereas lionesses select slightly smaller prey such as zebra and wildebeest. The black-backed jackal is a low-key predator in central Kruger compared to the big cats. It gets most of its dietary requirements from scavenging, although jackals in Kruger are known to have formed packs to hunt impala, steenbok, duiker and wildebeest calves.

Rhinos

Heinrich van den Berg

The Central Grasslands

 Habitat pointers:

- Mixed woodlands to the west of the Tshokwane – Satara main road
- Open grasslands with sweet grazing to the east of the Tshokwane – Satara main road
- Pockets of sweetveld around Orpen
- Open savanna grasslands around Satara
- Lebombo koppies around Singita Lebombo
- Olifants rugged veld between Satara and Olifants

The central grasslands have the highest lion population in Kruger. That's because of the availability of prey. The nutritious grasses support some of the biggest herds of zebra, buffalo, impala, giraffe and wildebeest found in Kruger. Lions may be spotted on any of the roads around Satara and they are often seen at dawn drinking at Girivana Water Hole 12km from Satara camp. The chances of coming accross a kill is far higher in central Kruger than almost anywhere else in the Park. The eastern half of the central grassland consists mostly of wide open basalt plains that support nutritious grazing and limited tree growth. The grasslands are contained to the east by the central Lebombo, which has its own unique ecosystem. The quality of grazing on the granite soils of the western grasslands is not as good as that of the basalt to the east. The western grasslands are more heavily treed, with pockets of bushwillow, knob-thorn and marula woodland. There are no major rivers running through the central grasslands, but there are a number of secondary watercourses, the main ones being the N'wanetsi, Sweni and Timbavati. Most of Kruger's larger raptors are found in the central grasslands, which have the biggest vulture populations in the Park.

BEST DRIVE IN THE CENTRAL GRASSLANDS
Orpen to Olifants via Timbavati Road:

The Timbavati Road tracks the river through thorn thickets, riverine bush and mixed woodland into central Kruger; stop at Leeubron, Timbavati picnic spot, Ratelpan and Roodewal. Game densities are not high but sightings are usually interesting. Allow four hours between Orpen and Olifants, including a stop.

CAMPS IN THE CENTRAL GRASSLANDS

Orpen	013 735 6355	See page 186
Maroela	013 735 6355	See page 186
Tamboti	013 735 6355	See page 186
Talamati	013 735 6343	See page 187
Imbali	031 310 3333	See page 191
Hoyo Hoyo	031 310 3333	See page 191
Hamiltons	031 310 3333	See page 191
Roodewal	012 428 9111	See page 193
Satara	013 735 6306/7	See page 198
Singita Lebombo	013 735 5500	See page 203
Singita Sweni	013 735 5500	See page 203

ORPEN GATE EXPLORER OPTIONS

- Main Road to Satara (H7); (48km; 2 hours) tar road; mixed woodlands leading into savanna grasslands; excellent game country; good for buffalo and lion;

- Talamati Drive (S140); (38km from Rabelais Hut and back again; 1,5 hours); dust road through mixed woodlands to upper catchment area of N'waswitsontso watercourse; very good sunset drive with many lion prides in the area;

- Timbavati River Road to Bobejaanskrans then on to Olifants (S39); (60km; 2,5 hours); dust road; one of the best drives in Kruger, a road of surprises with diverse species, habitats and geological zones along the Timbavati River; lots of good views over the riverine bush;

- Muzandzeni Road from Bobbejaanskrans to Tshokwane (S36); (65km; 2,5 hours); mixed bushwillow and acacia savanna with patches of dense woodland and several good water holes; good for raptors;

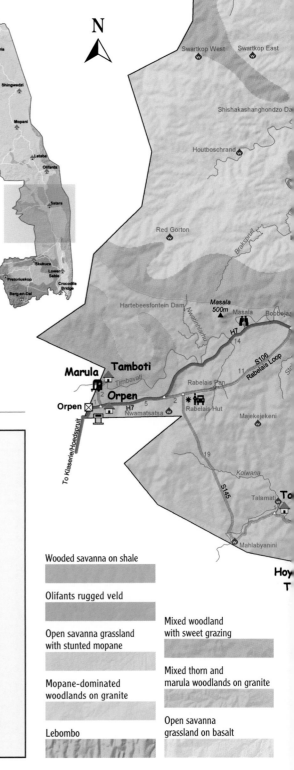

Wooded savanna on shale

Olifants rugged veld

Open savanna grassland with stunted mopane

Mopane-dominated woodlands on granite

Lebombo

Mixed woodland with sweet grazing

Mixed thorn and marula woodlands on granite

Open savanna grassland on basalt

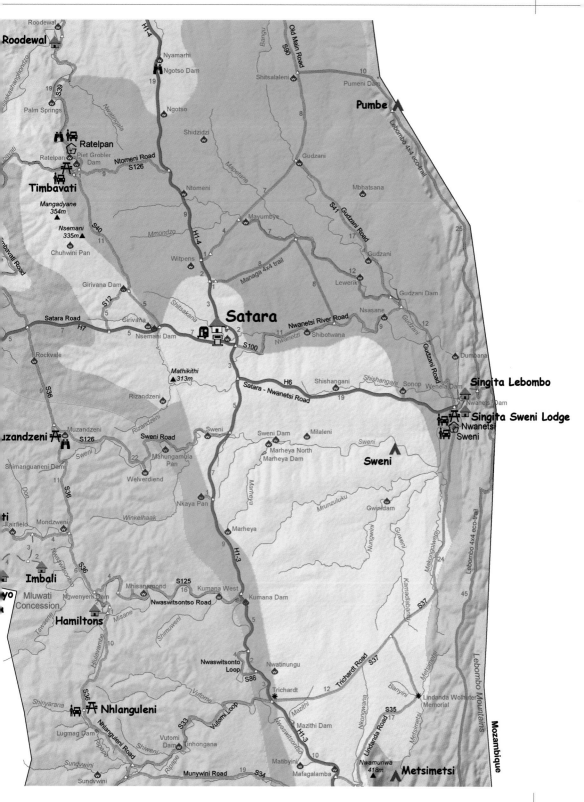

In the Orpen area, look out for

Animals

Lion

Black-backed jackal

Blue wildebeest

Buffalo

Impala

Birds

White-backed vulture

Senegal lapwing

Bateleur

Dark chanting goshawk

Black-bellied bustard

Orpen Gate

Orpen Gate leads one directly into lion country. The open grasslands stretching through to Satara and on to N'wanetsi are one of the best places in the Park to see lions and other predators. That's because of the large herds of grazing animals found here. With such a readily available supply of food it is not surprising that this is a popular environment for lions.

The reason for the abundance of game in this area is that Orpen sits on the edge of a continuous band of sweetveld that stretches from east to west across Kruger. Elsewhere in the Park the sourveld dominates the west, while the sweetveld is confined to the eastern plains.

Buffalo are found throughout the Park, but do particularly well in the central grasslands. There are approximately 31 000 buffalo in Kruger, living in herds of up to 250 animals. In times of stress they lose condition far more quickly than other grazers and are vulnerable to disease and drought – each adult requires around 21 litres of water a day. Kruger's buffalo were almost completely wiped out by excessive hunting and the rinderpest plague at the end of the 19th century but within 50 years their numbers had built up significantly. Buffalo suffered another calamity in 1992, when the drought almost halved the population. An estimated 15 000 buffalo died of hunger and thirst during this time.

Nigel Dennis

Buffalo

White syringa overlooking the Timbavati River

Africa Imagery

The Orpen sweetveld sits on gabbro rock, which forms intrusions such as Masala Koppie (500m) some 14km from the gate. The gabbro is similar to basalt in that it retains water and doesn't leach easily. The mineral-rich soils support nutritious grasses which are favoured by buffalo, zebra, wildebeest, impala and warthog. Because the grazing is good all year round, there are almost always animals visible from the road in the Orpen area.

Knob-thorn and buffalo-thorn are the most common acacias in the Orpen thornveld. There are also marula, round-leaved bloodwood and magic guarri in the woodlands, which become thicker along the drainage lines where large jackal-berries and sycamore figs occur.

Orpen to Satara

The most direct route from Orpen Gate to Satara is the tarred H7. One can include the Rabelais Loop dust road (S106). The closest water hole to Orpen Gate is N'wamatsatsa, 7 kilometres from the Gate. There are often buffalo here.

Two species of jackal occur in Kruger. The black-backed jackal is the more common and is often seen in the central grasslands. The side-striped jackal generally avoids the open plains and is more of a woodland animal that also favours the Lebombo. Jackals are usually solitary animals, scavenging by night and in the early morning. They are sometimes found in family packs and in such cases hunt impala and smaller antelope. They are particularly fond of ostrich eggs.

Nigel Dennis

Black-backed jackal

ORPEN, MAROELA AND TAMBOTI CAMPS

There are three small camps in the Orpen area – Orpen itself, Maroela Camp and Tamboti Tented Camp, the latter two being mainly geared for campers. The camps are close to the Timbavati River which enters Kruger just north of Orpen Gate.

Orpen is a small camp at Orpen Gate so is well-suited for late arrivals at the Park. The camp has 15 cottages, shop and petrol station. The proximity of the river means there is usually reasonable animal activity in this area, particularly late in the afternoon or early in the morning. Orpen offers some of the best night drives in Kruger. The Orpen area is usually reliable raptor and vulture territory. Cape vultures breed in the crags of the berg 50km due west near Strydom Tunnel, but often come into the Park to feed. The Bateleur is common as are most of the larger eagles.

Maroela and Tamboti are adjoining camps a few kilometres from Orpen Gate. They cater mainly for campers and caravanners. Maroela has 19 camping sites and two huts which can sleep eight people. There are communal ablution and cooking facilities. Tamboti is a camping site with permanent tents and caters specifically for people with disabilities. Reception for both camps is at Orpen Gate. There are no shops at the camps but there is a well-stocked shop at Orpen Gate. Both camps overlook the Timbavati River bed and are surrounded by wonderful riverine woodland with abundant bird life in the leadwoods, sycamore figs, acacias and bushwillows.

Orpen was named in honour of a major Kruger benefactor, Eileen Orpen, the wife of National Parks Board member JH Orpen, who purchased seven private farms in the area, totalling more than 60 000 acres (24 000ha) and then donated them to the Parks Board.

RABELAIS LOOP (S106) AND THE TALAMATI ROAD (S140)

Shortly after N'wamatsatsa Water Hole is the turn-off to Rabelais Loop (S106), a 12km dust-road detour off the main tar road (H7). Along the detour is Rabelais Hut which was once a ranger's post and the main entrance gate into central Kruger between 1932 and 1954. Rabelais was one of the original farms of the area, named after the French satirist. The ranger's hut has been maintained as a small museum.

Zebras never stray too far from water, but they never swim in it either. They prefer dust baths to clean themselves. Zebras can drink up to 14 litres of water a day, and they are most often seen at water holes

Nigel Dennis

Zebra

From Rabelais Hut, one can follow the S140 down south through the rolling mixed bushveld country towards Talamati. However, unless one is booked in at the small camp that overlooks a water hole, one has to drive back along the same road. The Talamati Road itself (S145) is good for game, particularly at the Fairfield Water Hole where giraffe and other browsers often emerge from the acacias for a drink.

THE SATARA ROAD (H7)

The Orpen-Satara Road usually has plenty of game in the pockets of thornveld within the mixed marula and knob-thorn woodlands. Thornveld is often an indicator of sweet grazing and there are usually herds of impala, zebra, wildebeest and buffalo along the road. In Shangaan folklore, zebras are a study in definitiveness. There is a proverb that goes, "We shall admit they are zebras once we have seen their stripes", which means "show me the proof and I'll believe you". The symbolism of the zebra has not been lost on politicians. Former South African foreign affairs minister Pik

TALAMATI CAMP

Talamati is a small bushveld camp in the mixed woodlands of the N'waswitsontso watercourse. In Shangaan *talamati* means "abundant water" which refers to the strength of the camp borehole. There are six self-catering cottages with no other facilities, although there is a public phone at reception. Talamati is on the edge of the N'waswitsontso wetlands which ensures there is usually good year-round birding. The sandy river feeds the Mluwati Concession before snaking its way down to Orpen Dam and on to Mozambique through the Lebombo. There are two bird hides at Talamati, one of which overlooks a water hole near the reception area.

SANParks

The Marabou Stork (*ghumba* in Shangaan) is known as the undertaker of the veld because of its superior scavenging abilities. It has a wingspan of 2,87m (9ft 6ins) and an unconfirmed report notes a specimen with a 4,06m wingspan, which makes it one of the longest-winged birds in the world. Marabous are believed to breed in Zambia and Zimbabwe and are summer visitors to Kruger.

Marabou stork

Michael Poliza

Central grasslands

Botha would enthuse at diplomatic cocktail parties how the new South Africa was like a zebra: it didn't matter whether one was white or black, both were an integral part of the body politic and could not survive without each other.

There are also usually large buffalo herds along the H7. Although they have a bovine appearance, they are one of the most dangerous animals of the African bush. Stevenson-Hamilton believed that buffalo were more dangerous than lion: "They are far tougher than lions, and far more solidly determined to get even with an enemy. In fact, a wounded buffalo bull will hunt his tormentor much as a terrier does a rat, and it is sufficient to say that, if he catches him, when the pieces come to be picked up they will be most conveniently removed in one or more sacks."

The best game spot on the H7 is probably around Nsemani Pan, 7km west of Satara. Nsemani is on a narrow strip of ecca shale which divides the granite

Heinrich van den Berg

woodlands of the west from the eastern basalt plains. The landscape is one of broken thornveld with rocky outcrops, such as Mathikithi Koppie (315m). Nsemani is probably the best place to see white rhino in the Satara area. Elephant, giraffe and kudu enjoy feeding on the surrounding Delagoa acacia and many-stemmed albizias, while steenbok and duiker find protection in the denser pockets of bush. Look out for steenbok around *Acacia tortilis* trees – they often feed on the dry pods that have fallen on the ground. The big carnivores often lurk on this stretch of the H7. Indeed tour guide Henry van Eck was lucky to survive a leopard attack at Nsemani in September 2003. The big cat apparently leapt into his open vehicle and mauled his leg before he managed to fight it off. Rangers later tracked it down and shot it dead. Official reports indicated the leopard may have been previously fed by tourists, thus becoming dangerously overly-familiar towards humans.

Qugunyan's Fortune

Somewhere in central Kruger lies an abandoned fortune of diamonds, gold and coins. The secret of its whereabouts was taken to the grave by a former Anglo-Boer War soldier whose initial discovery of the treasure eventually led him to the gallows. The story has its roots in the late 19th century on the Mozambican side of the Lebombo mountains. There, a chief called Qugunyan built up a substantial fortune by charging returning Shangaan mine workers a toll for crossing his land. At some point Qugunyan fell out with the Portuguese colonial authorities who dispatched an expedition to bring him to book. Qugunyan got wind of the plan and, entrusting his wives with his considerable assets, despatched them to stay with allies in the Pilgrim's Rest area. Qununyan died in battle and his wives never made it across the savanna grassland of what is today central Kruger.

Then in November 1900, during the Anglo-Boer War, a grisly discovery was made in the thick bush near the Olifants River. Writer Rob Marsh in *South Africa Weird and Wonderful* records how two Boer sympathisers riding through the bush to join Ben Viljoen's commando at the Crocodile River, came across a large collection of human remains. Among the sun-bleached bones were a number of rawhide bags full of diamonds, gold dust and an assortment of coins. The two men, Phillipus Swarts and a man named Jones, buried the treasure near the confluence of the Olifants and Blyde rivers, and went on to war. Jones was killed during the battle of Renosterkop and Swarts was captured and sent to St Helena as a prisoner of war.

After the hostilities ended in 1902, Swarts returned to Johannesburg where he enlisted the help of one Van Niekerk. Van Niekerk financed an expedition to the lowveld to search for the hidden cache and the two men set off in 1903. Swarts returned alone several months later saying that they had not been able to find the treasure and that Van Niekerk had disappeared in the bush. But, in a strange twist of fate several months later, Van Niekerk's widow recognised her husband's ring on the finger of one of Swarts's girlfriends, and reported it to the police. The police set up a search party and found Van Niekerk's skeleton in the bush near the Olifants River with a bullet in the back of his skull. They charged Swarts with murder and he was found guilty and sentenced to death. Apparently, he paid his lawyer with coins encrusted with soil and, before facing the hangman, told the investigating officer that the treasure was hidden in the bush to keep it out of the hands of the "damned British". Whether the police ever tried to find the treasure is not recorded, and to this date, the whereabouts of Qugunyan's fortune remains a mystery.

Xidzidzi the honey badger

The honey badger is a shy but ferocious little predator that is most active at night, foraging over areas of up to 35km between dusk and dawn. Known as the *ratel* in Afrikaans, and *xidzidzi* in Shangaan, this 12kg omnivore feeds on small mammals and reptiles, bird's eggs and roots. It is especially fond of honey, hence its name. It has a symbiotic relationship with the honeyguide. The little bird apparently leads the honey badger to bee hives, which the badger will then break up and the two animals will share the spoils. The honey badger has a tough, elastic skin which is one of its key defences against bee stings and mauling by predators. Although quick to retreat in the face of danger, the honey badger will react aggressively if cornered or attacked. Former Kruger information officer PF Fourie says he's heard of claims that a honey badger has killed a fully grown buffalo by severing its genitals with its teeth and claws.

THE MLUWATI CONCESSION

The Mluwati Concession is a 10 000-ha private reserve east of Talamati some 40km from Orpen Gate. It has three luxury camps which overlook the beautiful riverine bush of the N'waswitsontso and Mluwati rivers. Game drives may be done only in lodge vehicles.

The area consists of mixed woodland dominated by bushwillows and acacias, with swathes of open grassland. The grazing is mixed, with pockets of sweetveld and sourveld. The game-carrying capacity in this area is lower than the plains to the east because the grasses are less nutritious. The sweeter grass is to be found on the lower contours and so animals are most likely to be seen along the drainage lines and watercourses of this gentle rolling landscape.

The three Mluwati Concession camps are:

 ## IMBALI

Imbali was the original lodge in the Mluwati Concession. It is unashamedly upmarket, consisting of 12 luxury suites overlooking the N'waswitsontso River. The camp is built close to an excavated hunter-gatherer camp dating back several hundred years. Iron-Age artifacts found in the area have been built into special display units at Imbali, which is an aesthetic blend of stone and wood.

Brett Hilton-Barber

 ## HAMILTON'S TENTED CAMP

Hamilton's probably rivals Singita Lebombo as the most romantic place to stay in Kruger. It has six intimate luxury "tents" overlooking the N'waswitsontso Dam. Each "tent" has its own plunge pool, outdoor shower and private verandah. The aesthetic in the wood-and-canvas décor of the public area is early 20th-century safari. The camp is unfenced, and animals wander freely through it.

 ## HOYO HOYO TSONGA VILLAGE

Hoyo Hoyo is the most interesting architectural experience in the Park, offering a combination of traditional African culture with modern-day safaris. The earthy style of the camp is a blend of old and new. Hoyo Hoyo is a contemporary interpretation of a traditional Tsonga/Shangaan village. There are six luxury African fantasy huts overlooking the Mluwati River, each fitted with sophisticated modern finishings. The ethnic plushness of Hoyo Hoyo is a radically different offering from the traditional Kruger experience and will appeal to the more sophisticated and well-heeled.

None of the Mluwati Concession camps accept children under eight as guests unless the entire camp is booked out by a single party.

Imbali

Mfenhe the Baboon

Baboons are our closest relatives in the Park and the most advanced primates found in this environment. They live in troops of approximately 30 individuals and can range up to 14km in a day's foraging. Males are dominant and often move from troop to troop while females remain within the natal group. Intimacy is ensured through mutual grooming. Baboons often act as watchdogs for other animals because of their sharp sense of sight. Although they are mostly vegetarian, they have been known to kill small animals like impala lambs for food.

Baboon with baby on back

Michael Poliza

Timbavati River

Brett Hilton-Barber

Orpen to Olifants

The most direct route between Orpen and the northern camps of Olifants and Letaba is the highly-recommended Timbavati Road (S39). Alternatively one may take the road to Satara (H7) (see page 187) and then head north on the H1-4. (See page 205)

THE TIMBAVATI ROAD (S39)

The Timbavati Road (S39) is one of Kruger's best drives. It follows the Timbavati River for almost 50km through a diverse mix of thornveld and mixed woodland into mopaneveld over a series of different geological zones – granites, gabbro, ecca shales and basalt. Timbavati is derived from the Shangaan for "brackish water", yet this tributary of the Olifants is a reliable water source for game in central western Kruger. The plant and animal life along this road is interesting because it passes through so many different geological zones.

Elephant

Nigel Dennis

Animal numbers in this part of the reserve have increased steadily since the removal of the fence dividing western Kruger from the private reserves in the Timbavati area.

South of Timbavati Picnic Site, the road winds between thornveld and mixed bushwillow woodlands where, on an average day, the hornbills can outnumber the impala. It's interesting to note the relationship between rollers and bush shrikes along this road – rollers are more common in the thornveld further away from the river where the bush-shrikes dominate. North of Timbavati, the landscape becomes more broken as the road and river pass through Olifants rugged veld and the south-western mopaneveld.

Leeubron Water Hole on the S39 is rated by photographers as one of the top 10 sites for wildlife photography. Kruger's legendary "white lions" have been seen drinking here. Timbavati is a good picnic site to stop and rest. The turn-off is marked by a fine baobab. The picnic spot is at the extreme southern tip of the Olifants rugged veld, bordering on marula and red bushwillow woodlands. It overlooks the reedbeds and sandbanks of the Timbavati River. There

 ROODEWAL CAMP

Roodewal is a small, secluded private lodge on the Timbavati River, 44km north-west of Satara. It has a single bungalow and three cottages that sleep 19 people. The solar-powered camp is available only as a block booking. It is set among tall jackal-berry and Natal mahogany trees, and one of its features is a large game-viewing deck suspended between huge nyala trees overlooking the river. Each unit also has its own viewing deck. The camp has a fully equipped communal kitchen. There is no shop at Roodewal and check-in must be done when entering the Park. Guided walks and drives can be booked through Satara.

The White Lions of Timbavati

Timbavati is the name given to the Kruger's famous "white" lions. There had been itinerant reports of "albino" lions in the Park since 1928, but it was only during the 1970s that naturalist Chris McBride discovered two white lion cubs in the Timbavati Reserve bordering Kruger. They were captured and taken to Pretoria Zoo where both subsequently died. However, a few years later, there was another sighting of white lions, with confirmed reports of a great white male lion in the Tshokwane area. Since then, there have been numerous records of white lions being seen in the Park, and it is believed that this genetic phenomenon will surface from time to time in the future. The colouring of these white lions is not strictly albino – which is an absolute lack of pigmentation, but is a very light colour stemming from a rare gene that is found in both male and female lions. When lions carrying these genes mate, the result is a white cub or cubs. Lion reproductive patterns show that females are the constant element in a pride and that it is males that go to other prides to seek a mate. If the

SANParks

male lion mates with a female carrying the same recessive gene, then they will have a single – or several – white cubs in among the other tawny-coloured cubs in the litter. This phenomenon seems restricted to the Tshokwane/Letaba/Timbavati areas. Interestingly, in the same area, there have been validated reports over the years of at least three other "white" animals – a kudu, a buffalo and a giraffe.

White lion

are often elephant quite close to the site. However, as is the case with all other picnic spots, the feeding of wild animals has become a problem. Duiker walk out of the river bed to accept handouts, while glossy starlings, francolins and other birds have become beggars.

Cold drinks and firewood can be purchased at Timbavati and gas cookers can be hired. The site has reasonably decent ablution facilities.

The road north from Timbavati Picnic Site to Olifants can be very good for game, especially in the pockets of thornveld between the woodlands. One of the more interesting birds that occurs in this habitat is the kori bustard, which is the heaviest flying bird

in the world. Stop at the bird hide at Ratel Pan which overlooks the Piet Grobler Dam, while the Roodewal and Goedgegun Water Holes are also sometimes interesting. Piet Grobler, a grand-nephew of Paul Kruger, was the Minister of Land during the early 20th century who was responsible for much of the legislation governing Kruger, including the establishment of the National Parks Board (now SANParks). Roodewal is a big, red dolerite dyke that juts out of the lowveld floor above a well-shaded water hole. The rocks are part of a north-south ridge that divides the mopaneveld to the east from the mixed acacia woodland to the west. There is a noticeable decline in game numbers as the woodlands give way to mopaneveld.

Orpen to Skukuza

The most direct route between Orpen and Skukuza is the Nhlanguleni Road (S36) (see page 171), the dust road that bypasses Tshokwane and joins up with the H1-2 just north of Skukuza. Alternatively one can take the main road to Satara (H7), (see page 168) then south along the H1-3 (see page 175).

ORPEN TO TSHOKWANE (S36)

Four kilometres after Bobbejaanskrans is the Nhlanguleni Road (S36) that heads south through mixed bushwillow woodland on a two-and-a-half hour drive to Tshokwane. In Shangaan, *nhlanguleni* means "at the magic guarri". The gaurri is also known as the "toothbrush tree", because the ends of twigs fray into natural toothbrushes. The fruit is used as a purgative by local traditional healers.

This landscape is primarily sourveld and, therefore, not generous in game-viewing opportunities, although there can be sightings of buffalo, zebra, kudu and giraffe. However, it is a good road for seeing bateleurs and other birds of prey soaring high above the bush.

This is not a highly trafficked road, so it is a good choice if one wants to get away from other tourists. There are two get-out spots on this road at Muzandzeni and Nhlanguleni, which provide a respite from driving. Look out for Africa's fastest antelope, the tsessebe, around Muzandzeni. They are relatively rare in the Park and occur in isolated herds in the central and northern parts of Kruger.

Where the S36 is interesting, however, is that it feeds off into three smaller roads that follow riverine bush back into the lion country south of Satara. These are the S126 that follows the Sweni River, the S125, which traces the N'waswitsontso River back to the main Tshokwane-Satara Road, and the Vutomi

Loop. All three are good game-viewing roads because the mix of riverine bush and more nutritious grazing attract more animals, including predators such as lion and hyaena. The thorn thickets can be quite dense in summer, which makes game viewing more difficult. This whole area has been a traditional winter feeding ground for herds of impala, zebra and wildebeest.

The S36 also takes one into the Mluwati Concession area. (See page 191)

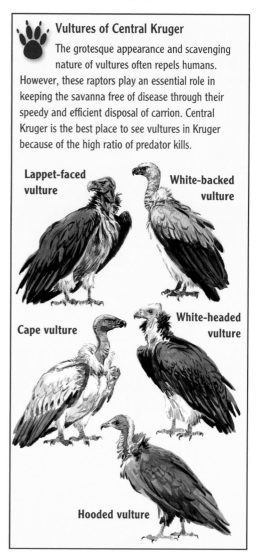

Vultures of Central Kruger

The grotesque appearance and scavenging nature of vultures often repels humans. However, these raptors play an essential role in keeping the savanna free of disease through their speedy and efficient disposal of carrion. Central Kruger is the best place to see vultures in Kruger because of the high ratio of predator kills.

Lappet-faced vulture

White-backed vulture

Cape vulture

White-headed vulture

Hooded vulture

Ancient predators of the African savanna

The open grasslands and mosaic woodlands of central Kruger are archetypal African savanna. This landscape underwent a major climate change at the end of the Miocene 5 million years ago, when global cooling led to a radical shift in weather patterns. The high rainfall that Africa enjoyed came to an end and the great tropical forests that had blanketed the continent slowly gave way to the relentless advance of the savanna. Over the next 3 million years Africa's fauna underwent a complete change. Forest-dependent species either died out or adapted to the more open landscape, while animals that evolved earlier in the Asian savanna made their appearance in Africa. This period is, of course, critical in the evolution of our own species. The aridification of Africa and the change in food-gathering patterns got our primate ancestors walking on two legs. Africa entered a further drier cycle at the start of the Pliocene, 5 million years ago, and this resulted in further extinctions, and evolutionary adaptations. Had one been able to travel through Kruger 2 million years ago, these are some of the predators you might have encountered in a landscape that would have been much more tropical and heavily wooded than the Park is today.

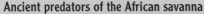

Sabre-toothed cat
(*Megantereon cultridens*)

Sabre-toothed cats (*Homotherium crenatidens* and *Megantereon cultridens*)
The sabre-toothed cats were distant cousins of the lion, which ultimately became the dominant species in this particular niche. They had large, specialised canines which were well adapted to killing, but bad for bone crunching. This may have led to their downfall as their large and elegant teeth were too delicate for a savanna lifestyle. *Homotherium,* in the fossil record between 5 million and 1,5 million years, was slightly larger than a lion and probably operated in prides in more open woodland. *Megantereon* was slightly smaller – about the size of a lioness – and preferred denser bush. *Megantereon* disappears from the fossil record about 500 000 years ago.

False sabre-toothed cat (*Dinofelis piveteaui*)
Dinofelis was as big as a lioness and had less-pronounced canines than the sabre-toothed cats. It was probably quite leopard-like in its behaviour, leading a solitary existence and hunting by night. *Dinofelis* was probably squeezed into extinction by the smaller and more versatile leopard which occupied the same riverine bush habitat. *Dinofelis* exists in the fossil record between 5 million and 1,5 million years ago. Leopard fossils dating back 3 million years have been found in South Africa.

Sabre-toothed cat
(*Homotherium crenatidens*)

False sabre-toothed cat
(*Dinofelis piveteaui*)

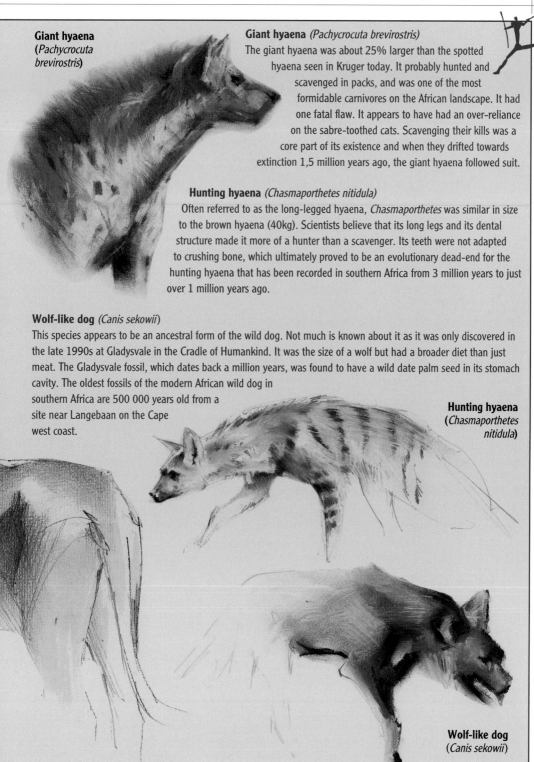

Giant hyaena
(*Pachycrocuta
brevirostris*)

Giant hyaena *(Pachycrocuta brevirostris)*
The giant hyaena was about 25% larger than the spotted
hyaena seen in Kruger today. It probably hunted and
scavenged in packs, and was one of the most
formidable carnivores on the African landscape. It had
one fatal flaw. It appears to have had an over-reliance
on the sabre-toothed cats. Scavenging their kills was a
core part of its existence and when they drifted towards
extinction 1,5 million years ago, the giant hyaena followed suit.

Hunting hyaena *(Chasmaporthetes nitidula)*
Often referred to as the long-legged hyaena, *Chasmaporthetes* was similar in size
to the brown hyaena (40kg). Scientists believe that its long legs and its dental
structure made it more of a hunter than a scavenger. Its teeth were not adapted
to crushing bone, which ultimately proved to be an evolutionary dead-end for the
hunting hyaena that has been recorded in southern Africa from 3 million years to just
over 1 million years ago.

Wolf-like dog *(Canis sekowii)*
This species appears to be an ancestral form of the wild dog. Not much is known about it as it was only discovered in
the late 1990s at Gladysvale in the Cradle of Humankind. It was the size of a wolf but had a broader diet than just
meat. The Gladysvale fossil, which dates back a million years, was found to have a wild date palm seed in its stomach
cavity. The oldest fossils of the modern African wild dog in
southern Africa are 500 000 years old from a
site near Langebaan on the Cape
west coast.

Hunting hyaena
(*Chasmaporthetes
nitidula*)

Wolf-like dog
(*Canis sekowii*)

SATARA CAMP

Satara Camp is an excellent game-viewing base in the middle of Kruger. Set in the flat, prime game-viewing knob-thorn and marula savanna plains, Satara is the second-largest camp in Kruger, and so accommodation is often available at short notice. Many Kruger veterans see Satara as the heart of Kruger because of the numbers of big game in the area and the fact that it is one of the best places to see lion in the Park.

Satara was originally designated farmland and was part of a privately owned belt that divided the old Sabi and Shingwedzi Game Reserves in the early 20th century. The camp's name originates from the notebook of an Indian land surveyor who numbered the original farm as 17 (*satra* in Hindi).

SANParks

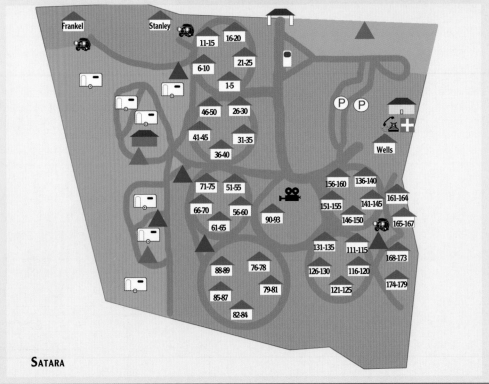

SATARA

It was made a ranger's post in 1910 and then became a tourist facility in 1928.

Unlike most other camps, it is not situated on a major river, although it is close to the confluence of the Shitsikana and Nwanetsi watercourses, which have well-developed riverine woodlands. The camp has a special African-ambience eating deck – the Nthuthwa ("giraffe" in the Shangaan language) Restaurant which specialises in traditional African meals. After most diners have left, this is a good place to listen for Satara's night sounds – the clink of fruit bats, owl calls, the whoops of hyaena, the screech of jackals and the occasional roar of lions.

Satara is also a child-friendly camp because of the amount of open space within the camp and the specialised game tours customised for young ones. It has a day area with a swimming pool.

One of Kruger's early rangers, William Walter Lloyd is buried at Satara, having died of a lung infection in 1922. His death is also the story of an act of extraordinary bravery on the part of a black ranger whose name is not recorded in the history books. Lloyd died in the middle of the night and the unnamed ranger took it upon himself to report the matter to Colonel Stevenson-Hamilton who was at Sabi Bridge (Skukuza) more than 70km away. The ranger ran and walked through the most dangerous lion-infested bush in the Park, reaching Sabi Bridge at 3am, less than 24 hours after leaving Satara. Stevenson-Hamilton immediately set out for Satara with the ranger. When they arrived, they found that Mrs Lloyd and her three small, barefooted sons had already buried Lloyd under a tree near their house (the first building in the Camp).

Stevenson-Hamilton reflected, "It must be difficult for people accustomed only to civilised surroundings to realise the position of women living far away in the African bush without neighbours, before the days of motor cars, and how they had to be prepared to face any kind of unexpected and sudden emergency."

Visits to Lloyd's grave can be organised through Satara reception.

IN THE SATARA AREA LOOK OUT FOR

Animals
Lion

Buffalo

Honey badger

Giraffe

Wildebeest

Birds
Red-billed buffalo-weaver

Red-eyed mourning dove

Ostrich

Kori bustard

African hawk-eagle

Satara and surrounds

Satara is good lion country and sightings of these magnificent beasts are possible on any of the roads around the camp. The surrounding area is at its best after good rains, which is why spring and early summer are prime game-viewing times. The vleis and pans in the surrounding sweetveld plains fill up quickly, attracting lots of birds

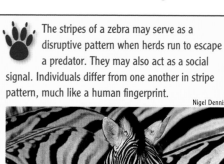

The stripes of a zebra may serve as a disruptive pattern when herds run to escape a predator. They may also act as a social signal. Individuals differ from one another in stripe pattern, much like a human fingerprint.

Nigel Dennis

Zebra

The duiker and steenbok are the only two antelope that are not strict vegetarians. Obviously, they are not hunters, but they will scavenge meat if they can. The common duiker is found throughout Kruger, but it prefers denser bush to open grassland. It has a distinctive zig-zag run if flushed from cover.

SANParks

Duiker

Girivana. Large herds of elephant are often seen at Girivana, named after a Shangaan chief who controlled broad swathes of central Kruger at the turn of the 20th century. It is rated as one of the top photographic spots in the Park because it is accessible to vehicles on three sides. This is also a favourite early morning drinking spot for lion.

All the big cats are to be found in the grasslands around Satara, which support large herds of zebra, wildebeest, buffalo and impala. There are also frequent sightings of elephant, giraffe and waterbuck.

Satara to the Lebombo

The grasslands to the east of Satara are rich in game because of the nutritious grazing associated with the underlying basalt. There are two main roads between Satara and the Lebombo – the tarred Satara-Nwanetsi Road (H6) and the Nwanetsi River Road (S100), which is a dust road.

SATARA N'WANETSI ROAD (H6)

The Satara Nwanetsi Road (H6) heads south-east from the rest camp through the open savanna grasslands along the Shishengendzini watercourse. There are water holes at Shishengendzini and Sonop, which is on the southernmost edge of the Olifants Rugged veld. As one moves eastward the bigger woodland trees are restricted to watercourses and the knob-thorn and combretum bush become increasingly stunted as a consequence of the drier climate. Although the H6 has sweet grazing along most of the route, this is not the most reliable road for seeing game. There are times when one comes across itinerant herds of buffalo, zebra, impala and wildebeest but often the landscape appears devoid of animal life. Wild dog sightings have on occasion been reported around Sonop Water Hole.

and a host of thirsty animals looking to put on condition after the tough, dry winter months. Warthogs are a Satara certainty and there are usually giraffe, buffalo, wildebeest and impala within a short distance of the Satara Camp.

The nearby water holes also attract the predators and the attendant flocks of vultures. On early-morning drives, look out for black-backed jackal making their way back to their lairs after a night's hunting and scavenging.

Two recommended water holes near Satara are Nsemani (see page 188) and

N'WANETSI RIVER ROAD (S100)

The N'wanetsi River Road (S100) is usually more interesting than the H6 because there is more riverine woodland along the road, and consequently a better chance of seeing game. There are more lion sightings reported along this road compared to the H6 a few kilometres to the south. Many of the grazers are found in mixed herds of wildebeest, zebra, impala and waterbuck, collaborating in keeping a look-out for dangerous predators.

Kruger author Wilf Nussey once watched a cheetah kill an impala right next to the road along the S100. He described how the cheetah, exhausted by the chase, was frightened off the kill by the arrival of several cars. In the confusion, a large leopard dashed between the cars, grabbed the fresh impala carcass and made off into the riverine bush, leaving behind a bunch of disbelieving tourists and a hungry, tired and disappointed cheetah.

The S100 marks the divide between the open grasslands to the south and the rockier Olifants rugged veld, which lies to the north. There are often herds of buffalo in the grassland around Shibotwana windmill

and Nsasane Water Hole. *Nsasane* is the Shangaan word for the umbrella thorn tree and was named after a nearby grove of these acacia trees. The N'wanetsi River Road joins up with the Gudzani Road (S41), which takes one south to the edge of the Lebombo Range towards Singita Lebombo and the N'wanetsi and Sweni Water Holes. A curious sight at Gudzani Dam is a regular fishing expedition by birds. Herons, egrets and hamerkops line up on the concrete dam wall to catch fish washed down the shallow spillway. This is a favourite water hole for waterbuck.

The Central Lebombo

The central Lebombo has a wide variety of animal life because of the different habitats. From far away the rugged hills seem featureless, but as one gets closer the nuances of these rhylotic koppies become apparent. This part of Kruger receives much less rainfall than the west, and this is apparent in the vegetation which grows on the stony soils. The red bushwillow is the dominant tree form but there is a diversity of plant life including many euphorbias and other succulents.

Hongonyi the blue wildebeest

The blue wildebeest – also known as the brindled gnu – is often seen in the open grasslands north of Satara, as well as the mopaneveld and the grasslands around Lower Sabie. Unlike the Serengeti where thousands of wildebeest come together for mass migrations, Kruger's wildebeest are generally non-migratory and usually occur in small herds of between three and six animals – although herds of up to 20 have been recorded. Wildebeest calves are usually born in summer and can stand within minutes of birth. They adapt from mother's milk to solid food within two weeks. Wildebeest are often found in association with impala, giraffe and zebra. They can go without water for days but prefer to drink daily. Other grazers often rely on wildebeest to find fresh grass and water.

Brett Hilton-Barber

Wildebeest

Hyaena

Nigel Dennis

N'WANETSI PICNIC SITE

N'wanetsi Picnic Site is a convenient lunch-time picnic stop in the central Lebombo. There is an open-sided thatched shelter overlooking the Sweni river gorge and a walkway up to a hut that has impressive views of the surrounding mountains and Mozambique. N'wanetsi is derived from the Shangaan description for "shimmering water". N'wanetsi used to be a private camp for senior government officials during the apartheid days. It was often used by the then Prime Minister Hendrik Verwoerd, who once complained during a five-day trip that he'd seen no lion. Lowveld author Piet Meiring recounts how, in desperation, ranger Gus Adendorff stole a wildebeest carcass from a pride of lion near Satara, loaded it onto his bakkie and secretly took it to N'wanetsi as lion bait. His ruse worked – 23 lion emerged from the bush to feed, giving Verwoerd a memorable last night in the Park, and an opportunity to use his new "cine" camera.

When fleeing a perceived threat, impala may perform a series of effortless leaps and bounds, a demonstration of fitness thought to signal to predators that the animal is in good condition and thus not worth the chase.

Impala

Wilderness Safaris

Mfene, the baboon, is a truculent, cunning and intelligent animal that will eat almost anything, including small mammals and birds. Baboons have even been known to hunt baby antelope. The major part of their diet, however, consists of plants, fruits and insects. They have a distinctive harsh bark, "Wa-hoo!", and their greatest enemy is the leopard.

Baboon

Nigel Dennis

SINGITA LEBOMBO

Singita Lebombo is the ultimate Kruger private experience. Located on a ridge in the Lebombo mountains, Singita Lebombo is unlike anything else in Kruger. Architecturally bold and contemporary, its style may best be described as modern African fusion, a cunning blend between Great Zimbabwe, Japanese zen and Georgia O'Keefe. The entertainment area, constructed of rock, wood and glass, offers stunning views over the dry, rugged mountains covered with euphorbias, and other plants suited to the arid conditions. The spacious rooms are designed for maximum privacy without compromising the view over the N'wanetsi river. Guests have a high level of personalised service, with rangers available at all times.

The 15 000-ha concession includes parts of the Lebombo inaccessible to the self-drive tourist. There is an interesting mixture of grassland and mountain habitat with particularly good birding. Singita Lebombo has a beauty spa of international standards, art gallery and shop. The lodge offers game drives and guided walks.

Brett Hilton-Barber

James Stevenson-Hamilton on lions: "They seem not only to be among the most intelligent of lower animals but also possess a well-developed sense of humour … of course, lion vary in temperament, just as do human beings. There are bold and timid, excitable and placid, good-natured and irritable individuals among them. Being what they are … it is wise not to take anything for granted in respect of their possible conduct".

Michael Poliza

Lions are rightly a symbol of vigour and power – they can mate over 40 times in a single day

N'WANETSI TO OLIFANTS (S41, S90)

The dust road between N'wanetsi and Olifants goes through open grasslands with stunted bush and into the stonier Olifants rugged veld. The first part of the route is known as the Gudzani Road (S41) which follows a watercourse of the same name. The Gudzani stream is a tributary of the N'wanetsi which, after summer rains, forms a number of pans that often attract large herds of grazers.

The Gudzani Road (S41) joins the Old Main Road (S90) between Satara and Olifants. There are sometimes eland at this junction. The game viewing along the Old Main Road is unpredictable until Bangu Water Hole, which is about an hour's drive from Olifants Camp. From Bangu to Balule, one is almost guaranteed to see elephant, particularly along the Olifants River watercourse.

N'WANETSI TO TSHOKWANE (S37) (TRICHARDT ROAD)

Sweni Water Hole is the best game-viewing spot along the S37, and it is conveniently located close to N'wanetsi Picnic Site. There is a bird hide at Sweni that has fine views over the Lebombo. The Trichardt Road from Sweni to Tshokwane heads across the eastern grasslands between the Lebombo range and the rather intriguingly named Makongolweni watercourse – "the place of the clitoris". *Makongo* is "clitoris" in Shangaan and is thought to have referred to a swimming pool in the stream reserved exclusively for the use of women from the communities that occupied the area before the Park was proclaimed. Game viewing along the S37 is reasonable in the vicinity of N'wanetsi and Sweni but, as one heads further south, the sightings become less reliable as the Olifants rugged veld gives way to the dry, open, stunted knob-thorn and marula grasslands. (See page 177)

Satara to Olifants

The most direct route between Satara and Olifants is the H1-4 tarred road. However, an interesting alternative is to take the S40 to Timbavati which goes through a wider variety of habitats. Another option is to take the Old Main Road (S90) through the eastern grasslands. (See page 204)

SATARA TO OLIFANTS (H1-4)

The H1-4 north initially goes through open grassland with shrub bushwillow and occasional marulas. Ngotso Water Hole about 20km north of Satara is the main water hole on the Olifants Road. It is a man-made dam fed by a vlei area that is favoured by elephant. It is usually a good birding spot frequented by the African fish-eagle. North of Satara, the magic guarri becomes less common, and in its place, are the *grewia* species – the raisin bushes. The H1-4 passes through a large swathe of open shrubveld and a series of pans along the Ngotso watercourse which is dominated by leadwoods. Many of these pans are too far

away to be interesting, but they attract a lot of giraffe and zebra to the area.

South of Olifants Camp, the landscape becomes quite rocky as the road starts dropping into the river catchment area. This area is known as Olifants rugged veld and is a transition zone between the woodlands of the south and the mopaneveld of the north.

Pioneer wives

The wives of Kruger's early rangers had it tough, living in the most primitive of conditions far from any luxury or social life. They were hardy. In the same year that Mrs Lloyd buried her husband at Satara, Mrs Ledeboer at Letaba spent two months in a leaky hut of mud and grass, single-handedly nursing her pneumonia-ridden husband and sick baby back to health, not seeing another person for that entire time. Ranger Cecil De Laporte frequently deputised for Stevenson-Hamilton during the 1920s and spent large stretches of time away from his wife who lived at their Crocodile Bridge quarters. Late one night, while Mrs De Laporte was on her own, a pride of lion got into the stables and attacked the donkeys. The infuriated former World War I nurse emerged from the house with guns blazing. She shot dead four lion and scared the others away into the darkness.

Red-billed mass action

There are more red-billed queleas in the world than any other bird. These nomadic little birds are among the most important bird species in Kruger in terms of how many there are and how much they eat. There are an estimated 37 million red-billed queleas in Kruger, occurring in nesting colonies of up to a million birds. Studies in Kruger show that quelea colonies, which feed in a six-kilometre radius from their nests, can consume up to 480 kilograms of plants and insects per hectare per day. Red-billed queleas are the avian equivalent of impala in that everything preys on them, including lion and crocodiles!

Red-billed quelea

Albert Froneman

Terminalia dawn

Brett Hilton-Barber

Kruger by night

There is more action at night in Kruger than during the day. Hunters take advantage of the cover of darkness to stalk their prey, while grazers and browsers often feed actively at night because their is less energy loss than during the day.

Late afternoon

Lions become restless; mothers play with cubs; pride energy levels rise in preparation for the night hunt; hyaenas emerge from their lairs; leopard get up from their day's rest; cheetah often hunt; wild dogs very active; impala move to the most open terrain around them; warthogs head for their burrows; baboons go to their roosts for the night; zebras seek a sleeping spot with minimal risk of ambush; rhinos become more active.

Evening

Lion and leopards begin hunting; hyaena hunt or scavenge; caracal are at their most active; cheetah settle down for the night; hippos emerge from rivers, often walking several kilometres away from water to graze, giraffe settle down to ruminate; impala rest as far from thick bush as possible; many antelope continue feeding; zebras settle down to sleep with one staying awake to watch out for predators; elephants browse; genets and civets do most of their hunting before midnight.

Late night

Lion and hyaena hunt; cheetah and wild dogs usually asleep; impala get up for a late-night feed; bushbabies very noisy, zebra sleep; elephant often sleep at this time, sometimes standing up; lots of animals often feed, including buffalo, wildebeest and kudu.

Pre-dawn

Lions often seen drinking at water holes or feeding on a kill; hyaena scavenge; prime hunting time for wild dog; cheetah – the most diurnal of the cats – get up to hunt; active time for serval which are also diurnal; impala rest.

Daybreak

Lions feed on the night's kill; hyaenas return to their dens; leopard often active for the first few hours of daylight before finding a good branch to rest on; impala feel safe enough to move back into wooded areas; hippos return to rivers to socialise and digest the night's food; cheetah hunt before the day's heat sets in; baboons wake up late.

Animal skins

Zebra

Giraffe

Wild dog

No two zebras have the same pattern of stripes. Which raises the question – is a zebra a white animal with black stripes or a black animal with white stripes? Scientists believe it is the former, as there is more white than black on the zebra's coat. No two giraffe have the same patterning either. Giraffe become darker as they get older. Almost all giraffe in Kruger are found south of Letaba, with very few populations in the north. Wild dogs also have individualised patterning. They may all look the same but the black spots on their backs differ from dog to dog. One of the most reliable places to see wild dogs in Kruger is the Phalaborwa Gate area.

Elephant

Brett Hilton-Barber

Olifants, Letaba and the Southern Mopaneveld

🍃 Habitat Pointers

- Olifants rugged veld south of Olifants camp
- Shrub mopane grasslands dominate the eastern half of the region north of Olifants
- Mixed mopane woodlands dominate the western half of the region north of Olifants
- Lebombo foothills along the eastern edge of the mopaneveld
- Pockets of riverine bush along the Olifants and Letaba rivers

The Olifants River is generally accepted as the divide between southern and northern Kruger. To the south the vegetation is dominated by bushwillow. To the north is the great expanse of mopaneveld and the start of elephant country. The transition zone between north and south is a unique habitat known as Olifants rugged veld, a broken landscape of black rocks with pockets of dense thorn and a tangled mixture of woodland trees. The other major river is the Letaba which meets the Olifants at a cutting through the Lebombo. There is far less game here than in the central grasslands and most of the animal activity takes place close to the rivers. Elephant are dominant but good lion and leopard sightings are often recorded along the Letaba River. Waterbuck are particularly prolific around Letaba. The rivers are important water bird breeding sites and some of the best birding in South Africa may be experienced along the northern banks of the Engelhard dam close to Letaba camp. There is a long tradition of human settlement in the broader Letaba River catchment and some of the artifacts from the Iron Age can be seen at Masorini Picnic Site near Phalaborwa Gate.

BEST DRIVE IN THE SOUTHERN MOPANEVELD
Engelhard Dam to Mingerhout Dam:

This drive includes over 20km of Letaba River frontage which is the centre of animal activity in the southern mopaneveld; the drive is particularly good in winter as animals tend to stick closer to water; take in Matambeni Hide and the Engelhard Dam wall for birding and Mingerhout Dam for animal watching. Allow five hours to and from Letaba Camp (return via the same route, as the S47 to the south of Mingerhout has large tracts of fairly featureless mopaneveld with few animals to be seen).

CAMPS IN THE SOUTHERN MOPANEVELD

Shimuwini 013 735 6683 See page 217
Boulders 012 428 9111 See page 217
Letaba 013 735 6636/7 See page 221
Olifants 013 735 6606/7 See page 230
Balule 013 735 6306 See page 232

GIRIYONDO BORDER POST (013) 753 5757

Gate times:

Summer (1 October to 31 March) from 0800 to 16h00
Winter (1 April to 30 September) from 08h00 to 15h00
Currently, only 4x4s are allowed across the border, and no vehicles that weigh over four tons. No commercial traffic is allowed through Giriyondo.

PHALABORWA GATE EXPLORER OPTIONS

- Phalaborwa Gate to Mopani (H14) 60km (2,5 hours); tar road; road tracks Ngwenyeni River through mopane and bushwillow woodlands; good for wild dogs, usually lots of elephant in mixed mopane woodlands north of Letaba River crossing;
- Letaba Road (H9) (51km; 2 hours); tar road through mixed mopane and bushwillow woodlands; stop at Masorini Archaeological Display; game more plentiful around Letaba Camp.

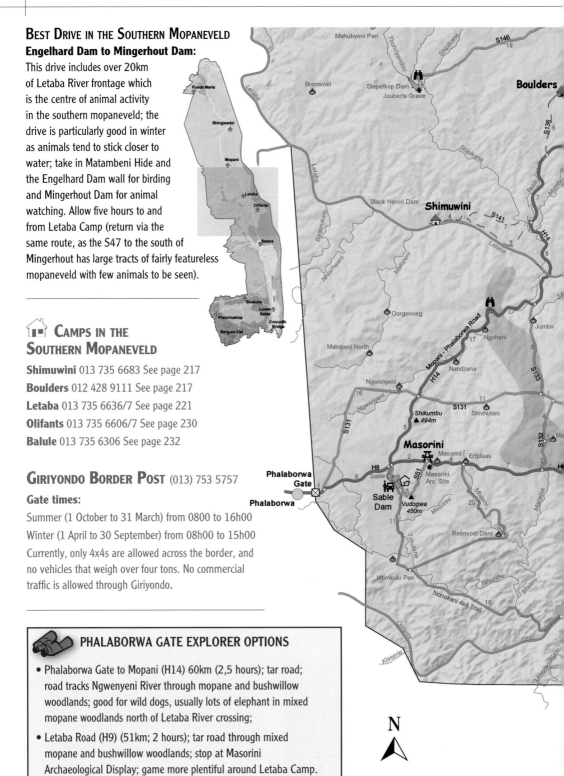

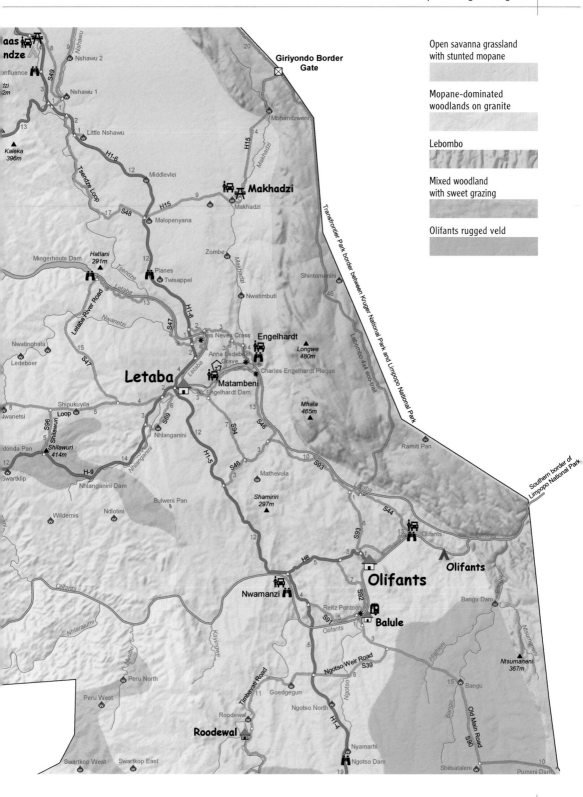

Open savanna grassland
with stunted mopane

Mopane-dominated
woodlands on granite

Lebombo

Mixed woodland
with sweet grazing

Olifants rugged veld

Phalaborwa Gate Area

The character of northern Kruger is entirely different from that of the south. This is because of the drier climate and the dominance of one main vegetation type – mopaneveld. These two factors limit the animal-carrying capacity of the land, so the variety and amount of game to be seen is not comparable to the area south of the Olifants River. Nonetheless, northern Kruger has its own magic, and the area between the Letaba and Olifants rivers, in particular, will not disappoint those seeking the full Kruger experience.

Phalaborwa Gate leads one directly into undulating woodlands of mopane trees mixed with bushwillows and acacias. Mopane grows as a tree or a shrub, depending on the climate and the degree of usage by elephants. Mopaneveld is the elephant's kingdom. More than half of the elephants in Kruger live in this environment, making use of virtually every part of the mopane – eating leaves, roots and bark and even twigs that have been burnt by fire.

Better than the South

Phalaborwa was settled by Sotho-speaking iron-working communities in the 16th century. The name literally means "Better than the south" because of the rich mineral profile of the area. Between 1800 and 1850, the baPhalaborwa were at the peak of their power under the chief Malatji, controlling a vast swathe of land between the Olifants and Letaba Rivers. Their influence waned as the ivory trade was wrested from their hands by João Albasini in the 1860s, and then, again, with the influx of European agricultural implements in the 1880s, which affected the viability of their smelting and forging businesses.

The underlying geology here is a mixture of granite and gneiss. In the Phalaborwa Gate area the granite juts out of the landscape in a series of distinctive koppies that have been used as navigational landmarks for centuries. There are the remains of many Iron-Age villages at the base of these hills.

The grass on the granitic soils in this region is a mixture of sweet and sourveld, but it is generally sparse because of low

Elephants in the Phalaborwa area

Brett Hilton-Barber

🍃 Mopaneveld – landscape of the north

Mopaneveld and mopane worm
Brett Hilton-Barber

Mopane (*Colophospermum mopane*) is the most common tree in Kruger. Mopaneveld, which is the environment dominated by mopane trees or shrubs, covers more than half the Park's total surface and dominates the central and northern areas. Mopane is a deciduous tree that varies in size in different localities – a major influence being climate, soil condition and elephant activity. The mopane tree is recognisable by its roughly grooved bark and, during winter and spring, by its roundish leaves which become golden-brown. Being rich in phosphate and calcium, it is an essential part of the diet of the biggest animal in Kruger – the elephant – and one of the smallest – the mopane worm (*Imbrasia belina*). During summer, aphids leave a sugar residue on mopane leaves and this is particularly relished by elephants. Mopane wood is sometimes used in furniture making because it is termite resistant. There are three main types of mopaneveld in Kruger:

- Mopane woodlands found on granite in the north-west of the Park – mixed in with acacia and bushwillows;
- Mopane shrubveld found on basalt in the north-east of the Park;
- Mopane thickets found on shales in the far north of the Park.

rainfall. The more palatable grasses are generally confined to the lower-lying areas, so the best game spotting is in the drainage lines and the contours along dry stream beds.

Look out for wild dogs on all the roads in the Phalaborwa area. These endangered animals avoid the lion-dominated central plains, restricting themselves to roaming in more marginal areas. There appears to

Among wild dogs, typically only the dominant – or alpha – pair breed.
Nigel Dennis
Wild dogs

Shifomhisi the eccentric and elusive poacher

One of Kruger's legendary eccentrics was a poacher called Shifomhisi. Originally from Acornhoek, just outside the Park, the Shangaan speaker moved into Kruger during the 1940s to pursue the existence of a wild man. He lived in aardvark holes on the banks of the Olifants River south of Phalaborwa and usually wandered around the veld completely naked, foraging on roots and trapping small animals. He refused to cut his hair or wash.

According to Kruger historians Kloppers and Bornman, Shifomhisi was an expert in concealment and managed to elude rangers through his cunning veld craft. If detected, they wrote, "he bolted with the speed of a tsessebe, leaping over bushes like an impala pursued by lion and seemed impervious to such things as thorns or fatigue".

However, once Shifomhisi began stealing from rangers' pickets, he provoked an organised campaign to capture him. A group of rangers tracked him down in the early hours of the morning to a hollowed-out anthill and tried to flush him out by throwing in burning sticks. Shifomhisi charged through the cordon into the night and disappeared. The rangers followed his tracks along the banks of the Olifants River and came upon him drinking at a pool. He made off into the bush but fell over a rock, injuring his leg and was captured by the rangers.

Shifomhisi was charged with poaching but was found mentally unfit to stand trial. He ended his days in a lunatic asylum.

Impala

Nigel Dennis

be a high concentration of African wild dog in the western mopaneveld between the Olifants and Letaba rivers. The best chance of seeing them is early in the morning which is their main hunting time. Stevenson-Hamilton believed wild dogs disturbed other animals more than any other predator in Africa. "A pack descending suddenly on a district, scatters animals far and wide...and it is not difficult to assess from the restless and uneasy manner of impala and other antelopes...that these bush pirates are on the warpath".

There are two get-out points within 10km of Phalaborwa Gate – Sable Dam and Masorini Picnic Site. Sable Dam, on the S51, is an exposed stretch of water within the mopaneveld. Although it was named after a herd of sable antelope associated with this area, these rare antelope are rarely seen at the dam. In fact they are rarely seen at all because of their preference for denser thickets. Sable and roan numbers appear to be declining in the Park, possibly due to the increase in the elephant population. There is a bird hide at Sable Dam that can be hired for overnight accommodation through Phalaborwa Gate. Lion frequently come to the water hole at dawn to drink, but the dam is generally not heavily trafficked by animals. Steenbok are a regular sighting in the surrounding bush.

Masorini Picnic Site, 10km from Phalaborwa Gate, is a convenient spot for lunch or just a quick toilet stop. It's at the foot of the big-bouldered Vudogwa Hill (439m), next to the remains of an Iron-Age village. Firewood and cold drinks can be purchased at the site, but one has to provide one's own food. Gas braais are available for hire. There are daily guided tours of the archaeological site every half-an-hour between 9am and 4pm, except on Mondays.

Phalaborwa to Mopani

The most direct route between Phalaborwa and Mopani is the H14, which is also the main access road to Shimuwini and Boulders Camps. The longer route is via Letaba Camp along the H-9 (see page 217) and then north on the H1-6. (See page 232)

PHALABORWA TO MOPANI CAMP (H14)

The Mopani-Phalaborwa Road (H14) passes Shikumbu Mountain (494m), which was occupied by the same 19th-century iron-making communities that inhabited Masorini. These hills served as landmarks of human habitation for anyone crossing the hot lowveld plains. Shikumbu is still regarded by many as a sacred hill associated with powerful *muthi*. Traditionalists in the area say that to point a finger at the granite mountain is to invoke bad luck.

The H14 tracks the seasonal Ngwenyeni stream ("place of the crocodile") and follows the riverine bush through the flat mopane bushwillow woodlands. There is usually animal activity around Nandzane Water Hole, which marks the confluence of the Ngwenyeni and Shicindzwaneni ("place of the ilala palms") watercourses. *Nandzane* is the Shangaan name for the caracal or rooikat, a medium-sized hunting cat with distinctive long and fluffy ears. There are some beautiful loop roads off the H14 along the stream bank. This is a recommended winter drive as there is usually a

Masorini Iron-Age site

Masorini is an Iron-Age archaeological site occupied during the 19th century by the Majola, a sub-group of the Sotho-speaking baPhalaborwa people. The Majola were iron smelters and forgers and probably traded metal, food and ivory products with other communities across the lowveld and as far as the Mozambican coast. The village has been partially restored and one can see the furnaces where smelting took place. The art of smelting was considered sacred and reserved only for men. If a pregnant woman was seen near a furnace it was deemed a particularly bad omen. From the artifacts and food remains excavated at Masorini, it appears that the residents grew and processed sorghum and supplemented their diet by hunting. No domestic animal remains have been found. Archaeologists believe the Majola were the last in a long line of people who occupied the site, which has evidence of human habitation going back more than 1 000 years.

Masorini site and Masorini artifacts

Brett Hilton-Barber

Letaba River

Brett Hilton-Barber

concentration of game in the bush along the watercourse where pools of water remain late into the dry season.

The Letaba River is one of the great bushveld arteries and it is worth stopping at the high-level bridge to study the surrounding area. There are often buffalo, giraffe, elephant, wildebeest, kudu and other antelope along the banks of the Letaba and the birding is usually good. In the north most animals are found in close proximity to the major rivers, particularly in winter when the pans dry up and the rain clouds disappear.

After crossing the broad, sandy bed of the Letaba River, the H14 continues towards the main Letaba-Mopani Road (H1-6) with turn-offs to Shimuwini and Boulders Bush Camps. Game viewing along the H14 north of the Letaba River is not particularly good until one passes the trio of granite outcrops of Tsale (450m), Kaleka (396m) and Ngodzi (472m), which signal the start of the sweeter grass of mopane shrubveld on basalt.

Termites

Termites are a crucial part of the savanna ecosystem in that they break down dead and decaying plant material and recycle it as nutrients. Scientists believe that termites consume over 50% of surface plant litter in the African savanna and that 20% of carbon produced in this habitat is due to termite activity. In Kruger termites are believed to eat about 20kg of plant material per hectare per year. In northern Kruger there are an estimated 1,1 million active termite mounds, or approximately a mound every hectare. The bigger termite mounds in Kruger have populations of over 200 000 termites. Besides their role in recycling energy, they are an important food source for many animals.

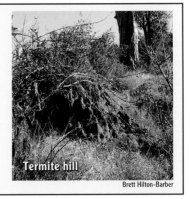

Termite hill

Brett Hilton-Barber

Phalaborwa to Letaba

The main route between Phalaborwa Gate and Letaba is the H-9 past Masorini (see page 215). Alternatively one can take the S131 dust road, a road of featureless mopaneveld usually devoid of human or animal traffic, save the odd elephant or two.

MASORINI TO LETABA (H-9)

For 20km after Masorini, the main road to Letaba takes one through fairly monotonous mopane flatland with not much game. There are, however, an extraordinary number of termite hills in this part of the Park. One will notice that the termite hills are at least 50m apart, because these insects are fiercely territorial. A termite mound can be occupied by successive generations of termites for centuries. During summer, one may be lucky enough to witness gatherings of eagles above the mounds, preying on high-flying termites, which are rich in protein. Another animal that feeds on termites is the rarely seen aardwolf ("earth wolf" in Afrikaans), a member of the hyaena family, which has such sensitive hearing that it can detect termite activity deep under the ground. Aardwolfs use their long tongues to lap up termites when they find them, and a single animal is capable of eating up to 300 000 insects during a night's outing.

SHIMUWINI CAMP

Shimuwini is Shangaan for "Place of the Baobabs" and there are some wonderful ancient specimens of these trees at the camp. The construction of the Shimuwini Dam changed the entire ecosystem of the area, introducing permanent water into the western mopaneveld, which has increased the amount of game in the area, particularly elephant. Waterbuck are common, while eland are often seen in the surrounding grassland. Shimuwini is one of the best birding camps in Kruger. It has 15 chalets and a central lapa that overlooks the Letaba River and the dam. The camp offers bush drives and guided walks. Firewood and ice are on sale at the camp but there is no shop. There are no electrical plug-points in the rooms.

BOULDERS BUSH LODGE

Boulders Bush Lodge is a private camp that takes its name from the surrounding granite koppies. It's an excellent birding spot because the five thatched chalets are on stilts. Each has its own deck at tree canopy level with views over the surrounding bushwillow and mopane woodland. The peaks of Ngodzi (472m) and Tsale (450m) can be seen from the camp, which is next to a stream and near a water hole. The lodge is available only as a block booking. It has no electricity – all lighting is solar-powered and cooking is on gas. It offers game drives and guided walks, but these have to be arranged when the initial booking takes place.

Each Kruger elephant pushes over up to four trees a day – sometimes to get at the leaves, sometimes for no apparent reason. Most trees resprout with only a fraction being killed. Naturalist Bob Scholes estimates there are about 300 mature trees per hectare in Kruger, and that elephants destroy one percent of Kruger's trees per year. The eastern grasslands have been worst affected with up to 60% of tree cover disappearing over the past 50 years.

Elephant

Michael Poliza

Palm Trees in Kruger

There are two main kinds of palm trees in Kruger – the wild date palm (*Phoenix reclinata*) and the lala (Ilala) palm (*Hyphaene natalensis*). The wild date palm is more common in the south of the Park on the banks of rivers and spruits. Primates and birds enjoy the clusters of yellow-brown fruit, while elephants eat the leaves and stems. The lala palm does well on the basaltic corridor, and is more abundant in the north, and there are some fine examples of these trees around Letaba and Shingwedzi camps. The fibre of both palms was traditionally used by Shangaan speakers for making mats and ropes and a fine alcoholic beverage can be brewed from the sap.

Brett Hilton-Barber

Lala palm

Shilawuri Hill (414m), is a great gabbro boulder which has been a lowveld navigational landmark for centuries. It marks the watershed between the usually dry N'washidzundzu and Nhlanganini watercourses. There is a loop road to Nhlanganini Water Hole which, when there is water, is inhabited by hippo.

Elephant and buffalo are often seen along the Nhlanganini creek, which is on the edge of a strip of sandveld. The diversity of vegetation here stands out noticeably from the mixed mopane bushwillow woodlands to the west and the shrub mopane to the east. Because of the variety of edible plants around, there is usually game to be seen. Look out for the pan-hinged terrapin at Nhlanganini. There are sometimes scores of these turtle-like creatures at this water hole. They are common throughout the Park, evading predators because of their ability to release a powerful odour that makes them smell like lions.

A distant relative of the zebra and rhino, the hippopotamus is generally a vegetarian, but has been known to steal meat from crocodiles.

A new species of baboon spider has been discovered near Letaba camp. Researchers found the new species during the 2003 spider survey in Kruger and to date it has not been recorded anywhere else in the world but in a patch of mopane acacia woodland near the camp. There are seven other species of baboon spider that are found in Kruger. The new species, *Ceratogyrus paulseni*, differs from the others in that it has a horn on its back. Baboon spiders are big and hairy with 16 legs instead of the normal eight. They are harmless to humans.

IN THE LETABA AREA, LOOK OUT FOR:

Animals

Bushbuck

Elephant

Leopard

Waterbuck

Vervet monkey

Birds

Verreaux's eagle-owl

Green-backed heron

Brown-hooded kingfisher

Red-headed weaver

Kurrichane thrush

Around Letaba

The area around Letaba has long been a site of human habitation. Archaeologists believe that some of the first Bantu-speaking people moving into southern Africa settled along the Letaba River from about 400 AD. They were metalworkers, farmers and traders who gradually displaced the nomadic San hunter-gatherers, incorporating them into their social structures or forcing them to more marginal areas. Over the next 1 000 years, successive waves of Bantu speakers migrated down the east African seaboard into southern Africa. In Kruger the main centres of occupation were along the Letaba, Limpopo and Sabie Rivers where there was a steady supply of game and water. Archaeologists believe that population numbers in Kruger varied according to

Apple-leaf – the rain tree

Apple-leaves are also known as rain trees because the ground beneath them is often moist. This is because of foamy secretions dropped by the froghopper aphids that sometimes infest the trees, feeding en masse on the leaves. Another explanation is that the apple-leaf comes out in flower ahead of the first spring rains and is, therefore, a reliable indicator to traditional farmers that planting can begin.

The flowers of the apple-leaf are a beautiful mauve-blue that are at their most colourful at the end of autumn, making the trees stand out in stark contrast to the dry veld.

The apple-leaf remains green even during very dry times and is a favourite with elephant, giraffe, eland and Lichtenstein's hartebeest. Most other browsers favour young leaves but find the older ones unpalatable.

Brett Hilton-Barber

Apple-leaf tree

climatic conditions and probably peaked at around 15 000 during the first millennium. Generally the area was marginal in terms of the cultural development of the subcontinent. Nonetheless, these communities had an impact on the landscape that was dramatically different to that of the hunter-gatherers. The pastoralists augmented their farming initiatives with hunting, often using fire and game pits to capture animals.

Letaba camp stands in a landscape of mopane shrubveld, based on basalt. Surrounding the camp, there are extensive mixed grass plains with a prevalence of apple-leaf trees among the mopane. Taller trees are restricted to the drainage lines and riverine forests where there are wonderful leadwoods, tambotis and nyala trees. The grazing is sweeter on the lower countours of plains.

The Letaba and Olifants areas have high elephant populations. In the past, there have been serious cross-border attempts at ivory poaching in this area. The worst period was towards the end of the civil war in Mozambique, between 1981 and 1983, when park authorities and poachers were engaged in a low-intensity war. Renamo rebels and the Mozambique government troops they were fighting both indulged in poaching as a sideline, infiltrating the Park through the Lebombo mountains and using automatic weapons to hunt elephant.

The discovery of a number of elephant carcasses at Shintomeneni, north of the Letaba River, marked the start of the two-year battle between the Park and poachers. In 1981 alone, 180 Kruger elephants were shot by poachers between the Letaba

Leopard

Albert Froneman

LETABA CAMP

Letaba, which means "river of sand" in Sotho, is one of Kruger's most pleasant camps. Set on a broad bend of the Letaba River near its confluence with the Nhlanganini Stream, the camp has wonderful views from the restaurant and recreation areas over the sandy river beds where elephant and buffalo regularly come to drink. The riverine bush around the camp stands in stark contrast to the sometimes monotonous mopaneveld of the north. The camp has tall, shady

Brett Hilton-Barber

trees, extensive lawns and a tame herd of bushbuck that wander nonchalantly between the rondavels. Letaba is known for its owls, in particular the African scops owl which calls regularly at night near the restaurant

Waterbuck are common along the Letaba River. They are the most water-dependent of antelope and their daily dependency on drinking makes them particularly vulnerable to lion. Letaba can bake in summer and get uncomfortably humid, but it does have very cool river views from the walkway and restaurant area. Elephant are a regular sighting along the river, and a visit to the camp's Elephant Museum is highly recommended for an insight into Kruger's "Magnificent Seven" and the emerging new generation of big tuskers.

Movie star Lee Marvin stayed at Letaba camp in 1975 for the filming of Wilbur Smith's "Shout at the Devil". Ranger Bruce Bryden, who was a stunt man in the movie, recalled that Marvin didn't really have to act much to be convincing in his role as a hard-drinking American hunter, as he was a naturally wild man who was "sloshed most of the time". Marvin and fellow actor Roger Moore set up a long-running poker game at Letaba, trading chips for R10 apiece, drinking Grand Mousseaux, smoking Cuban Hoyo de Monterrey cigars and listening to the sounds of the bush at night. No wonder Hollywood loves Africa.

Letaba is a large camp offering a variety of accommodation types, from camping to fully equipped guest cottages, and there are all the facilities of the larger camps, including an ATM machine. If one is overdone on animals there is a TV lounge and dartboard. Letaba is a good camp for kids in that the Elephant Museum has interesting displays, wildlife films are shown regularly and there is a children's activity programme during school holidays.

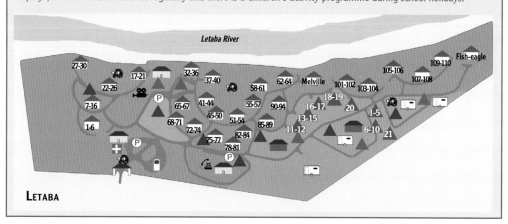

LETABA

The Magnificent Seven cemented Kruger's reputation as having some of the biggest tuskers in the world. However, the biggest tusks on any elephant found in the Park were not on any of the Magnificent Seven but were those of Mandleve, (which means "ear", as he had a distinctive notch in one of his ears). His tusks, each 2,71m long, weighed 69kg and 73,5kg respectively. Mandleve, who frequented the Skukuza area and was often seen near Kruger Gate, died a natural death in 1993, aged about 56 years old. There are three other tuskers that have become living legends: Duke, who frequents Duke's Water Hole area near Lower Sabie, Tshilonde, who lives in the Shingwedzi area, and Tshokwane, who is sometimes seen near the picnic site of the same name. Tshokwane's tusks have, unfortunately, broken off and have never been found.

SANParks

Tusks at Letaba's elephant museum

and Shingwedzi Rivers. This prompted a military-style response from the Kruger, which then began training its rangers in counter-insurgency warfare.

One of the first engagements between rangers and poachers during this "mini-war" was on a tributary of the Letaba River near Engelhard Dam. Rangers Ben Lamprecht and Ben Pretorius set up an ambush near a cache of ivory they found near the stream, and confronted the poachers when they arrived to collect their loot. The poachers ignored calls to drop their weapons and a shoot-out ensued. One of the poachers was shot dead and the others fled, giving Park staff a badly needed psychological victory. The stream where the gunfight took place was named Voorsitspruit (Afrikaans for "Ambush Stream").

Several other shoot-outs took place over the next 18 months and a number of arrests were made (including several Park staff

who had been working with poachers). The aggressive reaction to poaching initially contained the problem and then overcame it. By 1984, elephant poaching had been reduced to almost zero and the "mini-war" was over. The pendulum has now swung in the opposite direction, with the current elephant over-population raising the spectre of offically-sanctioned culling.

Engelhard Dam

The best way to experience Engelhard Dam is along the S62, which runs east off the Letaba-Mopani Road just after Letaba River Bridge and along the northern banks of the river. Game is usually plentiful in the area, especially in winter. Named after former US air-force bomber and later chairman of the Rand Mines Group, Charles Engelhard, the dam is a long stretch of water on the Letaba River that has some of the best birding in

The Magnificent Seven

Elephants have traditionally been hunted for their ivory, so those animals with great tusks have been prime targets for poachers and hunters. Kruger is famous for seven elephants with record size tusks that have become part of the Park's folklore. The term "Magnificent Seven" was coined by former Kruger head Tol Pienaar who borrowed the name from the 1960 Hollywood western of the same name. The biggest tusks ever recorded are from an elephant shot on the slopes of Mount Kilimanjaro in East Africa. One tusk weighed more than 100kg.

- Mafunyane (The Irritable One), whose perfectly matched tusks, each weighting 55,1kg, scraped the ground as he walked. Mafunyane had a fist-sized hole on the top of his head which was either from an old gunshot wound or a fight with another elephant, and this healed injury may have accounted for his bad temper. He occupied the Pafuri district and died of natural causes in 1984;

- João (named after the famous Portuguese ivory hunter João Albasini) had a left tusk of about 55kg and a right one of about 45kg before they broke off in 1984. He was frequently seen in the Shingwedzi area and survived an attack by poachers in 1982. Park authorities treated his AK-47 wounds, which appeared to have healed completely. He is believed to have died in 2000, but his body was never recovered;

- Kambaku ("Big Elephant") had a left tusk of 63,6kg and a right one of 64kg. He appeared to have the widest territory and was seen between Satara and Crocodile Bridge. He eventually was put down by rangers in 1985, after being shot and crippled by an irate farmer whose fields he'd strayed into outside the Park in the Crocodile River area;

- Ndlulamithi ("Taller than Trees"), had a left tusk weighing 64,6kg and a right one of 57,2kg, and occupied the area around Shingwedzi. He died of old age in 1985;

Mafunyane

- Dzombo (named after the Dzombo River near Shingwedzi where he roamed), had a left tusk weighing 55,5kg and a right tusk of 56,8kg. He was shot by poachers in 1983, but his tusks were recovered;

- Shawu (named after the Shawu River near Shingwedzi, which was his territory) had the longest tusks so far recorded in the Park (the left being 3,17m and the right being 3,06m), although they were not the heaviest (52,6kg and 50,8kg respectively). He died in 1982, possibly of complications from an old gunshot wound inflicted by poachers;

- Shingwedzi (named after the camp where he was often seen) had a left tusk weighing 58kg and a right tusk of 47,2kg. He died of natural causes in 1981, and was found in the Shingwedzi River bed on his front knees with his tusks embedded in the sand.

SANParks

Waterbuck

Nigel Dennis

The tree of mixed blessing

The tamboti (*Spirostachys africana*) is a tree of mixed blessing. On the one hand, it is poisonous to humans – eating meat cooked over a tamboti fire will result in severe stomach cramps (in some cases even death) – and the latex can cause skin blisters and diarrhoea. Sawdust from the tamboti (which makes excellent furniture) can cause blindness. However, porcupines love tamboti bark, the leaves are eagerly eaten by most of the browsers, and the fruit is a eagerly eaten by francolins, guineafowl and doves.

Briza

Kruger. It is surrounded by three different habitats – the rocky Lebombo range to the east, the surrounding mopaneveld and the riverine bush on the river banks. The confluence of the Makhadzi watercourse and the Letaba River is the site of the original ranger's picket in the area established by Leonard Henry Ledeboer in 1920. Ledeboer served as Letaba ranger between 1920 and 1929. At that stage, the area was called Hatlani, after a chief who had lived there. Ledeboer eventually moved his house to the northern banks of the Letaba, opposite the site of the present-day rest camp. He called his outpost Mondzweni, which, in Shangaan, means "at the leadwood tree".

Waterbuck are a common sight along the Letaba River, particularly where there are pockets of marshland. True to their name, these large, stoutly built antelope with distinctive white circles on their rumps, are never far from water. Natural history artist Charles Asterley Maberley observed that waterbuck may submerge themselves in water when fleeing predators, with only their nostrils protruding above the water. Lion are particularly fond of waterbuck, which have a strong scent, similar to the smell of turpentine. Other animals usually seen along the S62 include elephant, buffalo, impala and steenbok. Unlike most other antelope, the steenbok female is generally larger than the male.

There are two exceptionally good summer birding spots on the northern side of the dam – the Matambeni bird hide and the dam wall look-out spot. Among the Engelhard birds are all the herons, a variety of plovers, stilts, bee-eaters and storks and rarer species like the black heron and collared pratincole. Hippos and crocs are Engelhard residents, and there are usually elephant, waterbuck, impala and buffalo in and around the riverine bush surrounding the dam.

Engelhard viewpoint is halfway up Longwe Mountain (480m), the highest point in the Lebombo north of the Letaba River. Longwe takes its name from the Shangaan for a bag for carrying fruit, probably because of its bulky appearance. In the past Shangaan speakers referred to the entire Lebombo mountain range as the Longwe. The viewsite isn't positioned high enough up the ridge to be really rewarding.

LETABA RIVER LOOP (S47)

The Letaba River Loop north-west of Letaba Camp follows the river for 19km to Mingerhout Dam before cutting back southwards through the mopaneveld. In the spartan north, the best way to view game is to follow the rivers. Most herbivores don't stray much more than six kilometres from water, so the chances of interesting sightings are far greater along the Letaba than in the broad swathe of mopaneveld to the north. The S47 winds between the edge of the mopaneveld and the well-established

Martial eagles are among the heaviest flying birds in the world, weighing up to six kilograms and with a wingspan of two metres. They are found throughout Kruger and are particularly partial to leguaans as well as young antelope, mongooses and smaller birds.

Albert Froneman

Martial eagle

gallery forests of sycamore figs, tambotis and sausage trees that line the wide, sandy Letaba river bed. There are usually impala along the road and the browsers most often seen are elephant and kudu. There are usually waterbuck in the river bed.

Mingerhout Dam is a long, wide finger of water on the Letaba alongside an attractive, low range of well-wooded sandstone koppies. The dam wall is more than half-a-kilometre wide and the dam stretches several kilometres upstream. Hatlani (291m) is the highest of the koppies that mark the watershed between the Letaba and Tsendze rivers. Note how the bush around the koppies is a diverse, lush tangle of species

Matumi – the woodworker's friend

Mingerhout is the Afrikaans word for the matumi tree (*Breonadia salicina*) which is common along watercourses where they cut through rock. It has distinctive thin and pointy, shiny leaves and grows along rivers where the terrain is rocky. Outside the Park, many of the lowveld's tallest matumi trees were cut down after World War II to be turned into railway sleepers for the country's expanding rail network. Fortunately, the matumi is now a protected tree, following the wanton pillaging of lowveld matumis during the mid-20th century. Its problem is that it is a very durable wood that can be worked well – in central Africa it is the favoured tree for making dugout canoes, while, back home, it has a reputation for making good, solid building beams and parquet flooring. Local healers say a concoction made out of the bark is an effective treatment for stomach disorders.

Briza

typical of sandveld vegetation. Compare it to the somewhat mono-dimensional mopaneveld a few hundred metres away.

Mingerhout is a recommended winter game-viewing spot because it is a permanent water hole in a region where water is scarce in the dry season. There are usually crocs and hippos above the dam wall. Herds of animals usually come to the water from mid-morning until mid-afternoon when predators are at their least active.

The S47 south of Mingerhout is a dull drive. The tree mopane soon gives way to scrub mopane. There is rarely much animal activity along this road, nor on the S131, which is an alternative route back to Phalaborwa Gate.

The Letaba area is known for good owl sightings. Verreaux's eagle-owl and the pearl-spotted owlet are often seen on the roads in the area. Owls are regarded with suspicion in many traditional African cultures, as they are seen as the purveyors of evil. Nonetheless they are prized as ingredients for *muthi* because of their perceived wisdom, hunting skills and remarkable eyesight.

Letaba to Olifants

There are two main choices travelling between Letaba and Olifants. These are the main Letaba-Olifants tar road (H1-5) and the slightly longer Letaba River dust road (S46, S44). (See page 227)

LETABA-OLIFANTS MAIN ROAD (H1-5)

The drive between Letaba and Olifants camps along the main tar road (H1-5) takes one through relatively flat mopane shrubveld. Shortly before Olifants is Shamiriri, one of a number of northern-facing sandstone hills that form the watershed between the Olifants and Letaba rivers. From Shamiriri Hill (297m), one soon hits the Olifants River and one of the most beautiful stretches of the Park as the mopane gives way to Olifants rugged veld, and one is confronted by the lush, riverine forest of the Olifants River. There are often leopard sightings along this stretch of the road as these big cats hunt along the bush in the vicinity of the river and the koppies.

Just after the H8 turn-off is a particularly good stopping point overlooking the Olifants River on the west of the main road.

There is a magnificent sycamore fig with lots of bird activity, a number of jackal-berries and matumis closer to the water's edge. Buffalo and elephant are the most common big animals seen along here, while smaller herds of impala move along the fringes of the riverine bush.

LETABA-OLIFANTS RIVER ROAD

The Letaba River Road (S46 – S44 – S93) skirts the south bank of Engelhard Dam and tracks the Letaba River almost to its confluence with the Olifants. The views of the Engelhard from the south on the S46 were adversely affected by the 2000 floods that deposited large sandbanks along the river edge. These are now thick reedbeds which obscure the water from the road. Game viewing along this road is itinerant – often there may be no sign of animal life; at other times sightings are plentiful. The proximity of the river means there is usually some form of animal activity around, although the veld is scraggly and stony with sparse grazing that does not allow much carrying capacity. There are lots of patches of bare earth, unlike the mopaneveld where the grazing is more even.

The Letaba River road dips, and winds and climbs through the thickets, allowing occasional views of the river and the giraffe and hippo on the other side. Lion kills are often reported on the dust roads between Letaba and Olifants, their prey being mostly buffalo. It is best to do this road very slowly, not just to look for animals in the thickets but also to go easy on the suspension. A recommended stopping point is the Olifants get-out point which offers wonderful views onto the river below and the Lebombo range to the east. The Olifants River is one of the main breeding grounds of the rare saddle-billed and black storks which may sometimes be seen from the S44.

Giraffes have an extra strong and large heart, which is actually two to three times stronger than a human's heart, for pumping blood to the brain.

Nigel Dennis

Giraffe and impala

In the Olifants area look out for

Animals
Elephant

Lion

Hippo

Crocodile

Baboon

Birds
Martial eagle

Green-backed heron

Trumpeter hornbill

Black stork

Red-winged starling

Around Olifants

The landscape south of Olifants is unique to this part of Kruger – Olifants rugged veld is a rocky, wooded habitat that is a combination of knob-thorn, bushwillow woodland and Lebombo vegetation. The mid and lower slopes are clay soils on basalt, while the outcrops are the pinkish rhyolite that is the geological foundation of the Lebombo.

The sweet grazing is restricted mostly to the lower contours. An indication of the most palatable veld is the trees – leadwoods, sycamores and fever trees. Candelabra euphorbias and white kirkia trees dominate the higher contours where there is little grass. On the mid-slopes are the knob-thorns and bushwillows, interspersed with

River that divides the north from the south

The Olifants (Afrikaans for "elephant") River is a major dividing line between the north and the south of Kruger. To the north is mopaneveld, to the south the bushwillow and acacia species dominate. The earliest recorded use of the name is from 1869 when pioneer map-maker Vincent Whitshed Erskine referred to it as the "Oliphants". Previously the Olifants had a wide variety of names, including the *Lepelle* (Sotho) and *Rimbelule* (Shangaan).

Olifants River

Brett Hilton-Barber

purple-pod cluster-leaves and tree wistaria. Olifants rugged veld stretches from the main road to Olifants Camp (H8) and south-west to the Timbavati Picnic Site.

Around the Olifants rugged veld are a number of other ecosystems – the stunted knob-thorn savanna to the south, the Lebombo to the east and north, mopaneveld to the north-west and mixed bushwillow woodlands to the west.

As the name suggests, this terrain is favoured by elephants, which are attracted by the wide variety of trees.

There are usually more browsers than grazers in the Olifants rugged veld, and herd numbers are considerably lower than they are in the more open grasslands. Baboons and vervet monkeys are well adapted to this environment and hang out regularly around Olifants and Balule Camps. Listen out at night for the thick-tailed bushbaby which has a piercing, haunting cry.

Interesting drives around Olifants are to the N'wamanzi Lookout Point over the

There are eight species of mongoose found in Kruger, the most common being the dwarf, banded and slender mongooses. Kruger scientists estimating that for every 100 square kilometres there are 668 mongooses. They use termite mounds for shelter and feed mostly on insects. The rarest mongoose in Kruger is Selous's mongoose, which is found only in the Shingwedzi area in the north.

Michael Poliza
Elephant and calf

🏠 OLIFANTS CAMP

Olifants Camp is wonderfully situated on a high ridge overlooking the Olifants River about 10km upstream from its confluence with the Letaba. There are invariably elephants, hippos and crocs on the sandy river banks. The camp, which has dramatic views out over the mixed woodlands and the Lebombo Mountains, is well-positioned as a game-viewing camp because it sits between two river systems – the Letaba and Olifants – and three ecozones – the Olifants rugged veld to the south, which consists of knob-thorn and bushwillow in open grasslands, mopane shrubveld to the north and the rocky Lebombo foothills to the east. The varied habitat lends itself to a diversity of animals.

Olifants has a good reputation as a birder's camp – the density and diversity of the woodlands and the availability of water attract a lot of birds, while there are often great raptor sightings from the lookout deck as birds of prey – such as the martial eagle – use the thermal updrafts of the steep hill to get their "lift" into the skies.

The Olifants area is also famed for its trees. Lowveld cluster-leaf, raisin bush and mopane are common in the woodlands which, in spring, become very colourful with the emergence of the bright yellow flowers of the long-tail cassia which contrast with the weeping boer-bean's striking red flowers. There are a variety of rare aloes at Olifants, and the only accessible sesame bush in the whole of the Kruger Park grows just next to the petrol station.

Lanz von Horsten/Images of Africa

It is a large camp with more than 100 rondavels and a few guest cottages, but it does not have the variety of accommodation offered by Letaba. Where Olifants is exceptional is the range of activities it caters for, from mountain-biking and stargazing to the more traditional escapes of guided bush walks and drives. A backpacker's trail was introduced at Olifants in 2005 (see page 298 for details). There is no camping or caravanning at Olifants – the nearest camp that offers these facilities is Balule.

Olifants Camp has pioneered guided mountain bike trails in Kruger. The camp supplies two armed guides, the bikes, backpacks, snacks and water and can take a maximum of six participants. The options are full day, morning or afternoon rides.

Olifants has a day visitors' picnic site with a swimming pool.

Olifants Camp

OLIFANTS

Hippo

Olifants (off the H1-4); the Letaba River Road (S44), which has an excellent view spot over the Olifants as it enters the Lebombo; the Balule Bridge Loop (S92 and S91); Ngotso Pan on the H1-4); while one of the most beautiful landscapes in Kruger is the drive between the Olifants Camp turn-off and Shamiriri Hill on the H1-5 north.

Ngotso Pan is one of the best places in Kruger to get close-up photographs of hippo. The car park comes right to the edge of the water hole where hippo often cavort. Hippo once occupied every river in Africa but are now confined generally to game reserves.

The water hole at Bangu on the Old Main Road to Satara (S90) is worth visiting as giraffe, zebra, impala and buffalo often congregate here. From this point northwards, giraffe become less common as the acacia-veld gives way to

mopane. Acacia is the preferred diet of the giraffe and they are absent from most of the mopaneveld, with herds in the north concentrated mostly in the sandveld around Punda and Pafuri.

The S90 follows the Bangu drainage system through sweeping knob-thorn savanna grasslands. There are usually few other vehicles on this road so one has a real sense of isolation in the wilderness with views well into the distance. Game viewing in the north is always unpredictable, but there are often large herds of animals on the S90.

 Many antelope like impala, kudu and nyala have scent glands above their hooves known as metatarsal glands. When they sense danger, this triggers the release of a warning scent and alerts other animals in the herd.

231

The return of the elephants

Ivory hunters had shot elephants to the point of extinction in the Kruger area by the late 19th century. Indeed, when Stevenson-Hamilton surveyed what was then the Shingwedzi area in the early 20th century he thought that there were no elephants left at all. Unbeknown to him, a small herd survived in a secret, inaccessible gorge on the Olifants River where it cuts through the Lebombo Mountains. This was the ancestral population of the elephants one sees in Kruger today. Their numbers were boosted by a migration of elephants from Zimbabwe and Mozambique, who sensed the safety of the area once hunting had been outlawed. Today, there are about 13 000 elephants in Kruger, the biggest concentrations being found in the Olifants area with large herds also along the Letaba, Tsendze, Shingwedzi, Mphongolo and Shisha rivers. Smaller herds of elephant are to be found in the areas where they have been reintroduced – in the Timbavati, Sabie, Biyamiti and Crocodile River areas. During winter many elephants congregate in the Makuleke area in the far north.

Heinrich van den Berg

Elephant eye

BALULE CAMP

Balule Camp is a small satellite camp of Olifants Camp, 11km away on the banks of the Olifants River. It prides itself on offering an authentically rustic bushveld experience and is the ideal spot for die-hard campers. Balule Bush Camp has only six rondavels and 15 camping sites. There is no electricity and the evening light comes from paraffin lanterns. A curious feature is that none of the rondavels has any windows – only air vents. There is no petrol station, shop or restaurant. There is a communal kitchen with limited fridge space. The adjoining camp site is in a large grove of Natal mahogany, baobab and sausage trees. Guests need to check in at Olifants. Guided bush walks are available from Balule.

Letaba to Mopani

There is a single main road (H1-6) linking Letaba and Mopani camps, but there are a number of detours off this road including the Tsendze Loop (S48) and the Nshawu Loop (S50), which offers the option of bypassing Mopani en route to Shingwedzi. (See page 247)

THE MAIN MOPANI ROAD (H1-6)

There is usually excellent game viewing on the H1-6 between Letaba Camp and the Letaba River Bridge as the road closely follows the broad, sandy Letaba River bed. There are several loop roads off the H1-6 with expansive views over the river. Often there are baboons along this stretch of the

Tsessebe, impala and zebra

Albert Froneman

road, browsing in the trees, scrounging around on the ground or grooming themselves. Elephant and buffalo are usually seen drinking at the river during the middle of the day while at least one pride of lions is active in the area.

Stop on the Letaba River Bridge for a leg-stretch and to study the river banks and look at the water birds. One is allowed out of one's vehicle on the demarcated zone on the bridge, which was completely engulfed during the 2000 floods. The high-water mark of the floods has been signposted on both sides of the river and it is a wonder to imagine the volume of water that must have come downstream that fateful February.

The strong smell at the bridge is from a colony of free-tail bats that nest in the girders. They are usually seen only at twilight and are often hunted by rarer raptors such as the bat hawk and Eurasian hobby.

From Letaba Bridge to Twisappel Water Hole, the H1-6 goes through alternating tree and shrub mopane with large pockets of grassland. Twisappel Water Hole has a large surrounding vlei. This is the ideal habitat for waterbuck. Twisappel usually retains water in winter and is one of the main sources of dry season water for elephant, buffalo and other game in the southern mopaneveld.

North of Twisappel, animal sightings become less common as the carrying capacity

White rhinos are, of course, not white at all but are so called because of the misinterpretation of the Dutch word for "wide" which was used to describe the lip of the grazing variety of rhino.

Michael Poliza

White rhino

of the mopaneveld cannot support large herds of animals. That is not to say one won't see anything interesting. Keep a sharp look out on the H1-6 in the vicinity of the turn-off to Giriyondo Border Post (H15) for small groups of tsessebe. This is probably the best place in Kruger to see these rather awkward-looking, hump-shouldered antelope. Despite their ungainly posture, they are faster than any other antelope, and are capable of reaching speeds of over 100km/h over short distances. They are shy animals sometimes found in association with the zebra and wildebeest that are regularly seen along this road.

Another rare animal to look out for in this area is the roan antelope. It appears to be restricted to the eastern mopaneveld, whereas its 'cousin', the sable, is found more in the west. There are often scattered herds of roan north of the Letaba River, where they seek out the taller grasses in lightly wooded savanna. The law of unintended consequences has

Genet

Nigel Dennis

manifested itself in Kruger over the provision of water holes. Kruger managers now believe that the expansion of water holes in Kruger has been detrimental to roan antelopes in that it has favoured elephant, zebra and wildebeest which have displaced roan from their traditional territory.

The H1-6 continues along the flat, basalt plains dominated by shrub mopane. After soaking summer rains, a number of pans form in the area – the most prominent being the regular elephant drinking holes, Middelvlei and Nshawu. Be warned that one may see nothing for long stretches of this road, so a better alternative is to take the dusty Tsendze Loop Road (S48).

Tsendze Loop (S48)

The Tsendze Loop Road is a 17-kilometre detour off the H1-6 that provides some habitat variation by dipping out of the mopaneveld into the riverine bush along the Tsendze watercourse. The river twists and turns, which may account for its name. According to ethnographer HP Junod, it is based on the Shangaan *tsendzeleka,* which means "to ramble round like someone lost in the bush". There are usually plenty of elephant and buffalo close to the river. This road may be closed after heavy rains.

White rhino are usually associated with southern Kruger. However, a small population of these great grey grazers has also been established in the north, after a core group of 12 was released here during the 1960s. The highest concentration of white rhino in the mopaneveld is to be found in the flatlands between the Tsendze and Shingwedzi rivers.

South of Mopani, one can see the escarpment to the west (and the landmark hill of Masorini near Phalaborwa Gate), the Lebombo to the east and the Olifants Gorge in the Lebombo Mountains to the south-east.

War and whisky

Steinacker's Horse manned a number of pickets between Komatipoort and Makhadzi, which was then the northernmost camp. The regiment was established by the British to prevent the Boers from making contact with sympathisers in what was then Portuguese East Africa. However, the troops saw little combat and, in their only serious encounter with the Boers in 1901 at Fort Mpisane near Bushbuck Ridge, they were roundly beaten. For the most part, they occupied themselves by hunting, fishing and drinking, for which they were each paid 10 shillings a day. Records show that, of the 114 casualties suffered by the regiment, 35 were fatal and, of these, only 11 could be attributed directly to the war. Most deaths were caused by malaria, although the history books show that Trooper Smart was killed by a lion at Sabi Bridge, Trooper Chambers broke his neck when he fell off his horse south of Komatipoort and Trooper Gaines was caught by a crocodile in the Usuthu River in Swaziland.

Several members of Steinacker's Horse were recruited by Stevenson-Hamilton after the war. Among them was Harry Wolhuter, who wrote that the regiment supplemented its ration of tinned bully beef with venison and game birds, which the soldiers took delight in hunting. Other staples were tinned peaches, pickles and whisky. Excavations at the camp show that a "large and varied amount of alcoholic and liquid refreshment was consumed by the garrison", including rum, beer, schnapps, gin, wine, mineral water, soda and Rose's lime juice.

The Confluence is a scenic viewpoint along the Tsendze, while Mooiplaas Picnic Spot is a welcome refreshment stop well shaded by apple-leaf trees. Cold drinks and firewood are for sale and gas braais may be hired at the site, which has toilet facilities.

Letaba Camp to Mozambique

The route between Letaba Camp and the Mozambique border post of Giriyondo includes the main Mopani Camp road (H1-6) and the Giriyondo Road (H15).

Giraffe

Giriyondo Road (H15)

Allow about an hour-and-a-half to get from
Letaba to the Giriyondo Border Post, the
southernmost access point from South
Africa into the Limpopo National Park. The
Giriyondo Road (H15) follows the mopane
scrubveld over the Makhadzi watercourse and
through the flatlands to a gap in the Lebombo
that marks the border with Mozambique.

This road was first developed in 1903
by what was then the Witwatersrand
Native Labour Association to facilitate
the recruitment of Shangaans from
central Mozambique for the gold mines
of Johannesburg. In those days, labour
recruitment was a profitable business that
the authorities tried to regulate, with varying
degrees of success. The WNLA had a series

of rough-and-ready overnight camps every
25km between Massingir in Mozambique and
Gravelotte, which is just outside the Park
north of Phalaborwa Gate. From there, the
recruits were sent by rail to the Johannesburg
goldfields where they worked underground
mining the metal that has made Gauteng
Africa's richest commercial hub. There is
a tradition among returning Mozambican
mineworkers to this day that when they hear
the "bird of the lowveld" – the three-streaked
tchagra – they know they are halfway home.

Even if one is not going to Mozambique,
it is worth doing the 9-km trip along the
H15 to Makhadzi Picnic Site where a small
interpretation centre was built in 2003.
Makhadzi has extensive kitchen, cleaning
and ablution facilities, which makes it a

Nigel Dennis

good stop-off for anyone returning from Massingir Dam. Firewood, charcoal and cold drinks are on sale as well as some rather desperate-looking ornaments made out of tin cans and mopane leaves.

The picnic site is just beyond the Makhadzi River crossing where elephants often gather. Not far from the road along the stream is the site of a northern outpost used by Steinacker's Horse during the Anglo-Boer War. The remains of the camp were discovered during a field survey by rangers in 1996. Archaeologists began excavating the site in 1997 and many of the artifacts they recovered are housed in the Makhadzi interpretation centre, which also details the development of the Transfrontier Park and the ethnography of the area.

There are a lot of road humps between Makhadzi and the Giriyondo Border Post. What little game there is along this road is skittish, probably because of poaching in the past. The road passes through a gap in the Lebombo at Mbhandweni Water Hole, a creek in the Makhadzi River guarded by a fine old fig tree.

GIRIYONDO BORDER POST

Giriyondo Border Post is open in summer (1 October to 31 March) from 8am to 4pm and in winter (1 April to 30 September) from 8am to 3pm. Currently, only 4x4s are allowed across the border, and no vehicles that weigh over four tons. No commercial traffic is allowed through Giriyondo. Border telephone number: (013) 753 5757.

Kruger's giant

The elephant's trunk is more versatile than the limbs of any other animal – in the words of writer Richard Estes, it is an "all-in-one grasping, smelling, drinking, squirting, broadcasting tool" that is also used as a club if it attacks humans. Elephant trunks can be up to two metres in length, weigh as much as a rugby player and can hold up to 17 litres of water. Elephants can outpace humans – they are capable of charging at 40km/h for short distances. It is advisable not to go closer than 50m to an elephant in Kruger, and always be careful not to get between a mother and its offspring.

Elephant

Buffalo

Brett Hilton-Barber

Northern Kruger

 Habitat pointers

- Mopane woodlands to the west of the Mopani-Shingwedzi main road
- Mopane shrubveld to the east of the Mopani-Shingwedzi main road
- Impressive riverine forests along the watercourses of the Shingwedzi flood plains
- Lebombo foothills around Shilowa
- Transition from subtropical to tropical vegetation begins north of the Tropic of Capricorn

The northern expanse of mopaneveld north of Letaba to the Shingwedzi alluvial flood plains has fewer animals than most other parts of the Park. The carrying capacity of the veld is much lower than that of southern Kruger. The main road between Mopani and Shingwedzi divides the mopane woodlands to the west from the mopane shrubveld to the east. Elephant are the dominant browsers in the mopaneveld. The best game viewing in the north is around Shingwedzi, particularly Kanniedood Dam and the Mphongolo Loop. There are often large herds of buffalo around Mopani and lion sightings are not uncommon. Look out for rarer Kruger antelope such as the tsessebe and roan. They are often found between Letaba and Mopani camps, particularly near the Girioyondo border post turn-off on the H1-6. The north is a rewarding birding destination – there are sleep-over hides near Phalaborwa Gate and Mopani Camp, and important vleis east of Mopani, while the Shingwedzi flood plains are one of the country's top summer birding destinations. Shingwedzi is renowned for its big tuskers – most of the legendary Magnificent Seven inhabited the Shingwedzi flood plains. The northern Lebombo can be accessed via the Tropic of Capricorn Loop (S143).

BEST DRIVE IN THE NORTH

Shingwedzi flood plain drive (Nyawutsi bird hide to Babalala Picnic Site via the Mphongolo Loop):

This drive takes one from the edge of the Lebombo into the Shingwedzi flood plain system. There is wonderful riverine forest and birding at Kanniedood Dam and along the Mphongolo Loop. Stop off for refreshments at Shingwedzi Camp. Allow four-and-a-half hours including a stop.

 ## CAMPS IN THE NORTH

Mopani
013 735 6536 See page 242

Tsendze Camp Site
013 735 6536 See page 243

Shingwedzi
013 735 6806 See page 252

Bateleur
013 735 6843 See page 256

Sirheni
013 735 6860 See page 256

 ### MOPANI CAMP EXPLORER OPTIONS

- Nshawu/Tropic of Capricorn Loop (S50, S143, S144, H1-6) 44km; grassland drive on dust roads, best done early in the morning; often good birding along Nshawu watercourse but animal sightings are itinerant; allow 2,5 hours to and from Mopani Camp

- Mooiplaas (H1-6) 26km from Mopani Camp to Confluence and back; riverine bush and mopaneveld; stop at Mooiplaas for a braai (allow 3 hours, including a stop)

* Stapelkop Dam (S146) 38km dust road to and from Mopani Camp; wild drive through mixed mopane woodland; not many animals but a wonderful sense of isolation (allow 3 hours with 30 minutes at the dam)

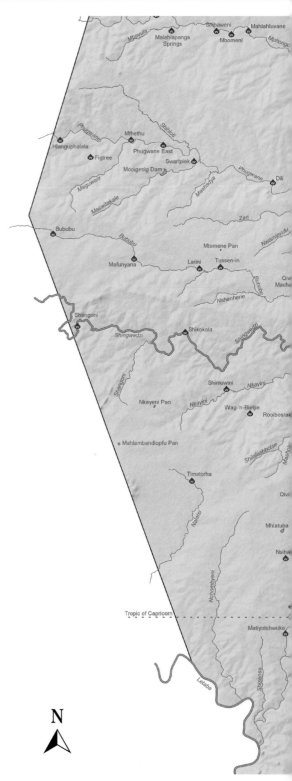

N

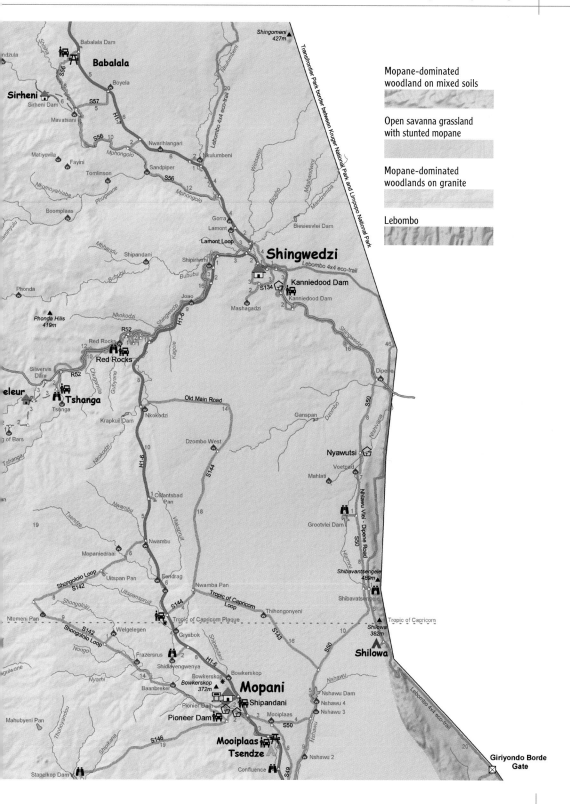

Mopane-dominated
woodland on mixed soils

Open savanna grassland
with stunted mopane

Mopane-dominated
woodlands on granite

Lebombo

MOPANI CAMP

Mopani lies south-west of Bowker's Kop, which has an impressive number of baobabs growing on its slopes. The rather stark face-brick aesthetic is quite a contrast to the quaintness of the thatched rondavel style of most of the other camps. Its biggest drawback is that it is not in a very game-rich part of the Park. Situated in the heart of the mopaneveld on the transition zone between granite and basalt, Mopani offers commanding views over Pioneer Dam, where skeletal trees protrude from the water. A sundowner on the wooden deck overlooking the dam is a highly recommended experience. There are several baobabs in and around the camp and the Mopani swimming pool has probably saved many an overcooked soul after a hot summer day's game driving.

Mopani has become an oasis in the dry mopaneveld since Pioneer Dam was built in the 1980s. The vegetation and birdlife have been radically altered by the introduction of a permanent water source in the north. One of the consequences has been the introduction of new species, including the collared (redwing) pratincole, which is now a regular at Mopani and Letaba, not having been recorded in Kruger before 1980.

During the construction of Mopani Camp, a lion attack nearly led to the death of ranger Kobus Botha. Botha and other rangers had been called by contract workers who had found a lioness in a building trench. The lioness retreated to a patch of long grass and hid, despite the rangers' efforts to flush her out. Then, without warning, it leapt out of cover and pulled Botha to the ground. Ranger William Ndobe remembers Botha screaming: "Shoot, shoot, shoot!" in a variety of African languages as he tried to fight the lioness off with his hands. Ndobe waited until he had a clear bead on the animal and pulled the trigger, killing the lioness with one shot through the head. Botha was pulled out from beneath the dead animal and airlifted to hospital, where he recovered from his wounds. Ndobe was decorated for his bravery.

Mopani has all the facilities of the large SANParks camps, including a restaurant, shop, and petrol station. The camp offers game drives and guided walks, which should be booked at reception when checking in.

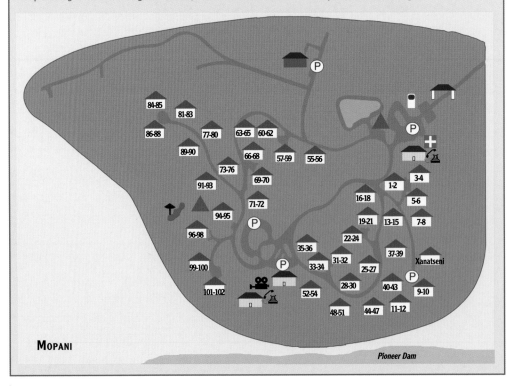

MOPANI

Pioneer Dam

In the Mopani area, look out for

Animals

Elephant

Waterbuck

Tsessebe

Hippo

Roan antelope

Birds

Reed cormorant

Southern carmine bee-eater

Grey hornbill

Broad-billed roller

Steppe eagle

Elephant

Albert Froneman

Around Mopani

The roads around Mopani Camp are not known for great sightings as the grazing in this part of Kruger is not very palatable. The dominant animals are elephant – which feed on the mopane – and buffalo, which literally have the constitution of an ox and can digest the coarse grasses. Choice sightings in the area are the rare roan and tsessebe antelope, which occur in small herds, sticking to the thicker mopane woodlands.

Mooiplaas Picnic Spot, 5km south of Mopani Camp, is a shady refreshment stop where cold drinks and firewood can be purchased and gas braais are available for hire. There are clean toilet facilities.

The most interesting sightings are most likely to be on the H1-6 south of Mooiplaas, where the road tracks the Tsendze River. There are a series of loop roads off the main road, the best being the drive to the Confluence, a viewpoint over a woodland gully and streambed. Lion are often active in the area late in the day, preparing for their night-time hunt in the riverine bush. Buffalo and waterbuck are their most favoured prey in this part of Kruger.

The Nshawu Road (S50) and Tropic of Capricorn Loop (S143) are also good options. The grazing in these areas is sweeter than the mixed woodland to the west of the camp and,

TSENDZE CAMPSITE

Tsendze Rustic Campsite is a rough-and-ready camping spot seven kilometres south of Mopani. The camp, shaded by old leadwoods, tree mopanes and apple-leafs, is designed for those who seek the more rustic side of the Kruger experience, those who want to "touch the earth lightly" according to SANParks officials. The facility has 34 camp-sites, two ablution blocks – with great "open-to-the-skies" showers – and two camp kitchens. Camp energy is either gas or solar powered and generators are banned, which means that noise levels are kept to an absolute minimum. Guests check in at Mopani Camp.

> ![paw print icon] Elephants produce a calf every four years or so after a 22-month pregnancy. They give birth, standing up, to calves that weigh on average 120kg! Elephant calf mortality is highest at birth.

consequently, the chances of seeing game are far better. A recommended day trip from Mopani Camp is to take the Nshawu road north-east to the Lebombo (S50), crossing the Tropic of Capricorn near Shilowa Mountain (382m) and stopping at the lookout point at Shibavantsengele, a few kilometres further on. It is not very high, but gives one a good view across the basaltic mopaneveld plains, which stand in stark geological contrast to the pink, stony rhyolite forming the Lebombo. The nearby crossing through the Lebombo into Mozambique was an ancient elephant highway and a route used by ivory hunters in the 19th and early 20th centuries.

A cave once used to store ivory has been discovered in the vicinity.

Just north of Mopani is Bowker's Kop, which has some magnificent baobabs on its slope. On one of these baobabs is carved the name of 19th-century hunter Miles Robert Bowker, whose party camped nearby in 1888. Among his fellow hunters were Fred and Harry Barber – distant relatives of co-author Brett Hilton-Barber. This intrepid group of adventurers used to undertake lengthy elephant hunting safaris from their Eastern Cape base right through northern Kruger into Mozambique and possibly as far as the Congo. The town of Barberton is named after the Barber brothers who discovered a gold reef near the site of the town in 1884, precipitating the first major gold rush in South Africa.

There is a water hole on the side of the road opposite Bowker's Kop where

Bowkers Kop

Brett Hilton-Barber

Waterbuck

Nigel Dennis

the Bowker and Barber hunters probably camped. There are sometimes sable antelope reported in the vicinity.

Just south of Mopani, at Shipandani, there is an overnight camping facility. Sited at the foot of a small hill, Shipandani was the original site of the area ranger's house. The house was washed away in the 2000 floods and has since been replaced by a bird hide, which can be hired for overnight camping through Mopani Camp (see page 240). The hide overlooks a narrow pool on the Tsendze River.

Stapelkop Dam is a 40-km round trip that is more interesting for birders than for those in search of animals. The S146 is a dirt road through the mixed mopane woodland, which does not support large numbers of game. The dam is an open expanse of water near a cluster of small granite hills. Just below the dam is the grave site of a 19th-century pioneer hunter, known only as Joubert. Joubert was an elephant hunter who supplied

Albasini's trading network with ivory. The circumstances of his death are not known.

Shongololo Loop (S142) heads north-west past Frazersrus Water Hole into the heart of the north-western mopaneveld. The road dips over a number of dry watercourses but there is usually little action in this generally featureless landscape, except perhaps at Ntomeni Pan which is almost on the Tropic of Capricorn. The S142 follows the Shongololo watercourse which, in turn, feeds into the Tsendze. Besides elephant sightings, this is not usually a good road for game viewing, and is recommended more for its wildness and sense of isolation.

Mopani to Shingwedzi

There are a variety of routes from Mopani to Shingwedzi, the main ones being the H1-6 tar road and the Tropic of Capricorn Loop (S143) which joins up with the Nshawu Dipane Road via Shilowa (S50). (See page 247)

Warthog

Nigel Dennis

MOPANI TO SHINGWEDZI (H1-6)

The H1-6 tarred road to Shingwedzi divides the western mixed woodlands from the open savanna grasslands of the east. The mopane trees vary in size according to the richness of the soil. There are lots of apple-leaf trees and leadwoods marking the watercourses. Small antelope are often seen around Bowker's Kop Water Hole which takes its name from the nearby hill with its baobabs and mountain syringas. (See page 244)

The mopane trees vary in size according to the richness of the soil, and the road passes a series of pans. One of the better ones is Shidayangwenya, 8km from Mopani

 The Tropic of Capricorn, a parallel line of latitude at 26 degrees and 30 minutes, is the southernmost point that the sun passes directly overhead at noon, which it does on the summer solstice, December 21 – the longest day in southern Africa. Although one is in the tropics north of this point, the first real tropical vegetation becomes apparent only in the Luvuvhu River area.

Camp. It is a long stretch of water among tall mopane trees, frequented by elephants.

The Shingwedzi Road crosses the Tropic of Capricorn just north of Grysbok Pan. One of Kruger's rarities to look out for here is Sharpe's grysbok after which the water hole was named. Sharpe's is one of Kruger's smallest antelopes and is extremely shy. It feeds mostly by night but does emerge during daylight when the weather is overcast. In Kruger it is found only in the extreme north of the Park.

The road to Shingwedzi passes through intermediate mopane with stretches of grassland. The main water hole along this road is Olifantsbad ("elephant's bath") Pan which, like most of the pans along this road, becomes really interesting only after good rains. Early summer thunderstorms result in millions of termites emerging from the ground in parts of the north, attracting a feeding frenzy of eagles, hawks, buzzards and falcons which gorge themselves on these high-protein delicacies.

North of Olifantsbad Pan, a small intrusion of gabbro thornveld marks the mini-escarpment between the Dzombo River catchment area and the Shingwedzi flood plains. The mopaneveld becomes visibly stunted as one moves into the eastern basalt plains. The grassland, in turn, gives way to mixed woodland as the road dips gently next to the Nkokodzi Stream into the alluvial flood plains of the Shingwedzi River system. The flood plains are marked by a stark change in the geological variety of the rocks, which have been deposited steadily in the watercourses over millions of years of flooding.

The H1-6 closely follows the Shingwedzi River for 15km before Shingwedzi Camp, and there is usually animal activity among the large leadwoods, figs and apple-leaf trees that line the river. There are inevitably elephants along this section of the road.

MOPANI TO SHINGWEDZI VIA SHILOWA (S50)

The S50 leaves the Nshawu watercourse (see Nshawu on page 241) and crosses the basalt flatlands of scrub mopane. This can be a rather featureless drive until one crosses the Tropic of Capricorn close to Shilowa Hill (382m). Between Shilowa Hill and the larger Shibavantsengele Koppie (489m), there is a pass that cuts through the Lebombo. This pass is believed to be an ancient elephant highway, used by generations of elephants migrating from Mozambique to their winter feeding grounds in northern Kruger. This migration route was disrupted when the Kruger eastern border was fenced in the 1960s and elephant populations in Mozambique were severely depleted by the civil war. However, the return of peace and the dropping of the fence as part of the Greater Limpopo Transfrontier Park initiative may see elephants reclaim their old road.

The elephant pass has also been used by humans for hundreds of years. The remains

Fraser of the Lowveld

One of the more eccentric characters in Kruger's history was Major AA Fraser, who was in charge of the Shingwedzi Game Reserve before World War I. Fraser, a tall, imposing veteran of the British army in India, had a knowledge of the bush that was matched only by his contempt for bureaucracy. Lowveld author Wilf Nussey described Fraser as a "powerful man with a great red beard, total impatience with administration and paperwork, superb marksmanship with rifle or shotgun, and a seemingly bottomless capacity for whisky". According to writer TV Bulpin, Fraser was a "real bushwhacker. He hated women but loved good guns and strong dogs".

Nussey records Fraser's somewhat unusual daily routine: "His practice was to get up very early, fish or hunt warthogs and go to bed after a late breakfast. He would rise again at about 6pm and spend most of the night working on his guns, mending clothing and reading the English country life magazine Field before getting a little more pre-dawn sleep." Fraser was always accompanied by a pack of dogs which, from time to time, acted as his bedding. During those rare occasions when Fraser had a guest, he would give over his bed and sleep on the floor cuddled up with his dogs, which, he said, kept him warmer than any blanket.

Despite his refusal to keep records, fill out forms or keep accounts, Fraser was appointed warden for Sabi Game Reserve in 1917. It was a short-lived experience. "When Fraser moved to Sabi Bridge," writes Nussey, "he took with him his pack of 25 dogs, answered no letters and so neglected his administrative duties that, when officials visited to find out what was going on, the office was so congested with cobwebs that labourers had to cut a way in."

 A rare fight between an elephant and a white rhino was recorded by Kruger rangers at a water hole near Shingwedzi in 1964. The cause of the vicious altercation was not evident, but both animals seriously injured each other. Ultimately, the elephant triumphed. The badly wounded rhino died of its injuries.

of an Iron-Age trading settlement have been found at the foot of Shilowa and there is archaeological evidence that ivory hunters and traders passed through it in the 18th and 19th centuries. Former Park head Bruce Bryden discovered a secret cave in the area that appears to have been enlarged through the intensive use of fire at some point in the distant past. The cave appears to have been used in the 1900s as a stash point for ivory and precious metals and may even have been used more recently by ivory poachers.

The S50 follows the Lebombo range northwards towards Shingwedzi. Two recommended stops along this road are the surprisingly large Grootvlei Dam on the Hlamvu Creek and Nyawutsi Bird Hide on the Ntshivana Creek. Nyawutsi – derived from the Shangaan word *nyawuti* which means "lion with a large mane" – is within a pleasant grove of tall trees next to a

> There is a Shangaan proverb that cautions people as to who they give their money to: "Do not tie your wealth to a hippo's leg", which means be careful that your money doesn't disappear like a hippo does when it ducks under water.

permanent water hole that occasionally attracts lion early in the morning. It is not favoured much by other game because the dense surrounding bush provides cover for lurking predators.

North of Nyawutsi, the road meets the Shingwedzi River at Dipene. Dipene was a dipping point set up to try to curb a foot-and-mouth disease outbreak in 1938. Migrants arriving from Mozambique were obliged to use the foot-bath before they could carry on into South Africa.

This 20-km section of the S50 road from Dipene past Kanniedood Dam to Shingwedzi Camp is one of the most beautiful drives in the Park. The lush riverine forest supports a great deal of animal life compared to the somewhat sparse pickings of the north-eastern mopaneveld. There are usually elephant, kudu and baboons on the river banks as well as nyala, which are not often found much further south. There are plenty of hippos in the bigger pools in the river and an abundance of crocodiles on the sandbanks.

Hippo

Nigel Dennis

Civet

Nigel Dennis

Around Shingwedzi

The Shingwedzi River formed the heart of the former Shingwedzi Game Reserve, which stretched from the Letaba to the Limpopo rivers. There was not much opposition to its proclamation in 1903 because of its remoteness and dubious commercial value. Even Stevenson-Hamilton believed that this vast stretch of mopaneveld was so wild that it was not fit for humans. That sense of isolation is still evident today and is one of the main attractions of northern Kruger.

The Shingwedzi flood plains have been shaped by millions of years of flooding and deep layers of rich soil have been deposited on the underlying basalts. These support the huge riverine trees that Shingwedzi is famed for – the Natal mahoganies, ebony jackal-berries, weeping boer-beans and sausage trees. The flood plains have good grazing, which means the area is rich with game compared to the surrounding mopaneveld.

The riverine bush has elephant, buffalo, nyala, kudu, duiker, monkeys and baboons and the shy Sharpe's grysbok. The main predators of the Shingwedzi flood plains are leopard, lion and hyaena. Packs of wild dogs are occasionally spotted around Shingwedzi Camp. The grasslands north of Babalala picnic site are reputed to be the best place in northern Kruger for seeing cheetah.

Shingwedzi is also renowned for its birding, particularly in summer when thousands of migrant birds arrive from central Africa and Eurasia. There are many water-bird nesting sites along the river, particularly around Kanniedood Dam.

The flood plains around Shingwedzi are among the best places in Kruger to see most of the rarer large antelope – the roan and sable, the tsessebe, eland and Lichtenstein's hartebeest.

IN THE SHINGWEDZI AREA LOOK OUT FOR

Animals

Elephant

African rock python

Spotted hyaena

Nyala

Kudu

Birds

Saddle-billed stork

Bennett's woodpecker

Collared palm-thrush

African fish-eagle

Eurasian golden oriole

SHINGWEDZI CAMP EXPLORER OPTIONS

(All distances are from Shingwedzi back to the camp):

- Mphongolo Loop (S56 and H1-7) (72km; 3,5 hours) tar and dust road through ancient Kruger forests and mopane shrubveld; lots of elephant and buffalo; often lion sightings;

- Kanniedood Dam (S143, S50) (20km; 1 hour): dust road along the Shingwedzi River; brilliant birding, lots of browsers in riverine bush; good sunset or sunrise drive;

- Red Rocks Loop (S52) (72km; 3,5 hours) dust and tar roads along Shingwedzi alluvial flood plains; good bush drive with itinerant game viewing.

Kanniedood Dam road

Brett Hilton-Barber

KANNIEDOOD DAM

Kanniedood (Afrikaans for "cannot die") Dam lies south-east of Shingwedzi Camp on the S50 and is one of the best drives of northern Kruger, as it follows the Shingwedzi River. The road has 10 loops off it, each of which should be driven along slowly, as there are remarkable bird and animal sightings to be had. The rare saddle-billed stork and other water birds are plentiful, while browsers such as nyala, bushbuck and kudu are regular inhabitants of the riverine forest here. Elephant, too, are common. It was in this area that Shingwedzi, one of the "Magnificent Seven", was found dead. He was discovered perched on his knees with his tusks stuck deep into the river sand. Baboon are plentiful and one may see lion and leopard in the vicinity.

Albert Froneman

African fish-eagle

SHINGWEDZI CAMP

The atmosphere of Shingwedzi reflects the rugged dryness of the north. Mopane trees dominate the large camp, which is situated close to the confluence of three major rivers – the Shingwedzi itself, the Mphongolo and the Madzemba. Shingwedzi, Shangaan for "the circle of iron", was built in 1933, and the original huts form the inner circle of the camp.

Shingwedzi has a variety of accommodation types, from campsites and small rondavels to family cottages. It has a swimming pool, petrol station, shop, restaurant, ATM and emergency breakdown service. There is a designated day visitors' area with a swimming pool and braai facilities.

The camp offers stunning views over the river and surrounding alluvial flood plains that are home to some of the biggest elephants in Kruger. Many of the Magnificent Seven elephants (see page 223) were Shingwedzi regulars and some of the new big tuskers can be seen in the river beds from the deck outside the camp restaurant.

In the 1930s and 1940s, before Shingwedzi was properly fenced, elephants used to wander right into the camp, much to the delight and consternation of those early tourists. In the 1940s, one large, bad-tempered bull was shot inside the camp after it had acted aggressively towards staff on several previous occasions. In that instance, there was no loss of human life.

However, one can never be complacent in an area where there are wild animals. A case in point was the 1992 tragedy in which a ranger was taken by a desperate leopard that climbed in through the open window of his guard house. Thomas Rihlamfu was a gate guard at Shingwedzi and, although diligent when walking outside, he assumed he was safe in the hut next to the main entrance gate. His movements appear to have been studied by an emaciated leopard which chose its moment to catch him unawares as he dozed inside his hut. His partly eaten body was found next to his bed one morning by the school bus driver who wondered why the gate wasn't open. The driver ran to find section head Louis Olivier – who had previously been decorated for saving a fellow ranger from a crocodile attack on the Sabie River. Olivier saw the open window, realised what had happened

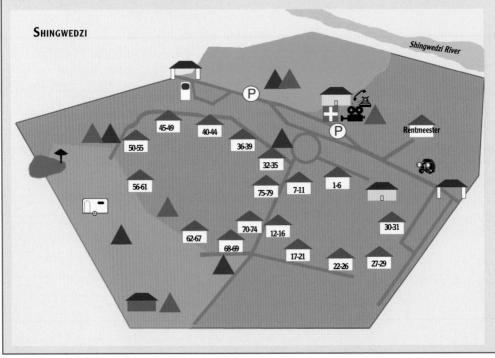

SHINGWEDZI

Shingwedzi River

Rentmeester

45-49
40-44
50-55
36-39
32-35
56-61
75-79
7-11
1-6
70-74
12-16
30-31
62-67
68-69
17-21
22-26
27-29

and ran out into the bush outside the gate. The leopard was right there in the grass. Olivier dispatched it with a shot. Like many of the other riverside camps, Shingwedzi has a continual parade of game along the river banks, even when the river dries up in winter. There are large herds of buffalo in the area and they drink daily in front of the camp when water is available.

One of the pleasures of staying at Shingwedzi is that there is usually animal activity close to the camp along the river past Kanniedood Dam (S50), which should be done at dawn or dusk, or preferably both. When the river flows, it acts as a magnet for water birds, which makes Shingwedzi one of the top summer birding spots in South Africa. There is a hide at Kanniedood but the birding is probably better along the river, as there is an interesting mix of woodland and water birds. In 1936 at Shingwedzi Camp ornithologist Leonard Gill discovered the first collared palm-thrush found in South Africa. The bird, which is considered a Mozambique resident, has since established itself at the camp, which is also noted for sightings of unusual raptors such as the Eurasian hobby and the bat hawk.

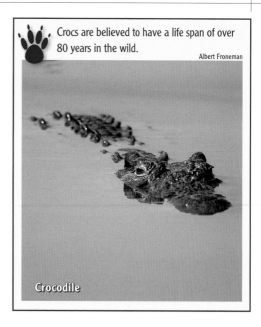

Crocs are believed to have a life span of over 80 years in the wild.

Albert Froneman

Crocodile

There is a bird hide further down the S50 at Nyawutsi, where one may get out of one's vehicle and watch over a small dam on the edge of the Ntshivana River, which divides the grasslands from the Lebombo. The continuation of this road takes one into the Tropic of Capricorn Loop. **(See page 243)**

RED ROCKS LOOP (S52)

The Red Rocks Loop (S52) follows the Shingwedzi River upstream into the mopane woodlands. It can also be accessed via the main road to Mopani (H1-6) which runs parallel to the road on the southern bank of the Shingwedzi. Both routes pass through robust riverine forest. This was the area frequented by two of Kruger's Magnificent Seven tuskers – João and Shawu. The Red Rocks get-out point is a beautiful place. Here, the Shingwedzi River crosses a band of Gubyane sandstone, and water erosion has created a series of potholes pitted in the smooth, reddish stone. Famed lowveld prospector, the American "Texas Bill" Lusk used to pan for gold regularly here between 1916 and 1920.

Brett Hilton-Barber

Buffalo

Albert Froneman

In the 1940s, the chairman of Kruger's Board of Trustees, Alfred Trollip and the Secretary, H Van Graan, had a close shave with a lion at Red Rocks. They were part of a small party that had been taken by an unarmed ranger down to the river bed when they heard a short, grunting noise behind them. They turned around to find a lioness staring at them from the edge of the bush about 50m away. The chairman noted the lioness's tail twitching from side to side before heeding the whispered suggestion that the party move quietly and purposefully back up to their cars. When they reached the safety of their vehicles, the ranger observed through binoculars that there was another lion, as well as three lionesses hidden in the bush close to where they had walked. It would have been one of life's supreme ironies if the Kruger trustees had ended up inside the lions they were committed to protecting!

The Red Rocks route ends at the Tshanga get-out point, unless one is going to Bateleur Camp on the edge of the Shingomane Dam. Tshanga is a very private spot set among large boulders. It offers sweeping views over the Tshanga River and the mopaneveld to the south-east. In Shangaan, *tshanga* means "cattle enclosure" and refers to old stone walls discovered near the site which are evidence of African Iron-Age human habitation in northern Kruger.

Shingwedzi to Punda Maria

There are few roads in the north, and the only link between Shingwedzi and Punda Maria is the (H1-7). A highly recommended game-viewing detour off this road is Mphongolo Loop (S56), which provides some relief from the mopaneveld by winding through magnificent riverine forest.

Kudu

Nigel Dennis

THE ROAD TO PUNDA (H1-7)

The Lamont Loop (S55) north of Shingwedzi has good views over the wide, sandy river bed, with elephant sightings almost a certainty. Much of the H1-7 goes through mopane scrubveld where there is often no game to be seen. The water holes at Nkulumboni South and Nwarihlangari are usually quiet.

MPHONGOLO LOOP (S56)

If one is travelling between Shingwedzi and Punda Maria, there is no excuse not to take the Mphongolo Loop (S56), which is one of the best drives in the entire Park. The detour is only 20km or so long, but one should set aside at least two hours for this trip because of the numerous loops that give one remarkable views over the river which is lined with some of the biggest and most beautiful

trees in Kruger. Among the giant jackal-berries, sycamore figs, nyalas and tambotis, a wealth of animal life is to be found, including large herds of buffalo and elephant. There are sometimes lion and leopard seen here.

Buffalo are notorious for their cunning and aggression when wounded. They are known to double back and ambush hunters who are pursuing them. In the case of lions, buffalo have been known to feign death to catch them off guard. They'll lie still, waiting for the right moment to leap up and thrash about with their deadly horns. Buffalo, kudu and nyala are most visible in winter here as this is the main source of water between the Shingwedzi and Luvuvhu rivers.

Duiker are common but far less visible than many other antelope – there is a Shangaan expression that, to go into hiding is "to make oneself a duiker".

SIRHENI CAMP

SANParks

Sirheni is a Shangaan word meaning "cemetery", after rumours that there is an elephant graveyard nearby. It is located in riverine bush on the edge of the mopaneveld some 54km from Shingwedzi on the northern end of the Mphongolo Loop. The camp, surrounded by established acacias, mopanes, silver cluster-leaves and leadwoods, overlooks the Sirheni Dam on the Mphongolo River. Guests have exclusive use of the hide at the dam which, according to camp staff, is often the site of kills. Staff say there is a leopard that lives near the camp, while lion and hyaena are sometimes seen in the area. If one is lucky one may see cheetah in the surrounding open plains, Lichtenstein's hartebeest, which is rare in Kruger, is often seen in the vicinity of Sirheni, which is also good for other rare antelope species such as sable and roan.

Sirheni is renowned as a birders' camp, with a bird hide overlooking the Sirheni Dam and the Shisha River Weir four kilometres away being two of the better birding spots in northern Kruger.

Sirheni has 15 self-catering cottages, and the camp offers guided bush walks and drives as well as a special botanical guide. Electricity is generator-powered and there are fridges in each of the units. There is no shop, although firewood and ice can be purchased.

BATELEUR BUSH CAMP

Heinrich van den Berg

Bateleur Bush Camp sits on the banks of the Mashokwe Spruit some 40km south-west of Shingwedzi at the end of the Red Rocks Loop road. It is a small, self-catering lodge with seven fully equipped luxury thatched cottages. It is the oldest, smallest and best equipped of the bushveld camps, with electrical plug points and limited TV reception.

Bateleur is on the edge of a thornveld intrusion into the mopane bushwillow woodlands and the camp is surrounded by tall trees and dense vegetation. There are two good dams in close proximity – Silwervis and Rooibosrant. There is a hide at Silwervis, which is a good game water hole with hippo and crocs and regular sightings of zebra, wildebeest, buffalo, tsessebe, bushbuck and nyala.

Camp specials are the black-backed jackal and caracal, while leopard are frequently seen in the dense bush along the watercourses.

Bateleur, named after the short-tailed eagle that is resident in the area, is an excellent birding camp. The dams attract large numbers of water birds and there are usually raptors circling in the skies overhead. Near Bateleur Camp is the hill of Shingomane which in the old days was the site of an initiation school for young Shangaan men.

Babalala to Dzundzwini (H1-7)

Babalala picnic site is next to a small water hole between the open mopane shrubveld to the east and the mixed mopane woodlands to the west. There are toilet and braai facilities at the picnic site and wood, ice and cold drinks are for sale. SANParks rangers say the grasslands around Babalala offer the best chances of seeing cheetah in the northern Park. Unlike most other carnivores, the cheetah rarely scavenges and will always try to find a fresh meal. Cheetah favour the open grasslands where they have the advantage of speed in catching their prey. Their non-retractable claws give them a grip on the ground for quick acceleration, while their broad tails help them steer. However, unless a cheetah catches its prey within half-a-kilometre, it will run out of steam and be forced to give up. Cheetah are at their most vulnerable after a high-speed chase, and have often been robbed of their prey by hyaena, lions and vultures immediately after a kill.

The tropical wetlands in the savanna north of Babalala are a key stopover for migrant water birds. The wetlands are part of the Shisha river system that, in summer, form a series of protected vleis which BirdLife SA has identified as an important habitat for some of South Africa's rarest birds. This is the place to break for a crake. The corn crake, African crake and more common black crake are all summer possibilities at Dokweni (Shangaan for "wishing for something"), Mawawi and Shisha West along the H1-7. (See page 268 for Dzundzwini Hill)

Fires in Kruger

Fire has occurred naturally on the savanna since time immemorial. Mostly, these have been caused by lightning strikes. Fires act as a cleaning mechanism for the bush, ridding the landscape of old grazing and dead trees. They also stimulate new growth. The Park policy is to allow natural fires to burn but to extinguish blazes that are started accidentally. One of the worst accidental fires in Kruger's history occurred in 2001 when 14 people died after being engulfed by a runaway fire while cutting grass.

Brett Hilton-Barber

Bushfire with baobabs

Antelope of the north

Eland

Nyala

Bushbuck

The riverine forest along the Luvuvhu River is the best place to see nyala in South Africa. They are tropical animals that look like a cross between a kudu and a bushbuck. They are the hairiest African antelope. The Luvuvhu River valley is also suited to bushbuck, rarely seen in Kruger because they keep to the thicker bush and browse mostly at night. The bushbuck males are known to be pugnacious animals that will turn suddenly on an attacker. According to former Kruger information officer PF Fourie, bushbuck have been known to kill leopards and even humans trying to hunt them. The northern sandveld is one of the best places to see eland in Kruger. Small herds are found in the drier areas away from the river. The eland is the largest African antelope and is one of nature's gentlest animals. It is the most frequently depicted animal in southern African rock art.

Impala

The Far North

Habitat pointers:

- Sandveld between Punda and Pafuri
- Dense mopane woodland around Punda
- Tropical riverine forest along the Luvuvhu and Limpopo rivers
- Shrub mopane to the east of the Punda-Pafuri main road
- Mountainous sandveld west of Pafuri
- Lots of baobabs

Albert Froneman

The far north of Kruger is unique. This is because it is in the tropics, and the geological base is sandstone rather than the granites and basalts that underlie the rest of the Park. Most of the extreme north-west of Kruger is classified as sandveld, which, as the name suggests, consists of very sandy, well-drained soils supporting a complicated mass of plant communities in which no particular tree or plant is dominant. Unlike other geological formations in the Park, some sandveld sediments are not part of the original landscape, having been deposited in northern Kruger by raging wind storms blowing in from the Kalahari several million years ago. The main features of the far northern landscape are the Limpopo and Luvuvhu River systems, the rugged sandstone mountains in the north-west and far more diversity than the mopaneveld. There is also a small, biologically significant ecosystem in the north-east known as the Nwambiya sandveld. Far northern Kruger lies on a fault-line known as the Limpopo Mobile Belt, which is the joint between the Kaapvaal Craton – the crust of the earth supporting South Africa – and the Central African Craton to the north. The hot springs in the Pafuri area are evidence of water being heated through cracks from deep below the earth's surface. The far north is the birding mecca of South Africa because it has so many Afrotropical species not seen further south. The far north is a long-standing winter feeding ground for elephant and there is a rich variety of game, particularly between the Luvuvhu and Limpopo rivers.

BEST DRIVE IN THE FAR NORTH
Luvuvhu River Drive to Crooks' Corner:

This is one of the most scenic drives in Kruger and especially good for birding. There is lots of animal activity in the riverine bush which is the favourite habitat for the nyala. Stop at the Luvuvhu River bridge, have a picnic at Pafuri and see three countries at Crooks' Corner.

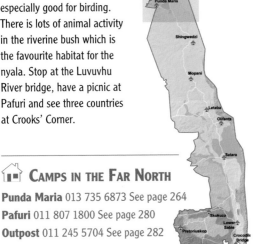

🏠 CAMPS IN THE FAR NORTH

Punda Maria 013 735 6873 See page 264
Pafuri 011 807 1800 See page 280
Outpost 011 245 5704 See page 282

PAFURI BORDER POST 013 753 5757

Gate times:

Summer (1 October to 31 March) from 0800 to 16h00
Winter (1 April to 30 September) from 08h00 to 15h00.
Commercial traffic is allowed through Pafuri border.

🔭 PUNDA MARIA GATE EXPLORER OPTIONS

- Directly to Punda Maria Camp, just over 10km from the gate; (tar road through sandveld and mopane woodland; allow approximately 30 minutes);

- Drive to Pafuri area, via the S60 to Klopperfontein (21km dirt road through tall mopane woodlands) and then 23km along the H1-8 (tar road through mixed mopaneveld and sandveld); estimated 2 hours' travelling time to Luvuvhu River Bridge;

- Head to Shingwedzi along the H13-1 to the main road (H1-7); tar all the way through mixed mopaneveld and grassland (75km to Shingwedzi; allow approximately 5 hours).

N

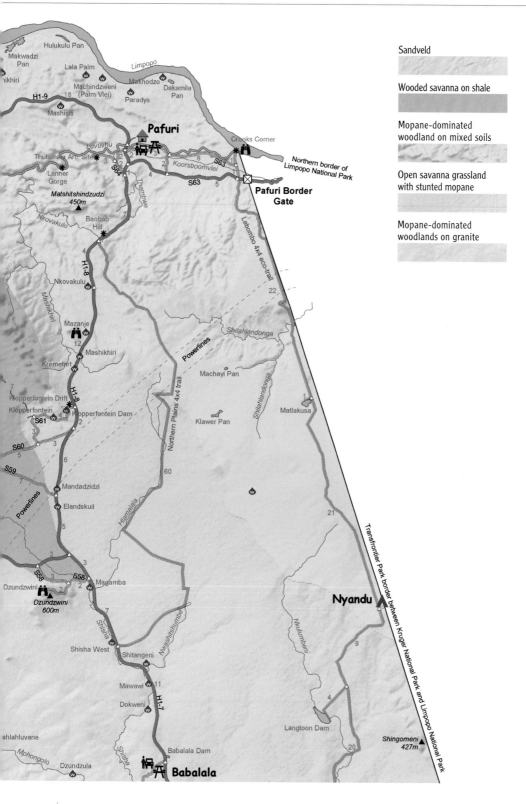

Sandveld

Wooded savanna on shale

Mopane-dominated
woodland on mixed soils

Open savanna grassland
with stunted mopane

Mopane-dominated
woodlands on granite

Animals

Sharpe's grysbok

Wild dogs

Zebra

Kudu

Elephant

Birds

Arnot's chat

Eastern nicator

Yellow-billed oxpecker

Grey-headed parrot

African harrier-hawk (gymnogene)

Punda Maria Gate

Punda Maria Gate is the direct access point into far northern Kruger from Gauteng. Set in mixed sandveld woodlands below Thulamila Koppie (not to be confused with Thulamela Heritage Site near Pafuri), Punda Gate has been upgraded to cater for the increase in tourist traffic to the north. The surrounding woodlands are a mixture of bushwillow and marula with a bit of mopane. There is a Day Visitors' Centre a few hundred metres along the H13-1, a recommended stopping point to acclimatise to the Park and learn about the natural and human history of the far north. Elephant usually browse along this road. Although there are lion in the area, they are not often seen.

Visitors' centre at Punda Maria

Brett Hilton-Barber

In 1981, three workers from Punda broke all the Park rules by arriving late at the gate from their weekend leave. They persuaded the guards to let them through and rode off into the dark on their bicycles on the nine-kilometre trip to Punda Camp. Only two of them arrived. The shocked survivors described how a lion had leapt out of the dark at the lead cyclist but missed him. The lion then went for the second bicycle – on which two of the men were riding. The man on the back – Louis Mathye – fell off as his terrified friend accelerated away, pedalling for his life. Punda's head ranger, Louis Olivier, and several assistants then raced back along the road and found a semi-mutilated black-maned lion tearing at Mathye's dead body. Olivier shot it at once. When they examined the animal, they found it had been starving to death – it was missing the lower part of its left hind leg, presumably caught in a snare – and had probably gone after human prey as a desperate option.

Around Punda

There are three main drives around Punda Maria – Mahonie Loop, the Klopperfontein road (S60, S61) past the mythologically rich Gumbandebvu koppies and the tar road (H13-1) between Punda Maria Gate and Dzundzwini Hill. (See page 268)

To the north-west of Punda Maria – in an area inaccessible to all except hikers on the Nyalaland Trail – are the remains of the 18th-century hilltop village, Makahane. This was named after a particularly ferocious chief, "Makahane the Brute" who had his enemies and petty offenders thrown from the cliffs to their deaths in the Luvuvhu River below. Makahane was murdered and buried here.

The Punda Maria sandveld has many of South Africa's rarest reptiles, such as the tigroid thick-toed gecko and the rough-tailed girdle lizard.

What's in a name
The name Punda Maria is a bastardisation of the Swahili word for zebra, which is *punda miliya*. The name of the camp was coined in 1919 by the first ranger in charge of the area, JJ "Ou Kat"Coetser, who named it after his wife, Maria. She apparently hated the rigours of living in such an isolated part of the country and had a predilection for striped dresses. Coetser, himself, was fired as a ranger for shooting animals and was eventually killed by a bull elephant near the Limpopo River. Stevenson-Hamilton never had much time for Coetser who he described as a "gasbag". The Parks Board renamed the camp and the gate as Punda Milia under the impression that it had been a spelling mistake and that zebra were the first animals seen in the area. After representations from Coetser's family in 1979, the original name was restored.

Albert Froneman

Lion with a kill

PUNDA MARIA CAMP

Punda Maria is an island of sandveld in a sea of mopane. It enjoys the highest rainfall in northern Kruger – an average of 650mm a year – and is renowned for its diverse vegetation and Afrotropical bird life. The camp retains the spirit of the times in which it was built. From being game ranger quarters, it was transformed into a tourist camp in 1933, and the original buildings have been maintained. It has the ambience of a small village and, because of its intimacy and isolation, people tend to be much friendlier towards each other than at other camps. Set against a ridge of Wyliespoort quartzite in a line of rolling hills that are the easternmost extension of the Soutspansberg, the camp is renowned for its birding.

There is a short, demarcated walk within the camp perimeter – the Flycatcher Trail – which offers a good sample of the bird life and vegetation of the area. Punda is a small camp with 22 two- and three-bed bungalows, two cottages that sleep four each, seven luxury tents and a camping and caravanning area. It has a swimming pool, shop restaurant and petrol station. Before Punda was established as a ranger's post it was the headquarters of an influential chief, Sikokolo. (See the Ivory Trail on page 267)

Brett Hilton-Barber

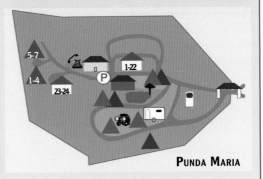

5-7
1-4
23-24
1-22
P

PUNDA MARIA

Grysbok

Nigel Dennis

THE MAHONIE LOOP (S99)

The 28-km Mahonie Loop (S99) around Punda Maria is a marvellous introduction to the sandveld. Named after the pod mahogany tree, of which there are many specimens in the area, the route is renowned for plants and animals that are rare elsewhere in the Park. There are trees such as the wild kirkia, the knobbly fig, the wild syringa, wild custard apple and myrtle bushwillow. Among the less common buck that may be seen along the drive are the rare, tiny suni antelope – the smallest in the Park – and Sharpe's grysbok. The suni, also known as Livingstone's antelope, inhabits the thicker sandveld woodlands. It often follows monkeys about, feeding off

Mahonie Loop

Brett Hilton-Barber

fruit and leaves dropped from the trees. This tiny, delicate antelope – which stands not much taller than a school ruler – is hunted by a wide variety of predators, including leopards, pythons and the larger birds of prey.

Among the less common birds to be seen is the bat hawk. Its presence here is not surprising, as in Kruger most of the bat species on which it is known to feed are associated with the Punda sandveld. Bats are more common than one supposes. Worldwide, there are about 850 bat species, which means one in every five mammal species is a bat!

Mahonie Loop has two notable water holes, Witsand and Matukwala. There is more likely to be animal activity at Witsand windmill during winter when water is scarce elsewhere. Birders should stop at Matukwala Dam and scan the surrounding woodlands for birds such as Dickinson's kestrel and

Haunted Hills

There is a great deal of folklore associated with northern Kruger. East of Punda Maria is Gumbandebvu Hill (576m), named after a chief whose daughter Khama was believed to possess great rainmaking skills. During years of drought, people from far and wide would bring gifts to Khama and implore her to bring rain. She reportedly would then slaughter a goat, prolonging its death cries so that the ancestors would hear the desperation of the people, and then climb to the top of the hill with bones and potions and implore the spirits to change the weather. Many people from this area today believe the hill is sacred and haunted.

the grey-headed parrot. For Kruger trivia fans, Matukwala dam was where ranger Gus Adendorff lost his small dog to a crocodile in the 1950s. There are often kudu on this road. Leopard and wild dogs have been seen on occasion.

Buffalo

Nigel Dennis

The impala lily

Despite its beautiful appearance, the impala lily *(Adenium multiflorum)* is deadly poisonous. The succulent shrub, which can grow up to two metres, is especially visible in winter when it flowers. It produces white flowers with delicate pink stripes and crinkly red margins that are very noticeable during the dry months, from May to September. It grows in sandy soils in rocky woodlands and open plains in the hotter, lower-lying regions of the Park. San bushmen used the sap from the impala lily to poison their arrows and to kill fish.

SANParks

PUNDA MARIA TO PAFURI

There are two main routes linking Punda Maria to the main Shingwedzi Pafuri road (H1-8). These are the S60 past Gumbandebvu Hill (see page 268) and the Punda Maria Gate road to Dzundzwini (H13-1), which is the most direct way to Shingwedzi.

PUNDA MARIA TO DZUNDZWINI (H13-1)

On the main road eastwards (H13-1) from Punda Maria Gate and Camp the landscape shifts from sandveld to tree mopane savanna and there are some wonderful stands of this tree and usually elephant to be seen. Shortly before the H13-1 joins the main Shingwedzi-Pafuri road (H1-8) there is a loop road that takes one to the Dzundzwini view site which, at 600m, is one of the highest points in the northern Park. At the foot of Dzundzwini Hill, at a beautiful spot under a giant sausage tree, is the site where JJ Coetser first had his camp when he was appointed ranger of the area in 1919. In 1836, when the voortrekker Louis Trichardt

The Ivory Trail

The "Ivory Trail" was the adventurer's road from civilisation into the elephant-hunting grounds of southern central Africa during the 19th and early 20th centuries. The trail left the Great North Road between Johannesburg and Zimbabwe near the present-day town of Polokwane and passed Soekmekaar, descending into the lowveld near Klein Letaba where there was a rough-and-ready place to sleep. From there, the well-worn path went east to the headwaters of the Shingwedzi River where there was a solitary store, which was the last place to get supplies before heading into the bush. The Shingwedzi River marked the start of lion country and, from this point on, people travelled only by day and built thornbush encampments at night to protect themselves and their stock from wild animals.

The Ivory Trail then passed the site where Punda Maria stands today. At the turn of the 20th century, it was occupied by a Shangaan-speaking chief called Sikololo who was known for his fortified gardens and his hospitality to travellers. Sikololo was under a permanent state of siege by wild animals desperate to raid his fertile gardens. In his book *The Ivory Trail*, TV Bulpin wrote that "Sikololo marshalled his defences with cunning and patience. His womenfolk beat drums all night when the crops were ripening and the place was littered with so many snares and traps that Sikololo himself, when leaving his hunt one moonless night, had come to grief in a pitfall and remained tangled in his own contrivances until morning".

Sikololo was also a fount of news and gossip about the wild lands beyond, providing valuable intelligence to passing hunters and traders. From Sikololo's place, the Ivory Trail wound through the mopane forests to a pleasant camping spot known as Senkhuwa after the wild figs (*nkhuwa*) which provided shade and nourishment. Today, the site is known as Klopperfontein, named after ivory hunter Hans Klopper who used to camp there regularly.

The next stop on the Ivory Trail was Baobab Hill from where the road wound down into the Luvuvhu River Valley to Makuleke Drift, the main crossing point. Once one arrived at Makuleke Store near Crooks' Corner, one was deep in elephant territory and the Ivory Trail then splintered into numerous bush paths that led one into Zimbabwe or Mozambique or along the Limpopo River. The Ivory Trail was used extensively by hunters and traders. Parts of it have now been developed into a self-drive tourism route.

Brett Hilton-Barber

Baobab Hill

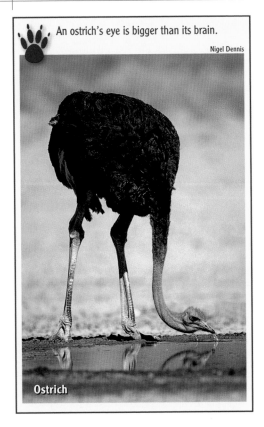

An ostrich's eye is bigger than its brain.

Nigel Dennis

Ostrich

passed by Dzundzwini, the area was densely settled under the control of the chief Matibee. He named the hill *Matibeetuijn*, Dutch for "Matibee's garden".

DZUNDZWINI TO SHINGWEDZI (H1-7)

The road south from Dzundzwini takes one through fairly flat, featureless mopaneveld. Although there are several water holes along this road, there is not much game because the grazing is mostly sourveld. A recommended get-out point is Babalala, where a thatched shelter has been constructed around an enormous sycamore fig. The open grasslands around Babalala are reputed to be among the best places to see cheetah and tsessebe in northern Kruger. This area is also known for its accipiters – birds of prey such as the black sparrowhawk and African goshawk. (See page 270)

PUNDA MARIA TO PAFURI (H1-8)

The best route from Punda Maria to Pafuri is to take the dirt road past Gumbandebvu (S60) which joins the main tar road (H1-8) near Klopperfontein. The road past the haunted hills has some of the best mopane woodland in Kruger. This is one of the best places in Kruger to see Arnot's chat, a localised bird species that is found only in the denser stands of tree mopaneveld. There is concern among some conservationists that this chat faces extinction because of elephant destruction of its habitat. Elephants and impala are usually seen along this very scenic stretch of the road.

The only intrusion into the wilderness area one encounters are the two huge pylon lines that carry electricity to South Africa from Mozambique's Cahora Bassa Dam.

Klopperfontein

Klopperfontein is the main centre of animal activity between Punda Maria and the Luvuvhu River. It is a transition zone between the mopaneveld and the sandveld, so there is a diversity of vegetation and animal life. The grazing is sweet because of the rich clay soils supported by ecca shales which are punctuated by a series of granite koppies, the highest being Matekevhele (482m) to the north-west of Klopperfontein Dam. *Matekevhele* in Venda means the "place of plentiful maize", which probably means it was a grain storage site in the 19th century. There is some mystery about these koppies as Kruger historians Klopper and Bornmen note that local people refused to spend the night nearby.

There are two viewing spots at Klopperfontein, which is named after the lowveld ivory hunter Dirk Klopper who frequently camped here. The windmill and the dam are both worth stopping at. Klopperfontein Dam is often visited by elephant and eland and, on occasion, lion have been seen here.

Klopperfontein Water Hole

Brett Hilton-Barber

There is a drift over the Klopperfontein Stream that was built by another ivory hunter, the legendary Cecil Barnard, who was known locally as Bvekenya ("he who swaggers"). Barnard's own journey was one of redemption. Once a poacher who had a hide-out on an island in the Limpopo River, he eventually became a game ranger.

During the height of the southern African conflict of the 1970s and 1980s, many mines were laid along the borders between South Africa, Zimbabwe and Mozambique. Former Kruger head ranger Bruce Bryden tells of his heartbreak at having to shoot an old bull elephant near Klopperfontein. It had been blinded and crippled by an anti-personnel mine. "How many elephant and other large game animals were killed or mutilated by mines during my time at the Kruger National Park

is known only to God. Certainly, we had to destroy quite a number of elephants in the northern areas after they had fallen foul of the mines laid so heedlessly in Zimbabwe and Mozambique. It was a terrible business; my blood boiled every time I heard or came across one of these landmine victims," he wrote in his memoirs.

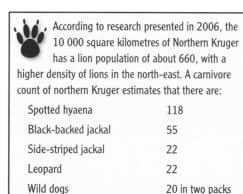

According to research presented in 2006, the 10 000 square kilometres of Northern Kruger has a lion population of about 660, with a higher density of lions in the north-east. A carnivore count of northern Kruger estimates that there are:

Spotted hyaena	118
Black-backed jackal	55
Side-striped jackal	22
Leopard	22
Wild dogs	20 in two packs

Rarer Raptors of the North

Far northern Kruger is known for its rare birds. Because it falls into the Afrotropical zone many raptors not seen elsewhere in South Africa can be seen here. Among the special raptors to look out for are Dickinson's kestrel, a small aggressive raptor, Ayres's hawk-eagle, a rare summer migrant, and Verreauxs' eagle, which nests in the sandstone cliffs of the Luvuvhu River Valley.

Ayres's hawk-eagle

Dickinson's kestrel

Verreauxs' eagle

Saddle-billed stork and elephant

KLOPPERFONTEIN TO PAFURI (H1-8)

The rocky granite ridge at Klopperfontein marks the start of the broken landscape of the broader Luvuvhu catchment area. The Shikuwa Stream rises at Klopperfontein and drops down to join the Matsaringwe which, in turn, joins the Luvuvhu near the Nyalaland Trail base camp on Kruger's western border.

The H1-8 heads north through gentle, undulating plains of shrub mopaneveld with views over the western edge of the Soutspansberg, until it reaches the landmark Baobab Hill.

This was a camp site for migrant labourers from Mozambique who were recruited for the Johannesburg gold mines. It was also used by hunters and ivory traders during the late 19th and early 20th centuries. From here, the road descends sharply into the Luvuvhu River valley through mopane

IN THE PAFURI AREA LOOK OUT FOR:

Animals

Leopard

Nyala

Elephant

Baboon

Bushpig

Birds

Racket-tailed roller

Narina trogon

Dickinson's kestrel

Pel's fishing-owl

Crested guineafowl

Pafuri Gate

Pafuri Gate is about six-and-a-half hours'
drive from Johannesburg and is the most
northerly entrance to Kruger. It is situated
in mopane woodland between the Limpopo
and Luvuvhu Rivers near Mabyeni Koppie
(386m). There are many fine old baobabs in
the surrounding landscape. The Limpopo
River runs in a parallel arc to the north
of the road, but is not visible. There are a
series of pans along the Limpopo which
are important feeding grounds in summer
for migrant water birds. Access to the pans
is restricted to guests at The Outpost and
Pafuri Game Lodge.

Albert Froneman

woodland until it levels off along the alluvial
flood plains. Here, the mopane trees end
abruptly and are replaced by the tangled flood
plain vegetation of thornveld and fever tree
forest which then give way to thick, riverine
bush on the river's edge.

From being almost non-existent, game
becomes quite plentiful in a short space of
time. The scenery in this area is exceptionally
beautiful, with dramatic sandstone koppies
and baobabs providing a visual counterpoint
to the lushness of the river area.

**PAFURI GATE
EXPLORER OPTIONS**

- Luvuvhu River drives (20km of river frontage
  between Nyala Drive and Crooks' Corner; dust
  road through thick, riverine forest; allow at least
  half a day);
- Main Road to Punda Maria (approximately
  70km along tar through mopaneveld and
  sandveld; allow for three hours of driving time).

Despite their bulk, eland are very good jumpers, with adults able to clear obstacles two metres high.

Pafuri Gate takes one directly into the northern sandveld between the Limpopo and Luvhuvu Rivers. This area is one of the most ecologically diverse parts of the Park, incorporating a variety of vegetation types and microclimates. The shrub mopane to the east of the H1-9 is one of the driest localities in Kruger. The vegetation here is intriguing as it is a mixture of South African lowveld and tropical African woodlands. Dominant trees in this part of the sandveld are the mopane, various bushwillow species, silver cluster-leaf and white syringa trees. They form a fairly dense blanket of vegetation

between the protruding sandveld koppies. There is not much game along the H1-9 until one gets closer to the Luvuvhu River where there is rich and diverse animal life.

Leopard are often seen near the Luvuvhu River bridge, which has engaging views over the river and surrounding forest. This is one of South Africa's best birding spots for rarities such as Pel's fishing-owl, Böhm's spinetail and the African finfoot and white-crowned lapwing. While driving around the Luvuhvu area, look out for the flood markers that show the high-water point reached by the floods of February 2000 that had such a devastating effect on Kruger.

The pans along the far eastern extent of the Pafuri region are home to an extraordinary ancient fish – the African lungfish (*Protopterus annectens brieni*). Lungfish

 The upside down tree

Brett Hilton-Barber

The baobab (*Adansonia digitata*) is southern Africa's most distinctive tree with its extremely stout, fleshy trunk and widely spreading crown. An African legend holds that a giant child of the gods once pulled the baobab out of the ground and then stuck it back upside down, which accounts for its root-like branches.

The baobab can grow up to 25m tall and has an astounding longevity – some trees in Kruger are believed to be well over 4 000 years old. The baobab has a particularly beautiful white flower that blooms in October and November. The tree has many uses. Elephant, kudu, nyala and impala chew on the bark, which has been used in traditional medicine to treat malaria, dysentery and bladder ailments. Baboons are very fond of the yellowish, oval fruit that has high Vitamin C and tartaric acid content. The fruit appears on the trees in late summer and turns brown in autumn. Sangomas prescribe a powder crushed from the seeds to stop hiccups in children. The fibrous bark is used for making ropes and fishing line.

Older baobabs often have hollowed-out trunks big enough for several humans to fit inside. Such trees have been used through the ages as hiding places, jails and places to store food and water.

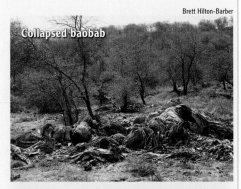
Collapsed baobab

Baobab

Africa Imagery

Land, humans and animals

Kruger was occupied by several indigenous tribes before it was proclaimed as a game reserve.

Most people in the area were removed by the authorities with little compensation. Because these removals generally happened before 1913, the cut-off date set by the South African government to settle land claims, there have been relatively few attempts at land restitution involving Kruger. One exception is that of the Makuleke community in northern Kruger. In 1969, this clan of Shangaan speakers, which had occupied the Pafuri land for generations, was forcibly moved from the area in the interests of consolidating Kruger.

In a historic deal forged with the South African government in 1998, a creative resolution was reached. Instead of insisting on the right to reoccupy the land, which would have compromised Kruger's wildlife heritage, the Makuleke clan agreed to enter into a private-sector partnership to develop new tourism facilities in the north.

A concession has been signed with Wilderness Safaris in which the Makuleke community will be involved in the development, staffing and servicing of new tourism facilities as well as sharing in their profit.

fossils have been found in the Karoo and have been dated back to about 150 million years. Unlike other fish, this species has lungs instead of gills, which makes it able to survive in mud when water dries up. This kind of fish may represent a time when aquatic creatures evolved into land-based animals. Park scientists have relocated individual lungfish to two other parts of the Park to try to safeguard the species against extinction.

Leopard territories are marked by scratches, faeces, urine and secretions. Male territories are larger than those of the female, and a male territory may overlap several female territories.

Albert Froneman

Leopard

Luvuvhu River

The Luvuvhu River is believed to have got its name from the Venda word for river bushwillow (*muvuvhu*). It forms the western boundary of Kruger between Punda Maria until just south of Pafuri, where it enters the Park through Lanner Gorge, cutting through Clarens sandstone, the uppermost sediment in the Karoo Sequence. The river winds through the sandveld into the alluvial flood plains before joining the Limpopo at Crooks' Corner. The forests on either side of the Luvuvhu – which include nyalas, large-leaved fever-berries, forest fever trees and sycamore fig trees – support a rich array of animal and bird life, while the sandbanks are often packed with crocodiles. Nyala, kudu, impala and baboons browse beneath the tall trees. Look out for leopards.

Brett Hilton-Barber

SANParks

Pafuri Picnic Site

Luvuvhu River

Pafuri Picnic Site

Pafuri Picnic Site is on the banks of the Luvuvhu River, surrounded by tall ana trees and thick riverine bush. There are toilet and braai facilities and one can buy firewood and cold drinks at the site. The picnic site exudes an air of tranquillity and the tall

Crocodiles mainly subsist on fish, but their prey will include any animal that ventures too close to the water, including humans. Female crocodiles nest on sandy shorelines, dry stream beds, or riverbanks. A female can lay 25 to 100 eggs, which she covers with sand, then guards until they hatch approximately three months later. Crocodiles are surprisingly good parents and, when the young start hatching, either parent may assist them to escape from their eggs by rolling them between tongue and palate. When in danger, an adult female crocodile may hold young crocodiles in her throat pouch for protection.

Crocodile hatching

Nigel Dennis

shade trees provide welcome relief from the hot sun, especially in summer. Ana trees are the only Kruger trees that lose their leaves in summer. It is a particularly nutritious tree, capable of producing up to a ton of pods which begin dropping in early summer. There are often nyala, kudu and impala at the Pafuri Picnic Site early in the morning, nibbling the fallen pods. To get a feel for the Luvuvhu landscape, spend at least an hour at this site watching birds, counting crocodiles, reading, relaxing or walking around.

Pafuri Picnic Site is something of a mecca for South African birders. Among the rarer birds that may be seen at Pafuri and along the Luvuvhu River are the thick-billed cuckoo, racket-tailed roller, Narina trogon and trumpeter hornbill. There is also an educational display about the nearby Thulamela archaeological site.

Dinosaur ancestors in Kruger

In 1995, hikers on the Nyala walking trail in the sandveld north of Punda Maria made a startling discovery. While examining a cache of stone tools exposed on the edge of a dry river bank, they came upon the fossilised remains of mammal-like reptiles. Several bits of petrified vertebrae were scattered over a small, mopane-covered hill. The fossils were identified as belonging to a large mammal-like reptile, the Euskelosaurus, which lived 200 million years ago in the pre-dinosaur era of the Triassic. Euskelosaurus was a plant-eating biped that probably waded through swamplands. It was about three metres high at the shoulder and 10 metres long. The remains of other Euskelosauruses have been found elsewhere in South Africa – notably in the Free State and the Karoo – but this site is believed to be richer in fossils than the others. Fossilised dinosaur remains are also believed to be in the sandstone in the Makuleke Reserve in Kruger, north of the Luvuvhu River.

Flooding in Kruger

In February 2000, the Kruger Park experienced floods of a magnitude that occurs only rarely. Tumultuous rains in the escarpment catchment areas of the lowveld rivers caused water levels to rise dramatically. Skukuza was swamped by water on February 7 in the worst floods in 50 years, but most of the damage was inflicted in the north, which caught the edge of Cyclone Eileen on February 24. The Luvuvhu burst its banks by 20m, killing hundreds of animals and washing away large trees and rocks. Approximately 200 tourists had to be rescued. The northern part of the Park had to be closed for eight months for rehabilitation operations. Helicopter pilots flying relief missions into neighbouring Mozambique reported that the 100km separating the mouths of the Komati and Limpopo Rivers was a single sheet of water that had displaced more than half-a-million people. Driving around the Park, look out for the 2000 flood-level markers that are to be found next to many rivers and in some camps. Although the 2000 floods caused the most damage to Kruger, they weren't as severe as the 1925 floods when the water levels were even higher. Kruger faced severe flooding in the late 1950s and mid-1970s as well. It is awe-inspiring how high the raging water can rise.

NEWS

February 13 2000

Movie pilots save flood victim from wild dogs

Chopper crews 'deserve medals', says destitute Parks Board director

MICHAEL SCHMIDT

A YOUNG man who was rescued from a pack of wild dogs in the Kruger National Park this week is the luckiest of 300 people who owe their lives to the heroics of two helicopter pilots as floods raged in the area.

The pilots were working for a film company making wildlife documentaries in the park when the Sabie River burst its banks. Dramatic footage shot from the air on Monday shows a man alone on top of a stone direction sign as the pack of hunting dogs eye him.

The man, whose identity has been established, is believed to be a South African guide for a group of German-speaking Swiss tourists who stranded when their vehicle was swept away.

They had been walking for several kilometres — which is dangerous because hippos came out of the river — when they found themselves cut off. "Said film director Gareth Haffies, who was in the chopper during the gruelling 5-hour rescue airlift.

"But the chopper is only a 5-seater, so we had to leave the person behind. When we returned 20 minutes later, we saw the guy we had left standing on a rock-pile road sign. He was surrounded by a pack of wild dogs — I think we got there in the nick of time. They were definitely in kill mode, and he was terrified.

"The pilot, Piet Otto, used the chopper to chase off the dogs when we landed. The man made a beeline for the chopper and dived in. He was pale and didn't say a word on the 10-minute trip back to his group. We never found out his name."

A hunting expert Dr Michael

Nyala rams

Africa Imagery

LUVUVHU RIVER DRIVE TO CROOKS' CORNER (S63)

The Luvuvhu River Drive (S63) to Crooks' Corner is undoubtedly one of the most beautiful drives in Kruger. The road follows the river through tropical woodland and there are many shady viewpoints overlooking the watercourse. The vegetation along the drive is diverse, ranging from dry thornveld and baobabs to lush riverine forest dominated by nyala trees, jackal-berries and figs. The ghostly green fever trees provide an eerie dimension to the riverine forest. These trees have roots that reach deep below the soil and are able to tap into underground water sources unavailable to most other vegetation. There are several loops along the S63, all of which are worth stopping at. The bird life at the water's edge is particularly abundant, often with uncommon species such as woolly-necked and yellow-billed storks, openbills and

Nyala doe

Brett Hilton-Barber

spoonbills. There are usually crocs sunning themselves on the sandbanks and pods of hippos in the larger pools.

The alluvial plains along the Luvuvhu River are home to most of the nyala in the park. Nyala are very localised antelope, and

277

Crooks' Corner

Crooks' Corner

Crooks' Corner got its name from the outlaws who lived there in the late 19th and early 20th centuries. Because of the three sovereign territories that met at the confluence of the Limpopo and Luvuvhu rivers – Portuguese East Africa, Southern Rhodesia and South Africa – it was relatively easy to avoid the law by hopping over into a neighbouring territory. It became a haven for ivory poachers, gunrunners and illegal tribal labour recruiters. Among the more infamous

Wilderness Safaris

of these was Stephanus Barnard, an ivory poacher known as Bvekenya ("he who swaggers"), who built many of the roads in the area. There was a trading store in the area owned by AlecThompson that was an important supply point and meeting place for the rogues who lived here. Crooks' Corner was a mine labour recruitment centre of dubious repute during the old Transvaal gold-mining boom of the late 19th century. TV Bulpin, in his *Lost Trails of the Lowveld*, noted that, among the hoodlums who found a means of livelihood in trading in humans were the two De Beer brothers. They were "among the best known loungers around Crooks' Corner. Proper wild men of the bush, they wandered around carrying little else save their rifles and a large bottle of Worcester sauce slung on a cord around their necks, they being uncommonly partial to that condiment with their venison".

in the words of James Stevenson-Hamilton, are "rather like a glorified bushbuck" with richer markings and a long fringe on the throat and back.

Besides the nyala, the animals one is likely to encounter here are kudu, impala and baboons. Although leopard are hard to see, a high proportion of these animals live

and hunt in the thick undergrowth of the Luvuvhu River.

The Luvuvhu River has a high population of crocodiles. These ancient reptiles feed mostly on fish and help control the balance of barbel in the rivers. Crocs often feed on other animals – a full-grown crocodile is capable of dragging an adult

The fig and the wasp

One of the most fascinating examples of co-evolution is that of the fig tree and a particular kind of wasp. Over 750 ficus species (19 of which are found in Kruger) depend on fig wasps of the family Agaonidae (Hymenoptera) for pollination. The tiny flowers of fig trees have an intricate maze of tiny scales that only the fig wasp with its spade-like head can negotiate. Fertilised female fig wasps –with specially adapted pollen sacs – leave their tree of origin and migrate to another fig of the same species with young fruit. They pollinate that tree and lay their eggs within the fruit. The fig tree has a chemical that protects the larvae. Male wasps then bore out the tree creating holes for the females to fly out and repeat the exercise.

Fig tree

Brett Hilton-Barber

lion or buffalo into the water. The biggest croc recorded in the Park was from the Luvuvhu River. It weighed 905kg and measured 5,5m.

The road ends under a large sycamore fig tree at Crooks' Corner, which is at the confluence of the Luvuvhu and Limpopo rivers. One can gaze across at Zimbabwe and Mozambique, and listen to hippo grunting in the pools below.

Pafuri Border Post Gate is a few kilometres from Crooks' Corner. It is one of the main entrances into Mozambique's Limpopo National Park. (See page 260)

NYALA DRIVE (S64)

Nyala Drive leads off the H1-8 (the main road between the Luvuvhu River and Punda Maria). The drive takes its name from the nyala trees and the antelope of the same name. The nyala is a dense, evergreen tree that fruits from late summer into early spring. Monkeys and baboons eat the grape-sized fruit off the tree, while fallen fruit is a favourite with elephant, impala and nyala. The nyala antelope looks like a shaggy cousin of the kudu, sharing the same vertical white stripes on its coat but without the dramatic curved horns. They are restricted mostly to dense river bush and are more common in northern Mozambique than South Africa or Zimbabwe.

Along this drive, there is a good chance of seeing Kruger's rarer antelope such as the solidly built eland, the most important animal in the San belief systtem. The crested guineafowl, with its curious "Afro-mop" scratches about in the bush on the side of the road, which winds through alluvial forest to the base of the Matshitshinadzudzi mountains where Thulamela is nestled. Visits to Thulamela have to be done with a guide and can be organised through Punda Maria, Pafuri Lodge or The Outpost.

Thulamela – Iron-Age kingdom

Thulamela, an ancient fortress overlooking the Luvuvhu River, was the political capital of an Iron-Age kingdom between 1200 AD and 1640 AD. The name is derived from the Shona phrase meaning "giving birth". Thulamela was "discovered" by a Park ranger in 1991 and much of the site has been restored. The rulers of Thulamela are believed to have controlled a far-reaching trading network between the Mozambican coast and the South African interior. Excavations have yielded traces of gold artifacts from Zimbabwe, glass beads from India and porcelain from China. Two skeletons were unearthed during excavations – a "queen" with gold and copper bangles and beads, and a "king" adorned with gold ornaments. Analysis of the "king's" skeleton indicates that he was probably murdered – stabbed through the stomach in approximately 1640 – and that Thulamela was abandoned soon afterwards. The two baobabs that loomed over the Thulamela meeting place are each believed to be more than 4 000 years old. The views from the top of this hill embody the sense of ancient Africa. Below, one can see the old elephant migration route through the surrounding hills and a magnificent baobab forest.

SANParks

Thulamela

🏠 PAFURI LODGE

Pafuri Lodge is the best way to experience the magic of northern Kruger. It is a prime birding location and there is a continual stream of animal traffic along the river in front of the camp. Older nyala hang around the camp to protect them from predators. The lodge aesthetic is Great Zimbabwe meets primitive luxury. Pafuri is a private safari lodge with 20 tented rooms connected to a communal deck and boma by a wooden walkway through an ancient riverine forest right next to the Luvuvhu. Six of the tents have

Brett Hilton-Barber

four beds, the rest have two. Each tent has its own intimate view over the river and the lush banks. The communal area is integrated into a grove of ebony trees and has an excellent viewing deck over the river. The first recorded "kill" at the camp was in July 2005 when a brown snake-eagle took a black mamba just in front of the communal deck to the awe and amazement of visitors waiting to be taken on a game drive. Pafuri Lodge offers morning and night game drives, trips to Lanner Gorge, walks, bush sleepovers and guided birding walks. There is no child restriction policy. Pafuri has its own airstrip, and charter flights from Johannesburg can be arranged.

Buffalo

Brett Hilton-Barber

Makuleke Reserve

The Makuleke Conservancy is the jewel of northern Kruger. The 24 000-ha private concession is located between the Luvuvhu River to the south and the Limpopo to the north. It is primarily a sandveld environment, distinguished by its central African vegetation, large alluvial flood plains and probably more animal and plant species diversity than anywhere else in Kruger.

Anti-poaching measures in 2003 and 2004 destroyed more than 1 000 snares and have eliminated illegal hunting. This has allowed the game to flourish. Lions, which were previously almost hunted out by cross-border poachers, have made a return.

Makuleke's big baobab

Brett Hilton-Barber

The area is a favourite winter grazing ground for elephant from Mozambique, Zimbabwe and elsewhere in Kruger. Leopard love the thick bush environment and prey on the nyala and impala that feed close to the river.

There is a large population of hippos and crocs at the confluence of the Limpopo and Luvuvhu rivers at Crooks' Corner. Among the more unusual sightings in the Makuleke Reserve are the eland and Sharpe's grysbok. The birding in the whole area is excellent, with specialities being the Pel's fishing-owl, black-throated wattle-eyed, orange-winged pytilia, African crowned eagle and racket-tailed roller.

One thing the Makuleke is not short of is baobab trees, which thrive in the basalt soils and dry, hot conditions. The baobabs give the Makuleke the feel of an ancient African landscape. Some of the bigger trees are more than 4 000 years old. They would already have been mature during the 13th and 17th

centuries when the Iron-Age Thulamela dynasty ruled the Limpopo Valley.

Baobabs are ecosystems on their own, supporting communal nests of red-billed buffalo-weavers and red-winged starlings as well as providing nesting holes and food – in the form of insects – for kingfishers, rollers, hornbills and mottled spinetails.

The Makuleke area is rich in human heritage. Co-author Lee Berger, who has been a heritage advisor to the Makuleke, discovered one of South Africa's earliest Stone-Age sites on the northern banks of the Luvuvhu near Crooks' Corner. Large stone hand axes from the site are believed to be approximately 1,5 million years old. The tool-makers were probably *Homo ergaster*, one of the earliest members of the genus Homo. This period in prehistory was a transitional one with a number of hominid species sharing the African savanna. The last of the gracile and robust Australopithecines (ape

Lanner Gorge

Gary van Rensberg

men) populations were still in existence but under pressure from the new, bigger-brained genus Homo, the first of our ancestors to master the art of stone tool-making. During the exploration of the Hutwini Hills, the low rolling ridge of hills south of the main Pafuri Gate road (H1-9), Berger and co-author Brett Hilton-Barber also discovered evidence of one of the world's oldest games – the maraba. On a flat rock, the professor found a "board" of regularly spaced carved-out holes. The game – a form of Chinese checkers using stones and holes, has been played in Africa since ancient times. Several other "boards" have since been found in the valleys on the lower slopes of Hutwini.

Hutwini also appears to have been an ancient burial ground with as yet unexcavated mounds found in the area. There are several rock art sites in shelters in the sandstone

 THE OUTPOST

The Outpost is a luxury lodge set high in sandstone hills overlooking the Luvuvhu River. Its design is contemporary, with a feel of steel and canvas and lots of space. It consists of 12 luxury stand-alone rooms, all with stunning views over the northern Kruger wilderness. The rooms are connected by a raised walkway. Besides the usual game drives and walks, The Outpost organises trips to Thulamela and Lanner Gorge along the Luvuvhu River.

The mighty Limpopo

The Limpopo River is Kruger's northern border as well as South Africa's frontier with Zimbabwe and, to the west, Botswana. It has its source near Johannesburg where it rises as the Braamfontein Spruit and the Crocodile River before joining Pienaar's River after Hartbeespoort Dam to become the Limpopo. The Limpopo zigzags in a 1 600-km arc across southern Africa before disgorging into the Indian Ocean at Xai-Xai in Mozambique. It was once one of Africa's mightiest rivers, larger possibly than the Congo River is today. However, a subcontinental tilt in the Angolan highlands aeons ago diverted much of its water into the Zambezi and Okavango Delta. In the next few million years the Limpopo is likely to become subsumed by the Luvuvhu River system which is geologically more active.

Limpopo River from Crooks' Corner

Brett Hilton-Barber

hills. The paintings depict human figures in some form of dance, and recognisable animals include elephant, eland and jackal. Berger and Hilton-Barber found stone tool manufacturing sites next to a narrow pass through the hills which appears to be an ancient animal highway. Early Stone-Age hunters probably used this pass to ambush game passing through. Among the animals they would have hunted are the extinct buffalo, *Pelarovus*, which had formidable horns up to three metres long from tip to tip.

The Makuleke Reserve has one of the most dramatic lookout points in all of Kruger. Lanner Gorge is a narrow, winding gorge where the Luvuvhu River has carved its course through sandstone cliffs over millions of years. The vantage point on the rocks high above the river offers sweeping views over northern Kruger and Venda, and the wonderful baobab-dominated sandveld. It was named by Kruger ranger Mike English because of the high density of lanner falcons nesting in the cliffs high above the water.

Lanner Gorge can be organised from Pafuri Camp, which also offers tours to the Thulamela Iron-Age kingdom site on the southern cliffs of the Luvuvhu. Lanner Gorge can only be accessed by guests staying at the two private lodges in the Makuleke Reserve.

During the past few centuries, the Limpopo served as a trading corridor into the southern African interior from Mozambique. Traders from the Middle East and Far East would stop off on the Mozambican coastline and barter or buy goods from traders who brought skins, salt and gold from the interior (see Thulamela on page 279). One of the main trading centres was the ancient city of Mapungubwe located at the junction of the Limpopo and Shashe rivers. Mapungubwe has been incorporated into a new Vhembe-Dongola Transfrontier Park which includes wilderness areas in north-western South Africa, south-western Zimbabwe and eastern Botswana.

Pafuri area landscape

Heinrich van den Berg

PART 3

WHAT TO DO IN KRUGER

Typical accommodation at Skukuza

Africa Imagery

Staying in Kruger

There are three broad categories of accommodation at Kruger:

- **Main Rest Camps:** all major SANParks rest camps have electricity, a shop, restaurant, petrol station, public phones, laundromats, braai and communal kitchen facilities as well as a first-aid centre. Many offer holiday programmes for children.
- **Luxury Lodges:** these are privately run five-star medium to small camps that are geared for comfort and indulgence, with excellent food, a high level of personal service and relaxation and beauty facilities. All are in concessions that are not accessible to self-drive vehicles;
- **Bush Camps:** these are SANParks smaller camps in more remote areas of Kruger; they are self-catering and do not have restaurants or shops. All units have braai facilities, fridges, cooking utensils and at least a two-plate stove. Some do not have electricity.

See page 314 for the Prime Origins Camp Quickguide. For all SANParks accommodation queries phone South African National Parks central reservations on (012) 428 9111. Luxury Lodge numbers and all other Kruger numbers are listed in this book on pages 314–317 and 320. Note that advance bookings are essential. Most luxury lodges do not take visitors who have not pre-booked, and most of the southern camps are booked up well in advance, particularly during school holidays.

PRIME ORIGINS TOP 5 GAME-VIEWING CAMPS IN KRUGER

- Skukuza
- Lower Sabie
- Satara
- Letaba
- Shingwedzi

Undoubtedly, the best way to experience the Kruger Park is to have one's own vehicle in which to travel around. This gives one the freedom to customise the trip according to individual requirements, be they to follow the game or to get away from everybody else. There are petrol stations at all the major camps and workshop facilities at Skukuza, Letaba and Shingwedzi. The following tips are tools for the journey.

Relax

A key to enjoying Kruger is to understand that time operates differently in the natural world. The rhythm of the bush is beyond human control and is dictated primarily by the cycle of seasons and the times of the day. During a 24-hour period, there are four main times of activity in the animal world – early morning, daytime, late afternoon and night. Much of the "action" happens either early in the morning or late in the afternoon and one should plan one's game drives around these times, and rest when the animals rest, which is during the middle of the day.

Choosing your Kruger experience

The three broad Kruger experiences are:
- Some of the best game viewing in Africa;
- Spectacular unspoilt landscapes;
- A sense of solitude in the wilderness.

It is possible to incorporate all three experiences into a single trip, but it's best to decide which of these is one's priority. For game viewing, plan your journey to include Skukuza, Lower Sabie, Tshokwane and Satara; for landscapes, Pretoriuskop to the rolling hills south of Skukuza; for isolation, head for the dirt roads of the mopaneveld in the northern part of the Park. Try to include riverine bush in any drive undertaken.

To maximise the Kruger experience, one must consciously adjust one's body clock and slow down. Remember, too, that the landscape is a fabric in which all the birds, plants and animals are like interwoven threads. Look for the points of connection.

Make use of get-out points

Make a point of stopping at the first get-out spot after entering the Park. Spend at least a quarter of an hour walking around, listening to the sounds, feeling the temperature, looking at the landscape. What trees are in flower? What kinds of birds are around? What is the weather doing? This is the best way to start adjusting one's body clock to get away from the rush of the outside world. While in the Park, plan journeys around get-out points – including picnic spots and camps. It breaks up the time spent in the confines of a vehicle and sensitises one to the different environments and scenery.

Africa Imagery

Shirimantanga get-out point near Skukuza

Water holes

In San (Bushman) mythology, the water hole is symbolically a midway point between the camp and the hunting ground. It is a place where friends are often found and enemies meet unexpectedly. It is the midway point between the water that falls as rain (representing the energy of the Creator), and the water that runs in the ground (the underworld). In short, the water hole is a place where things happen. Most kills in Kruger happen in the vicinity of water holes.

Africa Imagery

GAME-VIEWING TIPS

Step 1	Identify the species
Step 2	Determine group composition
Step 3	Try to work out the ages and sexes of the animals
Step 4	Watch the behaviour to understand the group dynamic

Within a group of animals of the same species, the most interesting relationships to watch are:

Adult males with everybody else	Asserting dominance and looking for mating opportunities
Juveniles with each other	The unselfish abandon of the young at play
Adult females with offspring	The most tender moments in the African bush

Drive slowly

There is one uncontested truth about enjoying Kruger – the slower one drives, the more one sees. Avoid the temptation to go fast when nothing much appears to be happening in the surrounding bush. Animals blend naturally into their environment and are missed easily if one is speeding. One should allow an hour for every 25km of road to take into account sightings and stops.

Stop at water holes

Stop at water holes, on river banks or at shade points overlooking watercourses, and switch off the engine. Wait and watch. Water plays a central role in governing animal relationships and, often, the most rewarding moments in the bush are those spent witnessing the passing pageant of animal life around water sources. Many kills happen at water holes as animals are at their most vulnerable when they are drinking.

Ditch the "checklist mentality"

The chances of seeing the "Big Five" in one single trip to Kruger are not good. One shouldn't put oneself through the stress of trying to do so. The lower one's expectations, the more one is likely to see. The beauty of Kruger is that it allows one to experience the totality and interconnectedness of the natural world. Good sightings should be events that punctuate one's experience of the Park rather than an end in themselves.

Get creative about impala

Usually, there's no shortage of impala in Kruger. One may see up to 30 different impala herds in a day – start differentiating between them. Are they bachelor herds of males or harems of ewes? How many are there? Are there young about? Are the antelope huddled closely together, which often indicates their awareness of danger? Or are they spread out? Are the impala grazing or browsing? What other animals are with them?

Use camps as education centres

There is a wealth of information in every camp, from the names of trees to environmental and archival displays. Each bit of information enhances one's subsequent drive. Camps are a good source of information as to what to look out

ESSENTIAL KRUGER

The tools for the Kruger experience are:

- Binoculars
- Insect repellent
- Torch
- Warm jacket for game drives (even in summer)
- Bottled water and snacks
- Camera and film (if you enjoy photography)
- Map
- Litter bag

All these items are available for purchase at the Park's shops.

for in an area. Most camps have at least one sightings board which can help one plan one's route in the direction of the last observed kill. Remember that lions will probably be at a kill hours after it has happened and scavengers may linger in the area for days.

Brett Hilton-Barber

Impala male

Hippo males in territorial clash

Nigel Dennis

"Any animal you watch is likely to be eating or searching for food, resting, scanning its surroundings to detect enemies or friends, or interacting socially, aggressively or sexually with others of its kind. Herbivores spend half to two-thirds of their time just eating and processing the large quantities of plant food they need to meet their bodies' growth and energy requirements. Carnivores avoid much of this drudgery by eating the herbivores; the high-protein diet gives them more free time, which they devote largely to loafing – or conserving energy, as ecologists and physiologists see it."

Richard Estes – *The Safari Companion, A Guide to Watching African Mammals.*

Respect wildlife and other humans

Most people have come to Kruger to get away from the noisy outside world and to experience African wildlife at its finest. Don't interfere with animals either by feeding them or driving too close to them. Animals always have right of way in crossing the road. At kills or sightings where there are several cars, one should take one's place in the queue, switch off the engine and enable everyone else to enjoy the experience, too. Human noise compromises the "wilderness" experience – especially jarring is music, the sound of cellphones and loud talking. One must stay in one's vehicle unless stopping at official get-out points – animals are used to vehicles, which have an accepted silhouette, whereas a human shape signifies that of a predator, which will cause alarm.

Share the experience

Ask people at camps or get-out points whether they have had any special sightings, and don't feel shy about sharing one's own experiences. Everyone is in Kruger for more or less the same reason, and there is a sense of camaraderie between people that doesn't exist outside the Park. Information gleaned from other visitors may be helpful in planning the next part of one's journey.

Brett Hilton-Barber

Animals have right of way in Kruger

Top 10 Kruger Drives

The following 10 drives are the authors' personal favourites and are placed in no particular order. They are chosen because of the beauty of the landscape, the likelihood of good game viewing – and birding – and the sense of place they convey.

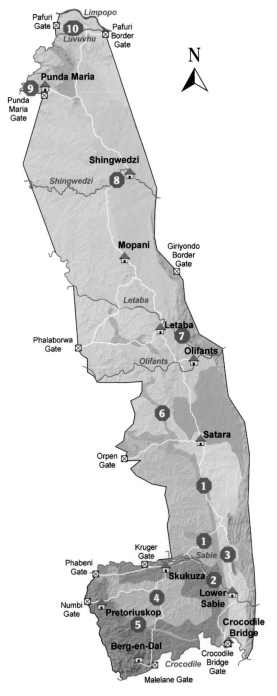

N

SKUKUZA TO SATARA
(H1-2, H1-3) 93km

The best chance of seeing lions in Kruger is on the Skukuza-Satara tar road (H1-2, H1-3) which climbs out of the Sabie River basin into the central grasslands. There are often elephant to be seen in the mixed woodlands at the N'watindlopfu River crossing and at the trio of water holes nearby.

A place to stretch the legs is at the Kruger Tablets get-out point. Tshokwane is roughly halfway between Skukuza and Satara and the only stop along the road where food and refreshments are available.

The Tshokwane area is usually good for game viewing because the convergence of mixed woodland, pockets of grassland, riverine bush and the Lebombo mountains attract a wide variety of animal species. The central grasslands begin north of Tshokwane. This is big-game territory with the largest herds of grazers in the Park and the big cats that feed on them. The grasslands around Satara are renowned for buffalo and lion sightings. Most of the big raptors are to be found here, too.

Allow at least five hours for this drive, including a stop-off at Tshokwane. (See page 149)

1. SKUKUZA TO SATARA 2. SKUKUZA TO LOWER SABIE
3. LOWER SABIE TO TSHOKWANE 4. MALELANE TO
SKUKUZA 5. VOORTREKKER ROAD 6. TIMBAVATI ROAD
7. OLIFANTS LOOP AND THE RIVER ROAD TO LETABA AND
ENGELHARD DAM 8. AROUND SHINGWEDZI – RED ROCKS
LOOP, KANNIEDOOD DAM AND MPHONGOLO LOOP
9. MAHONIE LOOP 10. LUVUVHU RIVER DRIVES

Skukuza to Lower Sabie
(H4-1) 46km

This road follows the Sabie River from the thorn thickets and mixed woodlands around Skukuza into the more open grasslands of south-eastern Kruger. It is a popular road for tourists and animals.

There are reputedly more leopards per square kilometre in this riverine bush than anywhere else in South Africa. The area around Skukuza is good for lion and hyaena sightings.

Nkuhlu Picnic Site is the only stop-off along this road and the terraced banks offer good views over the river and its resident hippo and croc populations. The N'watimhiri Causeway is a good detour off the main road. Larger herds of grazers become more evident closer to Lower Sabie as the bush becomes more open. Look out for cheetah and rhino in the thorn thickets closer to Lower Sabie Camp.

Birders should stop off at Sunset Dam, which is one of the main water-bird sighting spots in the south-east.

Allow two-and-a-half hours for this drive, including a stop-off at Nkuhlu. (See page 149)

Lower Sabie to Tshokwane
(H10) 40km

This is one of the most scenic drives in Kruger as it incorporates the Lebombo, giving wonderful views over the eastern grasslands. The road traverses a variety of habitats linked by stretches of grassland where one may see cheetah, lion, hyaena and the large herds of grazers they hunt.

The distinctive outline of Muntshe Hill stands out starkly above the lowveld. Mlondozi Dam lookout point offers good birding and views over the Lebombo and the eastern plains.

Some 25km north of Lower Sabie, the H10 hits the Lebombo and rises up above the grasslands. Nkumbe Hill (394m) is one of the best viewsites in Kruger. The road then descends quite rapidly into the mixed woodlands of the N'waswitsontso River basin where there are often elephant to be seen.

The area around Tshokwane is good for lions and other big game.

Recommended time, two-and-a-half hours, including stops at Mlondozi, Nkumbe and Orpen. (See page 149)

Brett Hilton-Barber

Stream crossings are often good game-viewing spots

Hyaena near Afsaal

Africa Imagery

VOORTREKKER ROAD
(H2-2) 35km

The Voortrekker Road from Pretoriuskop to Afsaal descends from the foothills of the lower escarpment. In the 19th century, transport riders used this route which was romanticised in the book *Jock of the Bushveld*. Near Ship Mountain there is a turn-off to where Jock is believed to have been born.

The dust road follows a line of sweetveld grazing through the sourveld of south-western Kruger so there is a better than average chance of good sightings of rarer game such as eland, white rhino and sable antelope.

There is a take-away restaurant and shop at Afsaal which has a picnic spot under a giant jackal-berry tree.

Allow two hours for this route, as it should be taken very slowly. (See page 115)

MALELANE TO SKUKUZA
(H3) 64km

The Malelane-Skukuza road rolls gently through the mixed woodlands of south-central Kruger, rising and dropping through a series of low ridges and shallow valleys that form the catchment area of the Crocodile and Sabie river systems.

The Malelane area is good for white rhino and many of the other grazers. Herd size is smaller here than in the eastern grasslands.

There are almost always animals in the more stunted veld south of Afsaal as the grazing here is particularly nutritious and hyaenas are regularly seen. Meals and refreshments are available at Afsaal.

Look out for lions between Afsaal and Skukuza. A good view site is Mathekenyane (Granokop). The road then descends gently into the Sabie River valley thorn thickets around Skukuza.

Allow for three-and-a-half hours, including a refreshment break at Afsaal. (See page 115)

TIMBAVATI ROAD
(S39) 59km

The dusty Timbavati Road follows the Timbavati River northwards, joining up with the main Satara road near Olifants Camp. The dust road and river wind through a mosaic of different landscapes in the game-rich grasslands of central Kruger.

Leeubron is a good water hole for lion sightings as they are attracted by the herds of impala, wildebeest, zebra and other grazers.

Cold beverages and firewood can be bought at Timbavati Picnic Spot but there is no take-way restaurant or shop. Interesting stops are Ratelpan, the Piet Grobler Dam and Roodewal Water Hole. Kudu, giraffe, elephant and other browsers are usually seen along this drive.

Allow three hours, including a stop at Timbavati. (See page 183)

Most of Kruger's elephants are found in the north

Africa Imagery

OLIFANTS LOOP AND THE RIVER ROAD TO LETABA AND ENGELHARD DAM
(S92, S91, H1-4, H8, S44, S46, H1-6, S62) 81km

The Olifants River traditionally marks the divide between southern and northern Kruger. The loop road from Olifants Camp south over the low-level bridge at Balule is heartland Olifants rugged veld. Unsurprisingly, there are usually plenty of elephant along the river edges of the Olifants. N'wamanzi get-out point offers good views. The dusty river road from Olifants to Letaba is a pleasant drive but game viewing is a matter of luck as the mopaneveld does not have the same carrying capacity as southern Kruger.

Engelhard Dam is known for its birding. One is likely to stop often along this route so allow four hours for a full experience, including a meal at either Olifants or Letaba Camps which have wonderful views from the restaurant areas. (See page 211)

AROUND SHINGWEDZI – RED ROCKS LOOP, KANNIEDOOD DAM AND MPHONGOLO LOOP
(S52, S56, S50) 170km round trip

The riverine vegetation and the water sustain large populations of elephant around Shingwedzi, where most of Kruger's largest tuskers have been recorded.

There are three compelling drives through the alluvial flood plains around Shingwedzi Camp. They are the Red Rocks Loop, Kanniedood Dam and the Mphongolo Loop. It is possible to do them all in a nine-hour day, but it is preferable to split them up over two days.

Red Rocks Loop follows the Shingwedzi River upstream for approximately 30km to the Tshanga Lookout Point and returns on the opposite river bank.

The S50 past Kanniedood Dam is a good game-viewing drive. There are often nyala and kudu browsing in the riverine bush and one should keep a lookout for leopard.

Lion

Africa Imagery

Mphongolo Loop, north of Shingwedzi, supports large populations of elephant and buffalo and the area is reportedly good for lion. There are wonderful riverine trees along this dust road. (See page 241)

MAHONIE LOOP
(S99) 28km

Mahonie (Mahogany) Loop around Punda Maria Rest Camp is a road for Kruger aficionados. It is a botanist's delight in that the dust road runs in a broad arc through sandveld foothills that support an intriguing mixture of trees and shrubs. The dust road is not a busy game road in terms of animal numbers. The more likely animals to be seen are kudu, impala, warthog and elephant. However, it is a road for rarities – such as Sharpe's grysbok.

The road has a good reputation among birders because it falls within the transition zone between subtropical and tropical birding environments and so there is a good chance of seeing species not normally seen in South Africa. This drive may seem a relatively short distance, but allow at least two hours in which to do it very slowly – best done at sunset or sunrise. (See page 261)

LUVUVHU RIVER DRIVES
(S63 and S64) approx 40km

The definitive far northern Kruger experience is the Luvuvhu River drive incorporating the Luvuvhu River Bridge, Pafuri Picnic Site, the road to Crooks' Corner and Nyala Drive.

The Luvuvhu River valley has extraordinary clusters of forests and river vantage points and no shortage of crocodiles that sun themselves on the sandbanks. There is a high traffic of water birds and raptors. There are usually nyala, kudu, impala and baboons in the riverine forests dominated by nyala trees. Most of the leopard in northern Kruger are to be found in these tropical river forests. Along the S64 there are dramatic sandstone koppies which are the site of the ancient Iron-Age kingdom of Thulamela.

Pafuri Picnic Site is a good braai area beneath the tall ana trees (cold drinks and firewood are for sale). Marvel at the February 2000 flood high-level mark which is recorded on the ablution blocks.

Although the road distance along the river is quite short, one can spend a whole day in this area and still not have enough. If under time pressure, allow four hours. (See page 261)

Organised game drives

There's no beating the freedom of driving oneself around Kruger. However, to deepen one's experience of the bush, the visitor should take advantage of the guided game drives offered by almost all of Kruger's camps. The best option is to go for the early-morning or evening drives. These are recommended because they enable the visitor to experience the bush during the transition zone between day and night, which is when there is a lot of animal hunting activity, and also because one has a guide on hand to explain elements of the environment and to answer any questions.

This is also a good time for spotting the smaller carnivores such as genet and civet which are hard to spot during the middle of the day. The sound of the bush is different at night, which is a time of both danger and respite. The best time to book for a camp-organised game drive is when checking into camp. The receptionist will be able to provide costs and other details and ensure the availability of seats for the preferred outing. Remember to take warm clothing on early-morning and evening drives as it can get chilly at this time, even at the height of summer.

Africa Imagery

The best organised game drives are early morning or early evening

Hikers on the Wolhuter Trail,
south-western Kruger

Heinrich van den Berg

Walking in Kruger

Most of the private and public camps in Kruger offer guided walks of a few hours through the bush. The early-morning walks are the best, and usually include breakfast. Bookings and payments may be made at the reception desk at each camp.

However, one of the best ways of experiencing the African bush is to participate in one of the organised overnight walking trails departing from a number of outlying wilderness camps. Hikers are accompanied by armed and experienced rangers. Each trail has a base camp, most of which have rustic, two-bed huts and basic ablution facilities consisting of reed-walled showers and flush toilets. There is a covered lapa which serves as dining and socialising area where simple meals are provided. There are three days of hiking with an average distance of 15km to 20km a day, with walkers returning to the base camp each

evening. There is a maximum capacity of eight people per hike. Participants must be reasonably fit and be between the ages of 12 and 60. No radios are permitted. Wilderness trails do not operate between November and February because of the heat. Hikers must check into the camp nearest the hiking trail (which are detailed below) before 15h30 on the day before the hike is booked for. They are then transported to the wilderness camp. Walks can be booked through central reservations at Skukuza at (013) 735 5139.

There have been three recorded incidents in Kruger's history where guides on walking trails have had to shoot animals to protect hikers. In none of the cases were any hikers injured. In 1983, ranger Trevor Dearlove's party came across three lions on a buffalo carcass during a walk on the Wolhuter Trail. The group was caught by surprise when an aggressive white rhino unexpectedly emerged from behind an anthill. It lowered its head and charged at the bewildered hikers, but Dearlove's reflexes were quick enough to raise his rifle and pull the trigger. The rhino collapsed in its tracks, 10 metres from the group. In the other incidents, a ranger shot dead another aggressive white rhino on the Bushman Trail and a charging buffalo was killed by a ranger on the Nyalaland Trail.

Wolhuter Trail

Situated between Berg-en-Dal and Pretoriuskop, the Wolhuter Trail takes one through the dramatic granite koppies and some riverine forests of the southern botanical biome in Kruger. It is named after the father-and-son team of Harry and Henry Wolhuter, who ran the southern section of Kruger for many years. There is an attractive dam at the base camp. A feature of the trail is the regular spotting of white rhino and reedbuck. Trailists meet at Berg-en-Dal.

Bushman Trail

The Bushman Trail Camp is north-west of Berg-en-Dal in a secluded valley close to the south-western boundary of the Park. Although it's only seven kilometres from the Wolhuter trail, it is an entirely different experience, focusing on rock art and other items of archaeological interest. Kruger has a rich, but largely unknown rock-art tradition that goes back several centuries. The landscape consists of dramatic granite hills and, because the walks are at a higher altitude than the rest of Kruger, there are many good views over the bush. Hikers meet at Berg-en-Dal.

Napi Trail

Napi Trail Camp is in the mixed bushwillow and knob-thorn woodlands between Ship Mountain and Skukuza and is well positioned in lush riverine bush at the confluence of the Napi and Biyamiti streams. The original

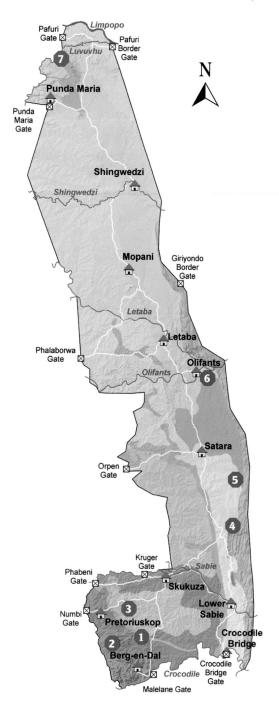

1. Wolhuter; 2. Bushman; 3. Napi; 4. Metsi-Metsi;
5. Sweni; 6. Olifants; 7. Nyalaland

Hikers studying spoor

Africa Imagery

SWENI TRAIL

Sweni Trail Camp is in the lightly wooded grasslands east of Satara close to the Lebombo. The trail camp overlooks the Sweni stream and provides inspiring views over the surrounding marula and knob-thorn savanna. This area is known for its high densities of predators and the animals they hunt. The Sweni Trail has a good reputation for extensive raptor sightings. Sweni hikers are fetched from Satara.

OLIFANTS TRAIL

Scenically, this is one of the most beautiful trails as it includes stretches of riverine forest, open savanna and the Lebombo Mountains. There are wonderful bush views from the base camp, which is on the southern bank of the Olifants River, some four kilometres upstream from where it joins the Letaba River. Part of the trail winds through the Lebombo foothills. The trail has a good reputation for game viewing, particularly lion. Hikers meet at Letaba.

NYALALAND TRAIL

This is the best trail for birding enthusiasts and botanists because of the variety of species found in the sandveld. Hikers meet at Punda Maria and are taken to the base camp north of Punda on the banks of the Matsaringwe stream near the Luvuvhu River. The walk takes one through a forest of baobabs and the northern botanical biome and includes the Makahanja ruins overlooking the Luvuvhu River. There are some spectacular views from the sandstone koppies, the most dramatic being the magnificent Lanner Gorge. There are some fossil sites on the trail. Hikers are fetched from Punda Maria.

camp was destroyed by fire and the new Napi A-frame huts have en-suite ablution facilities and offer wonderful views over the riverine bush. The walks wind through the undulating, picturesque woodlands and granite hills. Rangers virtually guarantee sightings of white rhino and buffalo, while elephant and lion are also commonly seen on this trail. Hikers meet at Skukuza.

METSI-METSI TRAIL

Metsi-Metsi is situated near the Lebombo behind N'wamuriwa Hill, north-east of Tshokwane. The base camp consists of A-frame huts nestled at the foot of the mountain overlooking a small water hole. A hide provides the ideal place to view many species of birds and mammals at close range. The landscape varies from undulating savanna to rocky gorges and ravines. The N'waswitsontso River, being one of the few permanent sources of water during the dry winter months, attracts an abundance of game – especially elephant. A great variety of wildlife, including black rhino and large predators, can be found here. Hikers meet at Skukuza.

Other walks in Kruger

RHINO WALKING SAFARIS

Rhino Walking Safaris offers luxury hikes in the 12 000-ha Mutlumuvi Private Concession 20km north of Skukuza. The hike takes a maximum of eight people, and no children younger than 12 are allowed. The three-night/four-day guided walk begins from the upmarket Rhino Post Game Lodge and follows elephant and rhino trails through the knob-thorn acacia savanna to Plains Camp which overlooks the Timbiteni Plain. Hikers need take only refreshments as all luggage is transported to Plains Camp, which is an eight-bed luxury tented camp with a well-stocked Africana library and a plunge pool. After overnighting at Plains Camp, hikers are taken on a number of paths through the bush with the option of spending the night at a rougher "sleep-out" camp in a raised platform in the trees.

For bookings, contact (011) 467 7407 or e-mail *alex@hartleys.co.za*.

The Rhino Post Lodge telephone number is 083 631 4956.

OLIFANTS RIVER BACKPACKERS TRAIL

The Olifants River Backpackers Trail is a special three-day hike designed for the fitter outdoor enthusiast. In fact, a prerequisite of the trail is a medical certificate showing the participant is in good health. Hikers have to be between the ages of 16 and 65. A maximum of eight participants per trail is allowed and the party is accompanied by two armed guides. The trail is an intense 42-kilometre walk along the broken hills and thorn thickets of the upper section of the Olifants River, upstream of the high-water bridge. It includes some of the finest riverine forest in Kruger with very old specimens of matumi, tree fuchsia, sycamore fig, Natal mahogany, mopane, leadwood and tamboti trees.

Hikers have to carry all their own gear including food, tent, sleeping bag and any other equipment needed during the four-day, three-night experience. Bookings and enquiries for the Olifants Backpackers Trail through SANParks Central Reservations on (012) 426 5117.

Brett Hilton-Barber

White rhino

Birding in Kruger

Kruger in its entirety is good for birding with the possible exception of the shrub mopaneveld in the north-east. Northern Kruger is renowned for its birding because of the number of tropical birds one sees, while the Lower Sabie and Crocodile Bridge areas in the south are also particularly rewarding. Generally, camps and water holes are the best places for birdwatching, but the richest birding experiences are probably on the guided wilderness trails. Among the most visible raptors are the steppe buzzard, bateleur, jackal buzzard and fish-eagle and the colourful species include lilac-breasted rollers, bee-eaters, kingfishers, weavers and starlings. Water birds abound along river banks and water holes, while the grey go-away-birds (loeries) and hornbills are a common sight in the bush. Essential equipment is a pair of good binoculars (7 x 35 and 8 x 48 are good).

White-fronted bee-eater

Nigel Dennis

PRIME ORIGINS' BEST BIRDING CAMPS

1. PAFURI 2. LOWER SABIE 3. SKUKUZA 4. SATARA

5. PUNDA MARIA

Taking young children into Kruger

The Kruger experience is not often appreciated by children under the age of eight, mainly because of the length of time one is stuck in a car and the limited opportunities for playing outside. For this reason, the south is more child-friendly than the north in that the distances are not so great between get-out points, the landscape is varied and the game more plentiful. Because of the hazard of malaria in summer months (October to March), it is not advisable to take children under the age of five into the Park.

If one is taking children to Kruger, it's best to choose camps which are less than an hour's drive into the Park. The most recommended are:

- Lower Sabie
- Berg-en-Dal
- Pretoriuskop
- Skukuza
- Orpen

do short game drives from the camp also make it conducive to taking small children. It has a large swimming pool set among the granite boulders, and an educational walk – the Sable Trail.

For entertainment value, the most child-friendly activities are offered at Skukuza where there are film shows and special educational activities geared for children. Skukuza has a large swimming pool and is geared to serving food fast for hungry little mouths. Toys and children's activities are available at the Skukuza shop.

In the north, the most child-friendly camps are Satara and Letaba because of their size and the fact that they are in good game-viewing areas which will alleviate the boredom children often experience during game drives. Satara and Orpen both offer specialised drives for children. The guided tours at Masorini archaeological site close to Phalaborwa Gate are also suitable for children.

Crocodile Bridge is probably the best gate to enter if you have young children. This is because of the likelihood of seeing large numbers of game fairly soon after entering the Park and the fact that it is only about an hour's drive to Lower Sabie which, like most camps, is a child-friendly environment.

Berg-en-Dal is child-friendly in that it has large, rolling lawns, a swimming pool and an educational trail in the camp – the Rhino Trail. The relative coolness of Pretoriuskop and the fact that one can

Brett Hilton-Barber

SANParks

Eating in Kruger

Traditionally the Kruger Park has not been associated with sophisticated culinary fare. South Africans are generally a nation of meat-eaters, and the standard evening meal in the Park is a braai (barbecue) under the stars. Sitting around a campfire, watching the flames and listening to the sounds of the night certainly adds to the ambience of the meal. Meat, vegetables, firewood and braai equipment are usually available at all shops in the Park and an outside cooking area is a feature of accommodation in the camps.

If you prefer not to cook your own meal, the main rest camps all have licensed restaurants and convenience food shops. You can't go too badly wrong by ordering a meat dish at a camp restaurant, but vegetarian and more complicated foods may be inconsistent in their presentation. Most of the restaurants offer venison – so, after watching animals during the day, you can eat them at night.

Many of the camps offer bush braais as part of an evening game drive. These are highly recommended.

If you can afford to be choosy about your food, the best meals are to be had at the private lodges. Most have internationally trained chefs who can transform basic indigenous recipes into stylish servings, and they have an array of offerings for more cosmopolitan palates. Private lodge restaurants are available only to patrons booked in at the camps.

Apart from Tshokwane and Afsaal, most of the picnic sites do not sell food but do have firewood for sale and gas cookers for hire.

Bush braai

Africa Imagery

Photography in Kruger

Despite the predominance of digital cameras, colour print film is available at most shops in Kruger. If you need slide film, it's best to purchase it before going to Kruger as it is increasingly rarely available. Digital video tapes are on sale at most shops.

According to renowned wildlife photographer Nigel Dennis, the following tips should be borne in mind:

- A camera with flash and a 70-200mm zoom lens is generally sufficient and a 100 ASA film is a good all-round choice for Kruger.
- On clear days, the best times for taking pictures are the first two hours of sunlight after dawn and the last two hours of daylight before sunset. The

Elephant

Heinrich van den Berg

light then is soft, and gives pictures a "glow". On overcast days, the opposite is true, with the best shooting time being from mid-morning to mid-afternoon. Using a flash on overcast days brings the subject up from the background.
- Turn off your engine before taking pictures as the vibrations can cause

images to blur. Likewise, when using telephoto lenses, make sure you have support for your camera so that your grip is steady.
- If you get close to animals, don't rush the pictures. The chances are that, if you're patient and persistent, you will get good-quality photographs.

PRIME ORIGINS' TOP WATER HOLES FOR PHOTOGRAPHY

- Sunset Dam near Lower Sabie
- Duke's Water Hole near Lower Sabie
- Girivana near Satara
- Leeubron near Timbavati
- N'watindlopfu between Skukuza and Tshokwane
- Bangu near Olifants
- Engelhard Dam near Letaba
- Kanniedood Dam near Shingwedzi
- Matjulu near Berg-en-Dal

PRIME ORIGINS' MOST PHOTOGENIC DRIVES IN KRUGER

- Crocodile Bridge to Lower Sabie (H4-2)
- Lower Sabie to Tshokwane (H10) – particularly Nkumbe lookout point
- Lower Sabie to Skukuza (H4-1)
- The scenic route around Berg-en-Dal (S110)
- The Fayi Loop east of Pretoriuskop (S14)
- Skukuza to Tshokwane (H1-2)
- The Timbavati Road (S39)
- The Balule Road south of Olifants

Skukuza shop

Africa Imagery

Shopping in Kruger

Shopping in Kruger has improved dramatically since the Parks Shops retail concession was awarded to a private-sector consortium led by Tourvest subsidiary Tigers Eye. The flagship stores are at Skukuza and Lower Sabie, which both stock a wide range of merchandise, from essential goods to luxury items, including souvenirs and curios, camera film and binoculars. Anything one needs for a pleasant stay in Kruger can be purchased here. There is a convenience store at Crocodile Bridge Camp that offers take-aways and snacks.

OPERATED BY THE PARKS SHOP

Skukuza	(013) 735 4126
Lower Sabie	(013) 735 0171
Pretoriuskop	(013) 735 5729
Berg-en-Dal	(013) 735 5729
Crocodile Bridge	(013) 735 6012
Satara	(013) 735 6328
Olifants	(013) 735 5883
Letaba	(013) 735 6314
Mopani	(013) 735 6530
Orpen	(013) 735 6079
Afsaal	(013) 735 8913

OPERATED BY THE COMPASS GROUP

Shingwedzi	(013) 735 6836
Punda Maria	(013) 735 5796
Tshokwane	(013) 735 5903
Nkuhlu	(013) 735 8900

Most of the private lodges have small shops where a limited range of jewellery, souvenir and gift items, crafts and curios are sold.

Conferences

Conference facilities are available from Skukuza (two venues), Berg-en-Dal and Shingwedzi. Bateleur and Letaba can cater for small groups.

For details on capacity, resources and bookings, phone (012) 428 9111 or fax (012) 343 0905.

Internet connectivity

Internet access is available at Skukuza and Satara.

Golf

Skukuza course is the only golfing facility in Kruger itself. It is a 72-par, nine-hole, 18-tee course a few kilometres from Skukuza on the road to Paul Kruger Gate. Built originally for Skukuza staff in 1972, it is now open to the public. The course is as close-to-nature as one gets, with beautiful bushveld trees, wonderful birdlife and views over Lake Panic. The course is not fenced in, so a round of golf often provides animal sightings. A lion once killed a buffalo on the first green and on another occasion, a honeymoon couple's golf game was interrupted by a pack of wild dogs chasing an impala across the course. Parks staff, however, do keep an eye on the area to keep dangerous animals away, and no golfers have ever been harmed by wild animals. Nonetheless, an indemnity form must be signed before teeing off. One should book early to avoid disappointment, and enquire about green fees when making reservations. Standard golf dress code applies. No caddies are available but there are golf trolleys for hire. The course is closed on Mondays. Tee-off times between 07h00 and 11h30 Sundays to Fridays.

Contact details (013) 735 5543
skukuzagolf@parks-sa.co.za

Africa Imagery

Skukuza golf course

4x4 Adventure Trails in Kruger

Day Trails

- Madlabantu (Man-eater); Pretoriuskop area; 42km through terminalia woodland and along the Nsikazi River into Big Five and rhino territory;
- Mananga (Wilderness) near Satara; 48km through knob-thorn, marula savanna in the central grasslands; many grazers; Big Five sightings, especially cheetah;
- Nonokani (Drive Slowly) close to Phalaborwa Gate; 46km from Masorini

Picnic Site south through mopane and bushwillow woodlands to Reenvoël Dam and then along the Olifants River back to Sable Dam;

- Northern Plains; Shingwedzi to Pafuri; 49km; begins at Babalala picnic site and goes east through mopane shrubveld and then into the baobabs of the sandveld;

Access is limited to six vehicles per day and a minimum of two per group is recommended in case of breakdowns. Conditions on

Lebombo 4 x 4 trail

Africa Imagery

the trails are sometimes challenging and, in extreme wet conditions, they may be closed down altogether. Permits are obtainable at the nearest camp or gate to the trail. There is no pre-booking. Drivers must start on the trail before 11h00 and be self-sufficient for the day as there are no ablution or other facilities available on any of the trails. Kruger officials recommend that each vehicle should have:

- At least five litres of drinking water;
- Enough food for three meals;
- A GPS instrument;
- A cellphone;
- First-aid kit;
- Fire extinguisher;
- Rubbish bag.

Only 4x4s with low-range capacity are permitted on the trails and drivers must stick to the designated routes.

LEBOMBO TRAIL

This is a five-day trail along the Lebombo from Komatipoort to Pafuri. The trail can accommodate up to eight vehicles at a time and all trips are under the supervision of armed rangers. The trail traverses the entire length of Kruger, crossing the Lebombo several times and snaking in and out of more than 30 different habitats. There are no facilities available on the trail and all vehicles must be self-sufficient. Bookings can be done through SANParks head office at (012) 426 5117; for further information see *www.parks-sa.co.za*

Lebombo 4x4 trail

Africa Imagery

Mountain Biking

Olifants is currently the only camp in Kruger to offer guided mountain bike excursions. The camp offers morning, afternoon and full-day rides with two armed rangers through the Olifants Rugged Veld of northern Kruger. Bikes, backpacks, snacks, water and helmets are provided. Each ride takes a maximum of six participants.

Book through Olifants Camp: (013) 735 6606/7

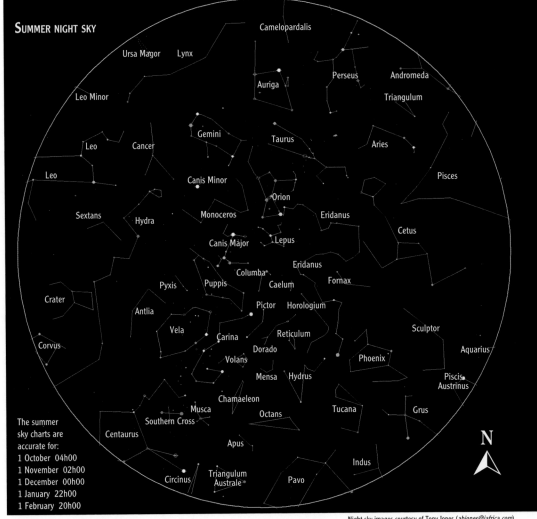

SUMMER NIGHT SKY

Camelopardalis

Ursa Major   Lynx

Perseus   Andromeda

Auriga

Triangulum

Leo Minor

Gemini   Taurus   Aries

Pisces

Leo   Cancer

Leo

Canis Minor

Orion

Sextans   Hydra   Monoceros   Eridanus

Cetus

Canis Major   Lepus

Columba   Eridanus

Crater   Pyxis   Puppis   Caelum   Fornax

Antlia   Pictor   Horologium

Vela   Reticulum   Sculptor

Carina

Corvus   Dorado   Aquarius

Volans

Mensa   Hydrus   Phoenix

Piscis
Austrinus

Chamaeleon

Musca   Octans   Tucana   Grus

The summer
sky charts are
accurate for:
1 October 04h00
1 November 02h00
1 December 00h00
1 January 22h00
1 February 20h00

Southern Cross   Centaurus   Apus

Indus

Circinus   Triangulum
Australe   Pavo

N

Night sky images courtesy of Tony Jones (*abjones@iafrica.com*)

Stargazing

One of the joys of Kruger is to be able to study the night sky without the interference of city lights. It is a humbling experience to consider one's insignificance in the face of the enormity of the universe. Our sun is part of the Milky Way galaxy, a small part of the ever-expanding universe, The Milky Way is a loose celestial spiral galaxy consisting of an estimated 100 000 million stars. Scientists estimate that it would take 100 000 years to travel at the speed of light from one end of our galaxy to the other – if one can indeed

talk about the "end" of galaxies. Our sun – which is an estimated 32 000 light years from the galactic centre of the Milky Way, rotates once around our galaxy every 225 million years. Olifants camp has introduced a night-time game drive that includes a study of the southern night sky through powerful telescopes. The experience has been dubbed the "Big Five, Big Sky Experience". The star-gazing trips are offered every day from late afternoon. Book through Olifants Camp (013) 735 6606/7

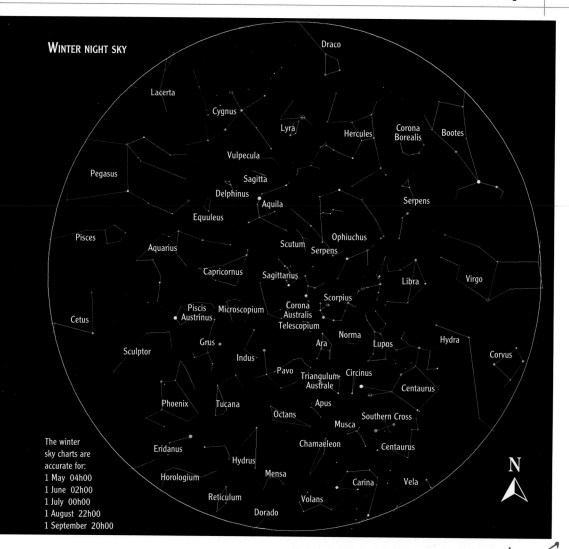

WINTER NIGHT SKY

Draco
Lacerta
Cygnus
Lyra
Hercules
Corona Borealis
Bootes
Vulpecula
Sagitta
Serpens
Delphinus
Aquila
Pegasus
Equuleus
Pisces
Ophiuchus
Aquarius
Scutum
Serpens
Capricornus
Sagittarius
Libra
Virgo
Piscis Austrinus
Microscopium
Corona Australis
Scorpius
Cetus
Telescopium
Norma
Hydra
Sculptor
Grus
Ara
Lupus
Corvus
Indus
Pavo
Triangulum Australe
Circinus
Centaurus
Phoenix
Tucana
Apus
Octans
Southern Cross
Eridanus
Chamaeleon
Centaurus
Hydrus
Musca
Horologium
Mensa
Carina
Vela
Reticulum
Volans
Dorado

The winter sky charts are accurate for:
1 May 04h00
1 June 02h00
1 July 00h00
1 August 22h00
1 September 20h00

N

Lonely hunter of the night sky

There is an old San hunting legend concerning the stars. There was a proud hunter (Aldebaran) who had seven sisters (the Pleiades). Aldebaran was a confident hunter who only needed one arrow to shoot his target. One day his hungry wives implored him to go out hunting and not to return empty-handed. Aldebaran came accross three zebra (Orion's belt), and shot at them. However, his hunting skill let him down and he missed all three animals. What was worse was that he could not retrieve his single arrow as it had landed near

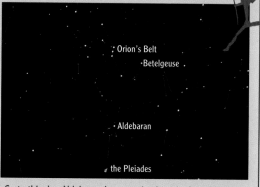

Orion's Belt
Betelgeuse
Aldebaran
the Pleiades

a huge lion (Betelgeuse) that had been stalking the zebra. So to this day Aldebaran has remained out in the cold night sky, too afraid to return home without food and too afraid to try and retrieve his arrow from the feet of the lion.

Lion

Michael Poliza

PART 4

QUICKGUIDES

Camp Quickguide

Camp	Size	Priv	Accom	Camping	Shop
Balule	Small	SANP	6 huts	Yes	Yes
Bateleur	Small		7 guest cottages	No	No
Berg-en-Dal	Large	SANP	23 cottages, 92 chalets & 2 guesthouses	Yes	Yes
Biyamiti	Small	SANP	20 chalets	No	No
Boulders	Small		5 thatched units		No
Crocodile Bridge	Small	SANP	20 chalets	Yes	Yes
Hamilton's Tented Camp	Small	Private	6 luxury tents	No	No
Hoyo Hoyo	Small	Private	6 luxury African fantasy huts	No	No
Imbali Main Camp	Small	Private	12 suites	No	No
Jock's Safari Lodge	Small	Private	12 suites	No	Yes
Letaba	Large	SANP	2 guesthouses; 10 family cottages; 5 budget huts; 50 bungalows; 30 river bungalows; 20 safari tents	Yes	Yes
Lower Sabie	Medium	SANP	60 chalets	Yes	Yes
Lukimbi Safari Lodge	Small	Private	16 suite	No	Yes
Malelane	Small	SANP	5 huts	No	No
Maroela	Small	SANP	Caravans and camping only	Yes	No
Mopani	Large	SANP	1 guesthouse, 12 cottages, 45 guest cottages, 45 bungalows	No	Yes
Olifants	Large	SANP	3 guest cottages, 2 guesthouses, 104 bungalows	No	Yes
Orpen	Small	SANP	12 huts, 3 family cottages, 40 tents	Yes	Yes
Outpost	Small	Private	12 luxury units	No	Yes
Pafuri	Small	Private	24 luxury tented units	No	Yes
Pretoriuskop	Medium	SANP	30 huts; 12 family bungalows	Yes	Yes
Punda Maria	Medium	SANP	2 cottages, 20 bungalows	Yes	Yes
Rhino Post Main Lodge	Small	Private	8 luxury units	No	No
Roodewal	Small	Private	1 family cottage, 3 bungalows	No	No
Satara	Large	SANP	10 guest cottages, 3 guesthouses, 152 bungalows	Yes	Yes
Shimuwini	Small	SANP	15 chalets	No	No
Shingwedzi	Large	SANP	1 guesthouse, 1 family cottage, 20 huts, 24 bungalows, 55 safari tents	Yes	Yes

SANParks online bookings *reservations@parks-sa.co.za*

Petrol	Laundry	Restrnt	Activities	Contact No
Yes	Yes	Yes	Morning, afternoon & late-night drives; morning & afternoon walk	013 735 6306
No	No	Yes	Morning and night drives; walks on request	013 735 6843
Yes	Yes	Yes	Morning & evening walks, morning drive & bush braai	013 735 6106/7
No	No	No	Early-morning and night drives; day walks;	013 735 6171
No		No	Morning & night drives, bush walks	013 735 6536
Yes	Yes	No	Night and early-morning drives	013 735 6012
No	Yes	Yes	Morning & evening game drives & birdwatching	013 735 8915
No	Yes	Yes	Morning & evening game drives & birdwatching	013 735 8915
No	Yes	Yes	Morning & evening game drives & birdwatching	013 735 8915 *bookings@imbali.co.za*
No	Yes	Yes	2 game drives & bush walks per day	013 735 5200 *reservations@jocksafarilodge.com*
Yes	Yes	Yes	Morning, mid-morning and night drives; early-morning and afternoon walks; sunset bush braai; elephant museum; wildlife movies	013 735 6636
Yes	Yes	Yes	Sunset and morning drives; early-morning walk	013 735 6056/7
Yes (diesel)	Yes	Yes	2 game drives, 2 bush walks	Reservations 011 888 3713 *lodge@lukimbi.com* Camp 013 735 8000
No	No	No	Early-morning and night drives; day walks	013 735 6152
No	No	No	None	013 735 6355
Yes	Yes	Yes	Morning and night drives, morning walks, sunset bush braai	013 735 6535
Yes	Yes	Yes	Morning, sunset and night drives; morning and afternoon walks; special river walk, mountain bike trail, star-gazing	013 735 6606/7
Yes	Yes	Yes	Morning and sunset drives; morning and afternoon walks, children's drive	013 735 6355
No	Yes	Yes	Morning, sunset and night drives; early-morning and afternoon walks	Reservations 011 2455704 *sue@klpg.co.za* Camp 013 735 8907
No	Yes	Yes	Morning, sunset and night drives; early-morning and afternoon walks, special guided photographic and birding drives	Reservations 011 807 1800 *Taniaj@wilderness.co.za*
Yes	Yes	Yes	Early-morning, afternoon and sunset drives; morning walks	013 735 5128
Yes	Yes	Yes	Morning and night drives; day walks; guided tour of Thulamela archaeological site	013 735 6873
No	Yes	Yes	Walking safaris, game drives and sleep-outs	Reservations 011 467 4704 *chipo@rws.co.za* Camp 013 735 8923
No	No	No	Morning & night drives, bush walks	013 735 6306
Yes	Yes	Yes	Morning and night walks, hiking trail, morning and sunset drives; children's drives; 4x4 trail	013 735 6306/7
No	No	Yes	Morning and night drives; day walks	013 735 6683
Yes	Yes	Yes	Morning, sunset and night drives; day walks	013 735 6806

Camp	Size	Priv	Accom	Camping	Shop
Shishangeni Main Lodge	Small	Private	22 chalets	No	No
Singita Sweni	Medium	Private	15 luxury units	No	Yes
Sirheni	Small	SANP	5 cottages; 10 family cottages	No	No
Skukuza	Large	SANP	16 family cottages; 4 guesthouses, 15 luxury bungalows, 61 bungalows (with kitchenette), 117 bungalows, 95 camping sites	Yes	Yes
Talamati	Small	SANP	15 cottages	No	No
Tinga Legends & Tinga Narina	Small	Private	8 luxury units each	No	No
Tsendze Rustic Camp	Small	SANP	34 camp sites	Yes	No

Gate times

Month	Gate opening & closing times	Sunrise Sunset	Temps °C
August	06h00–18h00	06h35 17h35	12–28
September	06h00–18h00	05h54 17h50	12–28
October	05h30–18h00	05hh22 18h02	16–32
November	05h30–18h30	05h00 18h22	16–32
December	05h30–18h30	05h00 18h33	18–34
January	05h30–18h30	05h19 18h52	18–34
February	05h30–18h30	05h42 18h39	18–33
March	05h30–18h00	05h57 18h13	18–33
April	06h00–18h00	06h11 17h41	13–28
May	06h00–17h30	06h26 17h19	13–28
June	06h00–17h30	06h40 17h13	9–26
July	06h00–17h30	06h42 17h23	9–26

Main Gates (closing times as above)			
	Jan–Mar	Apr–Sep	Oct–Dec
Open	05:30	06:00	05:30

Rules and Regulations

- Report to reception when arriving at your camp
- Booked accommodation can be occupied from 12h00 on the day of your arrival and must be vacated by 09h00 on the day of your departure
- Declare any firearms in your possession at the entry gate
- Don't get out of your car except at authorised get-out points and in camps
- Don't feed the animals or interfere with them in any way
- Observe the speed limit – 50 km/h on tar roads; 40 km/h on dust roads
- Don't remove anything from the Park
- Don't litter

Nigel Dennis

Warthog

Petrol	Laundry	Restrnt	Activities	Contact No
No	Yes	No	Game drives, guided walks	Reservations 011 463 3779 reservation@pinnaclecollection.com Camp 082 782 3736
No	Yes	No	Game drives, guided walks, health spa, art gallery	Reservations 021 6833424 reservations@singita.co.za Camp 013 735 5500
No	No	Yes	Morning, sunset and night drives; early-morning and afternoon walks	013 735 6806
Yes	Yes	Yes	Games drives, bush walks, wild life movies; shopping	031 735 4000
No	No	No	Morning and night drives, morning walks	013 735 6343
No	Yes	Yes	Customised game drives and walks, health spa	013 735 8400 reservations@tinga.co.za
No	No	No	None	013 735 6535

Distances

GATES AND CAMPS	Berg-en-Dal	Croc Bridge Gate	Letaba	Lower Sabie	Malelane Gate	Mopani	Numbi Gate	Olifants	Orpen Gate	Pafuri Gate	Paul Kruger Gate	Phabeni Gate	Phalaborwa Gate	Pretoriuskop	Punda Maria	Satara	Shingwedzi	Skukuza
Berg-en-Dal	•	149	234	113	12	281	97	219	213	453	83	110	285	92	415	165	344	72
Croc Bridge Gate	149	•	196	34	141	243	130	181	175	415	88	115	246	125	377	127	306	77
Letaba	234	196	•	162	226	47	216	32	117	218	173	200	51	211	176	69	109	162
Lower Sabie	113	34	162	•	105	209	95	147	141	380	53	91	213	90	342	93	271	43
Malelane Gate	12	141	226	105	•	272	94	210	204	444	74	102	277	85	408	156	333	64
Mopani	281	243	47	209	272	•	263	86	164	172	220	247	74	258	130	116	63	209
Numbi Gate	97	130	216	95	94	263	•	201	195	434	65	32	267	9	396	147	325	54
Olifants	219	181	32	147	210	86	201	•	102	250	158	185	83	195	212	54	141	147
Orpen Gate	213	175	117	141	204	164	195	102	•	335	152	175	167	184	297	45	226	137
Pafuri Gate	456	415	218	380	444	172	434	250	335	•	392	418	246	438	76	287	109	380
Paul Kruger Gate	83	88	173	53	74	220	65	158	152	392	•	50	224	60	354	104	283	12
Phabeni Gate	110	115	200	91	102	247	32	185	175	418	50	•	251	23	380	131	309	38
Phalaborwa Gate	285	246	51	213	277	74	267	83	167	246	224	251	•	261	201	119	137	213
Pretoriuskop	92	125	211	90	85	258	9	195	184	438	60	23	251	•	389	140	318	49
Punda Maria	415	377	176	342	408	130	396	212	297	76	354	380	201	389	•	245	71	342
Satara	165	127	69	93	156	116	147	54	48	287	104	131	119	140	245	•	178	93
Shingwedzi	344	306	109	271	333	63	325	141	226	109	283	309	137	318	71	178	•	271
Skukuza	72	77	162	43	64	209	54	147	137	380	12	38	213	49	342	93	271	•

Route quickguide

Route		Page
S50	Mopani to Shingwedzi via Shilowa	240, 242, 244, 247–248, 249, 250, 253
S50	Nshawa Loop	232, 250, 295
S51	Sable Dam	214
S52	Red Rocks Loop	250, 253–254, 295
S55	Lamont Loop	255
S56	Mphongolo Loop	250, 254, 255, 257, 295
S60	Punda to Pafuri	260, 263, 268
S61	Klopperfontein Loop	263, 268
S62	Engelhard Dam Drive	222, 224–225, 295
S63	Luvuvhu River Drive	277–279, 296
S64	Nyala Drive	271, 279, 296
S65	N'waswitshaka Road	144, 153
S79	N'watimhiri causeway	99–100, 109
S83	Maroela Loop	162
S86	N'waswitsontso Loop	176
S90	Old Main Road	204, 231
S91	Balule Bridge Loop	231, 295
S92	Balule to Olifants	231, 295
S99	Mahonie Loop	263, 264–265, 265, 296
S100	N'wanetsi River Road	201

Route		Page
S102	Bume to Randspruit Road	108
S106	Rabelais Road	185, 186–187
S110	Malelane to Berg-en-Dal	118, 305
S110	Matjulu Loop	114, 118, 120–121
S112	Rhino Koppies route	156, 157, 159, 161
S112	Stevenson–Hamilton Loop	127, 156
S114	Malelene to Skukuza	84, 107, 108, 114, 128–129, 130
S118	Mhlambane Loop	128–129
S120	Steilberg Loop	121
S121	Timfenheni Loop	128
S122	Muntshe Hill	102
S125	N'waswitsontso River Road	195
S126	Sweni River Road	195
S128	Old Tshokwane Road	101, 168
S129	Mafotini	168
S131	Letaba to Phalaborwa	226
S137	Duke's Water Hole Road	92, 94, 97
S139	Biyamiti Road	111
S140	Talamati Road	182, 187
S142	Shongololo Loop	245
S143	Tropic of Capricorn Loop	239, 240, 243, 250, 253
S146	Stapelkop Dam Road	240, 245

Nigel Dennis

Wildebeest

Directory

Kruger National Park: Private Bag X402, Skukuza 012 426 5000 *www.sanparks.org*

SA National Parks central reservations
012 428 9111 *reservations@parks-sa.co.za*

SANParks emergency call centre
013 735 4325

Camps
SANParks & Private (see page 314)

Gates
Crocodile Bridge	013 735 6012
Malelane	013 735 6152
Numbi	013 735 5133
Orpen	013 735 6355
Pafuri	013 735 8907
Paul Kruger	013 735 5107
Phabeni	013 735 5890
Phalaborwa	013 735 3547
Punda Maria	013 735 6870

Useful numbers
Avis Skukuza	013 735 5651
Breakdowns	013 735 4260
Conference queries	012 343 0905
Doctor	013 735 5638
Kruger Park Head Office	012 426 5000
Malaria Hotline	082 234 1800
Police (Skukuza)	013 735 9004
SAA Express	011 978 9000
Kruger Park Safaris	013 750 1112
Skukuza Airfield	013 735 4251
Skukuza Golf Club	013 735 5543
Skukuza Main switchboard	013 735 4000
Wilderness Trails	013 790 1480
Weather Bureau	082 233 9800

Cell phone coverage
Reception areas in green

References

Bushveld Trees, M Funston, Fernwood Press, 1996

Best Birding in Kruger, B Hilton-Barber and L Arthur, Prime Origins, 2007

Common Birds of the Kruger National Park, K Newman, Struik

A Dictionary of Kruger National Park Place Names, JJ Kloppers and H Bornman, (*SA Country Life 2005*)

Field Guide to the Cradle of Humankind, B Hilton-Barber and Prof L Berger, Struik, 2005

Field Guide to the Mammals of the Kruger National Park, Heike Schutze, Struik 2002

A Game Ranger Remembers, B Bryden, Jonathan Ball, 2005

Getaway Guide to the Kruger National Park, C Ewart-Smith, Sunbird, 2005

Guide to the Ecozones of Kruger, Jacana

The Kruger Experience – Ecology and management of savanna heterogeneity, edited by J du Toit, K Rogers and H Biggs, Island Press, 2003

Kruger – an African Eden, B Scholes and N Dennis, Struik

Kruger National Park, Dr L Braack, Globetrotter, 2000

Kruger National Park Questions and Answers PF Fourie (*SA Country Life 1978*)

Kruger – Portrait of a National Park, D Paynter and W Nussey, Macmillan South Africa

Kruger's Rivers, Dr Andrew Deacon, Custos, 1994

Let's Visit the Kruger Park, R Bigalke, Afrikaanse Pers Boekhandel, 1960

Lost Trails of the Lowveld, TV Bulpin, Howard Timmins, 1951

Making the Most of Indigenous Trees, Fanie and Julye-Ann Venter, Briza

Memories of a Game Ranger, H Wolhuter, Shuter and Shuter

Our National Parks – National Parks Board publication 1955

Roberts' Birds of South Africa, VII Edition, PAR Hockey, WRJ Dean and PG Ryan, (John Voelcker Bird Book Fund)

Sappi Tree Spotting, Lowveld, R Grant and V Thomas, Jacana 2004

The Safari Companion, Richard D Estes, Russel Friedman Books, 1999

South African Eden (The Kruger National Park 1902–1946), J Stevenson-Hamilton, Struik

Vutlhari bya Vatsonga – the Wisdom of the Tsonga-Shangana People, HP Junod, Sasavona Books

Wild Life in South Africa, James Stevenson-Hamilton, Cassel and Co, 1947

Wildlife and Warfare, J Carruthers, University of Natal Press, 2001

Nigel Dennis

Bushpig

Index

Page numbers in **bold** provide fuller information.
Page numbers in *italics* indicate illustrations.